In Song and Sorrow

The Daily Journal
of Thomas Hart Benton McCain
86th Indiana Volunteer Infantry

Edited by Richard K. Rue
and Geraldine M. Rue

Augmented by stories from
86th Regiment Indiana Volunteer Infantry, 1895
by James A. Barnes, James R. Carnahan
and Thomas H. B. McCain

Indiana's Roll of Honor, Volume I, 1864
by David Stevenson

Indiana's Roll of Honor, Volume II, 1866
by Theo. T. Scribner

Library of Congress
Catalog Card Number
98-70280

ISBN 1-57860-19-7 (Hardcover)
ISBN 1-57860-020-0 (Paperback)

Manufactured in the United States of America

Use of the diaries of Thomas Hart Benton McCain
by special arrangement with
Robert S. McCain and Michele A. McCain, Owners

Table of Contents

INTRODUCTION

Thomas Hart Benton McCain was born in Clinton County, Indiana, on January 24, 1839 to Hugh and Minerva McCain. After public school he attended the well-known Thorntown Academy. After completing the course there he taught school during the winter season and in the summer worked as a printer for the *Citizen of Lebanon* newspaper.

He was among the first to enlist after the Civil War broke out, entering as a 7th Corporal in Company I of the 86th Indiana Regiment.

T. H. B. McCain started his remarkable journal before the regiment was mustered in, and continued with an entry nearly every day of his service, including the days following his capture at Stones River.

Even though McCain was captured in his first battle, he did not miss any action. The Eighty-sixth went into winter quarters near Murfreesboro, and he rejoined them there after being paroled.

The Journal is a complete reflection of McCain's physical, mental and spiritual experience in the Western Theater. From the very beginning it is evident that Thomas Hart Benton McCain is an ardent Christian. The patriotism he felt for his country and his "insulted Stars and Stripes" appears to be just as strong and sincere as his faith in God, and he gives a good deal of consideration to them in his daily writing.

The words you read here are the words that Thomas Hart Benton McCain wrote over one hundred thirty years ago. Except in a very few instances, the punctuation has not been standardized. The grammar, the misspellings, the incorrect dates, the misunderstandings are preserved. Very few meanings are changed by incorrect spellings in the diary. But beyond this, it has been our decision as editors, and the publisher's decision also, to publish the journal in its entirety. It seems necessary to take McCain's experience as a whole - to see empty and uneventful days as well as exciting ones. Our wish is that this sensitive, intelligent, idealistic young man's experience be shared with the reader in as full a form as is possible.

This writer has been a student of the Civil War for over forty years. I have considered it beyond my wildest dreams to ever find such a treasure as this diary, much less have the opportunity to study it and transcribe it at my leisure. For this opportunity I am deeply indebted to T.H.B. McCain's great grandson, Mr. Bob McCain of Ft. Myers, Florida and his wife, Michele. I only hope that sharing this diary with others gives a small part of the enjoyment I felt when I read it.

Included in the book are passages from *86th Regiment, Indiana Volunteer Infantry,* a regimental history written by Capt. James R. Carnahan, Capt. James A. Barnes and McCain, and published by McCain's Journal Publishing Company.

Other stories are from *Indiana's Roll of Honor, Volumes I and II.*

After the war, T. H. B. McCain reentered the field of journalism, first publishing the *Delphi Journal*, and a short time later, the *Lebanon Patriot*. In 1868 he tried to operate a newspaper in Murfreesboro, Tennessee, but at the time it was no place for a "Republican" newspaper. His family heard that he had just missed being tarred and feathered and given a ride out of town on a rail.

He spent some time as editor of the *New York Star* before returning to Indiana and becoming editor, co-owner, and later owner of the *Crawfordsville Journal* and the Journal Publishing Company,

In 1867 he married Salome Longley, daughter of Mr. and Mrs. A. H. Longley. They had two sons, Arthur A. McCain and Fred T. McCain. He died May 1, 1898 at his home on Wabash Avenue in Crawfordsville.

Richard K. Rue (1935-1997)

FOREWORD

From *86th Regiment, Indiana Volunteer Infantry,* abridged

During the winter of 1860-61 seven of the Southern states undertook to secede from the union. Soon other states from the South joined in the movement and attempted to set up an independent government. They took possession of the arms and treasure of the United States, and finally Fort Sumter, near Charleston, South Carolina, was fired upon, and the garrison, after a stubborn fight, was compelled to surrender. This firing upon the United States flag and upon United States soil was the open declaration of war against and upon the Government, and this was to be met. Abraham Lincoln at once issued his proclamation for 75,000 volunteer soldiers for a term of three months.

In response to the President's call, Indiana Governor Oliver P. Morton issued a proclamation April 16, 1861 calling upon the "loyal and patriotic men of this State, to the number of six regiments, to organize themselves into military companies, and forthwith to report the same to the Adjutant General (Lewis Wallace), in order that they may be speedily mustered into the service of the United States."

The two proclamations had hardly been flashed over the wires until the State of Indiana had more than filled her quota, and her regiments were hurrying from peaceful homes into fields that were to be made far more glorious, by their deeds of valor, than any battlefield of the old world where the wars had been waged for conquest or hate, at the command of a despot, and by soldiers of fortune or force.

From North to South, from East to West within the borders, the sons of Indiana responded to the call. They came from all walks of life, farm boys and professionals, students and bankers, from every village and city, leaving all prospect for future comfort for the hardships, danger and death that awaited them in their new lives as soldiers.

Scarcely 300 men in the entire state had ever stood in military ranks, or ever had a single drill in the manual of arms. Not more than ten of the number had ever held a rank above captain, and none had ever commanded a battalion or regiment. These men were speedily equipped, and without any delay for preparatory drill were put on board trains and sent to the front to engage in active campaign life.

The United States was ill-prepared to outfit 75,000 men, so at first, each State provided uniforms and arms for the men recruited within its borders. Governor Morton convened the legislature in special session and recommended that "one million of dollars be appropriated for the purchase of arms and munitions of war..." The legislature at once authorized a war loan of two million dollars, and appropriated half for general military purposes, $500,000 for arms and the remainder for other purposes, including the State Militia.

The "Three Months Men," regiments organized under the President's first call, were numbered from six to eleven and were sent to the front immediately. Another call, this time for 42,034 volunteers, was issued May 3, 1861. Enlistments had continued at such a quick pace that the regiments returning from the first three months found the quota filled. Those regiments then re-enlisted, and before another call was issued by the President, they had all been accepted by the War Department, mustered in, and had returned to the front. Another enlistment call was made on July 1, 1861 for 500,000 men. Under this call, Indiana furnished two regiments of infantry for twelve months service, forty-seven regiments of infantry for three years, four companies of infantry for three years, three regiments of cavalry for three years, and eighteen batteries of artillery for three years.

Another call was issued, and by the end of 1861, Indiana had mustered into service regiments six through fifty-nine, and eleven batteries of light artillery. Additional calls in 1862 sent forth thirty-seven additional companies of infantry, two of cavalry, nine of artillery. Each of these regiments had their full complement of men - 1,000 each. By the end of the war, Indiana alone had furnished 208,367 men. Of this number, 24,416 were killed or died of disease.

The Eighty-Sixth Volunteer Infantry Regiment was recruited in response to the President's call on July 1, 1862, for 300,000 more men; 21,350 from Indiana. The month had not passed away until each of the ten companies of the regiment was in "Camp Tippecanoe."

When the Civil War broke out T. H. B. McCain enlisted as a 7th Corporal in Company I of the 86th Indiana Regiment. After a service of several months he was promoted to the office of sergeant major, and during the last year of the war he served as first lieutenant of the company, being captain in effect, as the captain was serving as a member of the staff.

Thomas Hart Benton McCain in 1865 (*left*) and in 1896.

A

Daily Journal

kept by

T. H. B. McCain

while in

the volunteer service

commencing

the 23rd of August, 1862,

the time

of his volunteering

in defense

of the insulted

"Stars and Stripes"

A.

Daily Journal

kept by

S. H. B. McCain

while in

the Volunteer Service,

Commencing

the 23rd of August 1862,

The time

of his volunteering

in defense

of the unsullied

"Stars and Stripes"

Man is transacting History each day he lives, but as time rolls on it is forgotten with the "buried past". Much may be learned from unwritten history but more may be learned from that which is recorded. The errors of the past may be seen and corrected. I trust that which I write in this little volume will not only be history, but will point out the many errors of my life and lead me in the future to correct them.

T. H. B. McCain

Man is transacting History each day he lives, but as time circles on it is forgotten with the "buried past." Much may be learned from unwritten history but more may be learned from that which is recorded. The errors of the past may be seen and corrected. I trust that which I write in this little volume will not only be history but will point out the many errors of my life and lead one in the future to correct them.

S. H. B. McCain

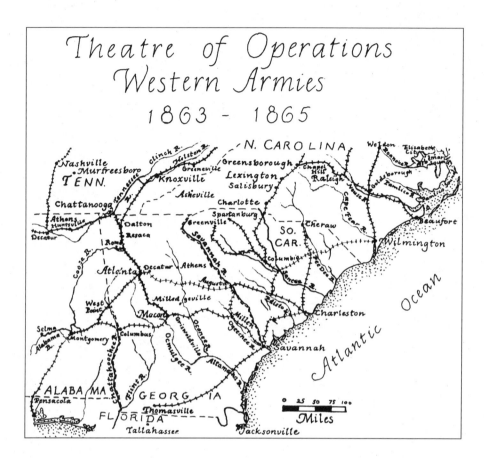

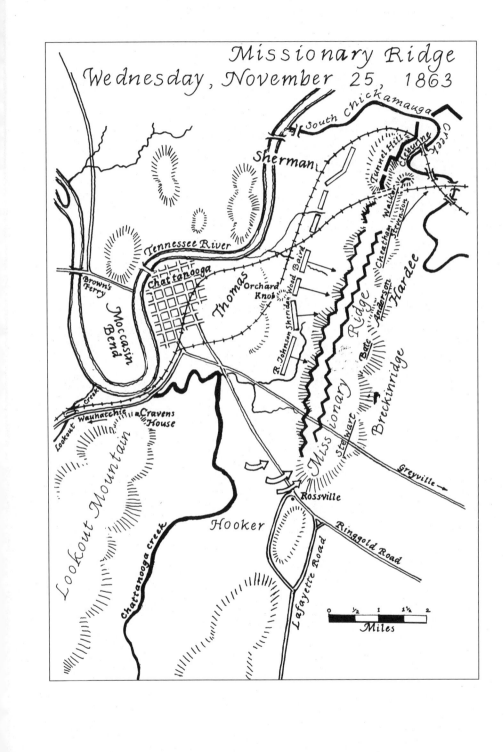

Missionary Ridge
Wednesday, November 25, 1863

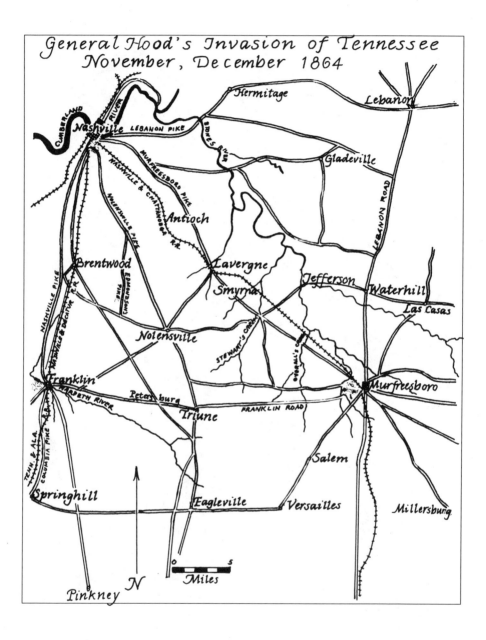

General Hood's Invasion of Tennessee
November, December 1864

Miles

N

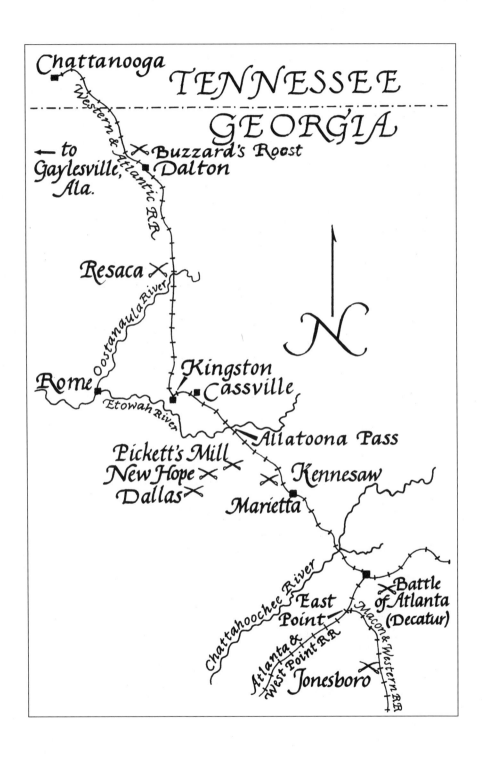

Chapter One
From Home to Kentucky

Saturday August 23 1862
Today I enrolled my name as many. The many brave volunteers to go in defenses of our common country. I enlist under Capt. W. C. Lambert of Stockwell, Ind. Am in the 86th Regiment Ind, Vols, I go simply from a sense of duty not because I want to go. May I put my trust in God that my life may be preserved and return safely to loving friends at home. Went into camp. Because of the "noise and confusion" I did not rest well the first night.

Sunday August 24th 1862
In company with my associates went over to the city of Lafayette and attended church at "Eastern Charge" M E Church. Att class meeting in the morning also at S School in the afternoon. Partook of the hospitalities of Bro. Snyder whom I shall long remember. Returned to camp in the evening.

Monday August 25th 1862
Started early this morning for home. Welcomed by father, mother, sisters & brothers. Spent a few hours in company with them after which I bade them farewell it may be to meet them no more again on earth. If I should not be permitted to meet them here I hope to meet them in heaven. 'Tis hard to part from friends with whom we have mingled since infancy and go to brave the dangers and storms of the battlefield. Hard indeed must be the heart that could bid old associates and scenes of infancy farewell without shedding a tear. Came back to Thorntown. Several ladies had called to see me. I bade them farewell. Spent the ballance of the evening in company with Mollie, Annie Frank and Charley.

Tuesday August 26th 1862
Making preparations to make my final departure from T--. Annie wrote several songs that I might engage in singing to cheer the long and weary hours of the camp. Again I bade my many dear friends in Thorntown farewell. I am now this evening in "Camp Tippecanoe." Having sent a note in the morning to some lady friends in Colfax they met me at the train and as a token of their regards they presented me with a ripe "mush-melon." God bless the girls - may they be ornaments to the circle in which they move, emblems of piety and virtue and finally be saved in that country where there are no

wars. Returned to camp Tippecanoe. Found the camp alive and the boys as noisy as ever.

86th Regiment, Indiana Volunteer Infantry, abridged

CAMP TIPPECANOE

Camp Tippecanoe was on high, rolling ground, which, with its superior drainage made it an ideal location for a military camp. Soldiers were billeted in three-sided sheds made from undressed boards from the saw mill. The camp in general was very scantily furnished with the most necessary articles for convenience or comfort. The bunks were not even supplied with straw.

No events transpired in Camp Tippecanoe at Lafayette that were of particular importance in the military history of the regiment. However, on a Sunday night a depredation was committed which was distinctively and positively not military.

On that morning it was discovered that the sutler's tent was laid low. His tent and goods gave the only evidence that a cyclone had struck the camp. The whole matter was easily explained. The Hoosiers were getting ready for a campaign and had tried their hands on the sutler's tent and goods.

The establishment gave evidence of their prowess. It was evidently of pillage and had been well executed. The man attending to the stock of goods had gone to town during the night. Some of the vigilant, riotous spirits of camp had observed this and soon collected from the quarters others equally bold and turbulent as themselves to complete the work contemplated.

Who organized the raid or led the raiders is not known positively, but certain it is, that the work was artistically done; for if ever a sutler's tent was stretched flat and his goods strewn to the four winds, here was the time and place. Had it been pursued, it would not have been difficult to identify those few men who were ever ready for such deeds. One of the leading spirits of the raid on the sutler was a member of Company H. He was one of the bravest men in the regiment and finally gave his life on the field of battle.

Wednesday August 27 1862

Slept on the ground last night and caught a severe cold in consequence of which I feel much depressed. Much surprised this afternoon on meeting with my old friend Josey Foxworthy. At night he preached to the regiment. This is the first opportunity or indeed the first religious exercises held in camp since I came. Loud and sweet were the songs of Zions that ascended from the many voices assembled on the green this evening, The exercises were closed with prayer by Capt Lambert.

Thursday August 28th 1862
Last night in consequence of my cold I was quite unwell and did not rest well during the night, Frank and I went out to the city to return in one hour and a half. Dispatched our business in a hurry and returned at the appointed time, Soon after we came back was ordered on company drill. 'Tis eventide, On every side I hear a commingling of noises. Some talking, some reading, some singing and sorry to say some playing cards. This afternoon our Captain took us to the river to bathe.

Friday August 29th 1862
This morning my name was called to go "on guards" the next 24 hours. "On Guard!" For the first time I am called in the physical struggle to stand at the outer posts of the camp to give the alarm of any danger either of internal factions or external foes. A startling illustration of our moral warfare I need to keep the outposts of my moral nature well quartered against the many demoralizing influences of the camp. Many amusing incidents occurred while at my post at the wicket gate. Today received the appointment of 5th Corporal.

Saturday August 30th 1862
This morning at 6 o'clock I was relieved from my post by the relief guard. Went over to the city and accidentally met with little Billy Watkins. Wrote home. Drew some clothing.

Sunday August 31st 1862
Again the Holy Sabbath dawns. Not as I have seen it in other days so brilliant yet not withstanding all the din and confusion it seems a holy time. The sacrifices many young men have made - have given up their peaceful homes. Sabbath and Sanctuary privileges for the hardships and privations of a soldier's life. My mind reverts back to the many pleasant seasons of the class meeting, of the congregation and of that dearly loved place the Sabbath School. Can I forget my little Sabbath School class? Can I forget Hattie, Mattie and the two Annies? My prayer is that they may grow up to be useful women. Frank

and Dick and I have passed out the guard lines and are now reclining our weary bodies on the slope of a hill. To the east is heard the rumbling noise of the camp. O how refreshing to breathe once more the pure atmosphere of heaven! While visiting here Dick and Frank go to sleep. Now all is still save the soft winds gently sighing through the branches of the trees. O what a sacred hour this is while writing. Meethinks I hear the bells calling the good to the house of God. Can I write without thinking of home? My heart grows weary with this thought! O that I had language to express the emotions of my heart. Let God's will be done not mine. Affection's tear is silently dropped yet I sternly bear the sorrows of leaving home with all its beloved associations. I ask that should I meet them no more on earth that I may meet them in heaven. A refreshing shower made glad our camp this afternoon. Rev. Mr. Snepp a United Brethren minister preached to the soldiers this afternoon. Good order prevailed. Later in the evening a general row seemed inevitable caused by the "demon whisky."

86th Indiana Regiment, Volunteer Infantry, abridged

Hairs

*I*n referring to the hardships of diet in Camp Tippecanoe, it is not meant to insinuate that the Commissary of Subsistence at the camp failed to do its full duty in furnishing rations. All certainly had plenty to eat, indeed, much that none wanted, and yet ate it -- reluctantly it is true, but ate it all the same. There was plenty of bread and meat and an abundance of good water. The bread was fairly good baker's bread. The meat was excellent. What then was the trouble, may be asked. The difficulty of mastication and the deglutination were not directly referable to the quality of the bread or meat, or any of the solid foods issued, nor were they occasioned by the quality of the drinks. The malignant imp that presided over the appetite and almost defeated the plan of subsistence was not in any of these articles originally, but it was over and in all these before they were finally and fully prepared for the palate. It ruled in camp everywhere - that is in Camp Tippecanoe.

To be more explicit, the different companies of the Eighty-sixth upon their arrival in camp had issued to them a lot of coarse white hairy blankets, the like of which had never been seen before or since. They could hardly be called woolen, but were composed of coarse stiff hairs which were ever ready upon a touch to desert their place in the original fabric and cling with wonderful tenacity to the place of their adoption. In these blankets the boys stood guard at night. They threw them around their shoulders in the chill of cool evenings; they slept in their bunks wrapped in them, and consequently they were literally covered from head to foot with these foul, unsightly hairs. Like the effects of original sin they were ever present.

Clothing was covered with them; nose, eyes, mouth, and ears were filled with them. An hundred Esaus spat and sputtered from morning until night, and from night until morning again to free their mouths of these persistent abominations. There were few or no vessels yet provided which could be used for transferring the rations from the regimental commissary department to the company quarters. Therefore these blankets came readily into use: for rations we had to have. Thus at a very early date there was a very general and liberal admixture of these blanket hairs with all rations drawn to be used by the companies. The crop was an unfailing one, an abundant supply.

By this double use of the blankets the hairs were generously and even copiously distributed everywhere; no place or person was slighted. The bunks were full of them; the rude tables were festooned with them; the bread was dressed and robed with them; the meat was well covered with coarse white hairs. They invaded the sugar; tin plates were ornamented and embellished in various designs by these long, stiff, tickling, unwelcome nauseating hairs. The coffee cups were likewise wreathed and fringed in fantastic dressings with them. In short, not a drinking or cooking utensil of any kind could be found about the company quarters of that camp but what was fully decorated with these white-robed conquerors.

With a persistence that seemed born of intelligence they were ever present - conquering time and space and the palates of hundreds of sturdy lads and strong men, showing no favors to any. The boys were at first disgusted, then angry, then both disgusted and angry, then disgusted, angry and sick, for the gorge of every man did not fail to rise in rebellion against such treatment, as every well-fed, well-treated, and cultivated stomach should do. Yet this or a similar experience may have in one sense been necessary and beneficial in proving the boys' stomachs and preparing them for that which was to come, for although these constituted their last and only ration of edible blankets they suffered many hardships and sore trials of the stomach and palate during their term of service. This was, however, their worst and most trying experience of the palate while they remained in camp at LaFayette.

Monday September 1st 1862
Last night I acted as assistant Corporal on account of the uproar in camp. I finished up my work just as a heavy rain was approaching. This morning the air feels fine, the sky clearer. Three hours on drill this morning. Cool in the evening.

Tuesday September 2nd 1862
Clear and cool this morning. Frank came in from Thorntown last night bringing with him some of the necessaries of life sent us by the ladies of Thorntown. Went to the junction to bring them in. At noon partook of the "goodies" sent us in company with Col. Hamilton and others. Procured a pass to go home as the regiment will leave in the morning. Left "Camp Tippecanoe" for the train. Got aboard and arrived at Colfax where I met several lady friends. Through the kindness of two of them I was relieved of a walk which I was compelled to make to Thorntown by they taking me in a buggy. On our way stopped at W.A. Haworth's. Remained about half an hour after which we resumed our journey. The night was pleasant which made it agreeable buggy-riding especially when in company with ladies. Arrived at Mr. Cones' about ten o'clock where we were kindly welcomed. Glad indeed to see Thorntown though been gone but a week.

Wednesday September 3rd 1862
Arose this morning considerably refreshed after a night's good rest. As the regiment will pass through today preparations are being made by the citizens to furnish the soldiers with refreshments. The train came in and with it came the soldiers. They were well entertained and the 86th Regiment Ind. Vols will long remember Thorntown. I got aboard the train and bade Thorntown farewell! It may be the last time I will see it. Arrived at "Camp Murphy" in the afternoon and pitched tents. All is noise and confusion. Moving "duds" is new to us but I presume we will be fully initiated ere long into the mysteries of war.

86th Indiana Regiment, Volunteer Infantry, abridged

CAMP CARRINGTON

The regiment was next moved to Camp Carrington (also called Camp Murphy at times) near Indianapolis, where they were officially mustered in on the fourth day of September, 1862. They were given their uniforms and

---

equipment and introduced to "the Union soldier's abomination" - hard tack, the army cracker.

They received their Enfield rifles and became fully acquainted with their use and care. From tip of bayonet to butt of stock no portion or part escaped the closest scrutiny and examination. Only a little drilling was done.

A little incident occurred at this camp before the men had drawn arms. It showed the mettle of the Hoosier boys and that they intended to do what they believed to be their duty.

The camp guard had been established and strict orders given to the guards to allow no one to cross the guard line except at the gates with properly signed passes. Of course the raw recruit thought this order meant just what it said, and accordingly supposed that no one was to be allowed to pass in or out over the line, be he a private or Major-General, not knowing that field officers were by military rules excepted.

Well, General Carrington was riding round on a tour of inspection and thought to ride into the camp of the Eighty-sixth. He rode up to the guard line and naturally supposed that the guard had been properly instructed and knew sufficiently of military matters to admit him. But he had struck the wrong man.

Attempting to cross, the guard halted him, but he rode up quite near to the guard and informed him who he was, and that he was entitled to pass - to enter camp at will notwithstanding the instructions from the Colonel to allow no one to pass in or out. But no, the guard was firm and insisted he could not pass into camp over his beat. The General became impatient and attempted to ride forward into camp regardless of the guard's threatening attitude and warnings to keep off.

Now came the fun. The guard, quite as determined as the General, seized the bridle rein of the General's horse, reined him back upon his haunches and struck the General a heavy blow on the left arm and shoulder with a stout cudgel with which the guards were then armed.

The General now thoroughly aroused spurred his charger forward, causing him to break away from the guard and so rode into camp. This little episode was witnessed by many of the boys who scarcely knew what to make of it. The General himself was very much excited, asked the company to which the soldier belonged, his name, and sought his Captain and then Captain Hamilton.

All expected to hear him severely denounced and perhaps ordered a

> severe punishment for his gross blunder. But on the contrary, the General commended him highly for his great firmness in doing that which he believed to be his duty and recommended that he be promoted to corporal immediately if there was a vacancy, and if not, as soon as a vacancy occurred.

Thursday September 4th 1862
This morning is beautiful. This camp is all astir. Great excitement caused by the news from the 55th regiment. I hear that several Thorntown boys are badly hurt among whom are Howard Cones and Will Martin. Today was mustered into the service of the United States by the mustering officer, Capt. Simonson.

Friday September 5th 1862
Taken by surprise this morning by the arrival of Champion and Howard Cones from the Richmond battlefield after a march of 98 miles through the woods having escaped from rebels. Very warm day drew arms at the arsenal.

Saturday September 6th 1862
Frank and I had pictures taken together. Met with many old friends in town among whom were Jas. H. Smith. Visited the "American" office once more. Returned to camp and found the regiment on battalion drill. In the afternoon received $25.00 bounty money. Heavy rain storms in the evening which makes camp life disagreeable.

Sunday September 7th 1862
While the camp is all confusion in the bustle of receiving wages, received $15.00 in addition to that I received yesterday. Sent home $40.00. How unlike is a Sabbath morning to a Sabbath morning in camp. The many pleasant scenes of home usher into my mind which makes one feel lonely. Rainy afternoon. The 86th Regiment struck tents and at about sundown bade farewell to "Camp Murphy" and took the train for Cincinnati. Arrived in Cincinnati about 1/2 past 2 o'clock in the morning. Tumbled down to sleep in the C & I R.R. depot. After sleeping a couple of hours marched to the 5th Street market where we were served to a Soldier's breakfast consisting of boiled ham, bread and coffee.

Monday September 8, 1862
Having partook breakfast we were marched back to the river. Here for the

first time I had the pleasure of seeing a steam boat. The regiment crossed over the river on a pontoon bridge, I am now on the sacred soil of Kentucky! Boasted Kentucky! The land which has reared some of our best statesmen! Marched through Covington and out to "Camp Mitchell." In consequence of the heat and not yet inured to soldier life I fell by the wayside, I succeeded however, in getting in a milk wagon and riding to camp. Soon after getting to "Camp Mitchell" we were drawn up in "line of battle" as it was reported that the enemy were in a short distance of our lines. Slept on our arms during the night.

Tuesday September 9th 1862
Slept on the hillside last night but it being so steep I slid down and toward morning I found myself about ten feet below. "Marching orders." Immediately in line and soon on the way to some point we knew not where. After marching about 8 miles in circuitous route we halted in a open field on the east banks of the Licking and about three miles from Newport. Entirely fagged out. I laid down and was soon fast asleep.

Wednesday Sept 10th 1862
This morning I am tired, hungry and thirsty. Hearing of a well about a half mile distant I go in search of water, I have often heard of boasted Kentucky - of her lofty hills and fertile plains, of her gushing springs and pure rivers but what I have so far seen it is rocky, barren and unfruitful. There are no springs, no cool water like we have in Indiana. When I came back the regiment had orders to change positions in an expected attack by the enemy. They moved to an elevated position on the left bank of the Licking. Supperless we were ordered to lay on our arms during the night to be awakened at 3 o'clock.

Thursday September 11 1862
I go into the city of Covington and pay 15 cents for a breakfast that when at home it would have made me sick to even have looked upon the table. We return to the intrenchments and were immediately ordered to "fall in." The order was passed from officer to officer to load. Indications are that a battle was near at hand. I see looking along the line that not a few are "shaking in their boots." Couriers at all times are coming in riding at full speed. What messages they bring is kept from the private soldier. It may be that the rebels are near at hand and they may be some distance. Though our pickets have been driven in at one or two points I commit myself into the hands of Him who knoweth all things. His will not mine be done. Night comes but no enemy. Ordered to the intrenchments but the order was countermanded and

I am permitted to lie without the ditch. Soon a heavy rain comes up and we roused from our slumber to huddle together. To protect us from the rain as much as possible.

Friday September 12th 1862
Feel rather wet this morning on account of the rain last night, Our tents are across the river. If they had been here we would not have been in them as we were ordered to lie near the intrenchments. During the day I assisted in pitching tents with the intentions of taking a good night's rest.

Saturday September 13th 1862
Had the extreme felicity of resting well last night in a tent for the first time since I came on the "sacred soil." The weather is quite cool. I have written several letters today, most of them, however, have been written for those who cannot write to friends at home. Drilling in the manual of arms, after which Mr. Rash and I go to the Licking to bathe. I feel at least 50 per cent better. One great cause of sickness in camp is the manner in which soldiers keep themselves. It is now Saturday night, We are collected in our bunk singing some of the dear old songs of home, some of which are very applicable especially the "Pleasures of War" & "We Conquer or Die."

Sunday September 14th 1862
Again the holy Sabbath dawns bright and beautiful. How different is a Sabbath in camp to a Sabbath at home. Rev. Mr. Harker, our chaplain preached to the regiment today. It was soul reviving to hear the messages of Divine Truth. The sermon touches the hearts of many, no doubt, reminding them of the good that were assembling at the respective places of worship in their native State. Closed with prayer by Capt Lambert. It was then announced that there would be prayer meeting at 4 o'clock, but, there was none on account of orders received to march. Gov Morton and Henry S. Lane were in camp today.

Monday September 15th 1862
All quiet in the regiment this morning, The news of an expected attack however, excites a few. Wrote home. All around me the soldiers are writing to friends at home. In the afternoon in company with Lieut Doster and others I go to the Licking to bathe. This is a narrow but deep stream and at the place where we were it was still being the back waters of the Ohio. Went to rest as usual, but were soon awakened by the alarm that the enemy were

rushing on to attack us. Immediately jumped into the intrenchments and there remained till morning.

Tuesday September 16th 1862
When I arose this morning casting my eye along the intrenchments many were they who had been slain by Morpheus during the night. It looked as though he had gained a complete victory, One by one they arose, thus proving that the work of King Morpheus was not serious.

Wednesday September 17 1862
This morning I was put on as "Corporal of the Guard." Received a letter from John King, the first received since I came here from home. Glad indeed, to hear from home. Quite a windy day. The commissary shanty was blown down. A man was severely hurt by the casualty.

Thursday September 18 1962
Today writing letters to friends at home. Foxworthy, Mollie, Annie, father and mother. As I was on Guard duty yesterday I am exempt from drill today. Saw Gen New.

Friday September 19th 1862
This morning while I write I am seated on the hill side which slopes to the south. Far away as far as the eye can reach the meandering stream wanders through nature's hall.   On either side is one continual range of hills methodically delineated in deeper hues and in more variegated aspects than any of the noble designs of the talented Raphael or Angelo could display. The fog which for a while dims the beauty and sublimity of the Licking, will, as the golden orb approaches the zenith clear away. So it is with soldier life at this time, The fog of rebellion which for awhile dims the beauty and sublimity of free government, will, as the hosts of freemen from the north approach, clear away. Another stir this afternoon in consequence of the order to cook three days rations.

Chapter Two
In Pursuit of Bragg

Saturday September 20th 1862
Early this morning had orders to march. Immediately the usual bustle commenced and every one were asking the question "Where are we going?" Tents are struck, baggage packed and off we started, Before reaching the guard lines of the camp ground the regiment was ordered to halt. After waiting patiently "in line" all day the order "forward march" was given. By this time it was dark. Marched through Covington and down by the river's side. The "Forest Rose" and "Dunleith" were waiting for us. The left wing of the regiment took the "Forest Rose" while the right took the "Dunleith." So I was quartered on the hurricane deck. Rested well during the night.

Sunday September 21st 1862
Again it is the Sabbath morning. Much rather would I prefer being at home where I could enjoy the blessings of a peaceful life, I could there enjoy the privilege of attending church & Sabbath School. But instead of this I am bound down the river somewhere unknown to me. Proudly the steamer glides from shore and we bid adieu to Covington and Cincinnati. The first town on the river is Lawrenceberg, after which we pass Aurora, Rising Sun, Warsaw, KY., Stark, Vevay, Ghent, KY. Carrolton, Ky., Madison and Hanover. When the boat reached Hanover it ran against a sandbar and was compelled to remain there 'till morning.

Monday September 22nd 1862
Fun this morning, "Wade to shore" was the order given by the Capt of the boat. Immediately many of the soldiers waded to the Indiana shore, I visited Hanover College. The building is a beautiful structure situated on the north bank of the Ohio about 400 feet above high water mark. Very tired when I reached the top of the hill but was conducted through the college by the janitor whom I took to be a gentleman. I learned there were about 25 students in attendance. The boat was towed over about 12 o'clock. I took passage in the window of the pilot house where I am now writing. The first little town is Marble Hill where it is said round stones are quarried. Majestically the proud ship moves on meeting in her course several steamers among which are the "Bostona", "Forest Rose" and "Emma Duncan" and others. No doubt steam boat traveling is pleasant where a person is comfortably quartered but going as soldiers and faring as soldiers is not at all pleasant. Arrived at Louisville at sunset but were ordered across the river to

a camp near Jeffersonville which is called "Camp Gilbert." I lay down this evening with the tooth ache, headache and heart burn and not very well generally.

Tuesday September 23rd 1862
Pitched tents this morning in "Camp Gilbert." Jesse D. Bright is said to own the farm. All day long I have suffered intensely with the toothache, This evening I had the tooth extracted which threw me into a violent fever and headache. The regiment is again under marching orders, but I am unable to go. Draw knapsacks. All is confusion getting ready to start. It is reported that the enemy are marching upon Louisville. I do not, however, credit the report. But, should it be the case the city will never be surrendered to them. Never while a single guard of patriots remain to impede their progress. Never while there is a drop of patriotic blood to be spilled by the advancing bayonet of the foe and along with the last life struggle to their knees to impede their forward movement.

Wednesday September 24th 1862
Arose this morning feeling much better though passed a very uncomfortable night. Went down town and breakfasted, Wrote home. As yet I have received no word. Why it is I cannot tell. Some fault in the mail perhaps. In the afternoon I took a stroll down the river. Came to the penitentiary. Through the kindness of Mr. Miller the Warden I was shown through the building, I learned from him that there were about 20 convicts. I saw the youth and grey haired sage, but a majority of them were middle-aged men. Most of them were busy. All kinds of manufacturing is carried on but cooperage seems to be the principal business. As I came away I was impressed with the conviction that I would much prefer to wear a soldier's uniform than be uniformed with a convict's garb, though to speak the truth so far as hardships are concerned the soldier far surpasses the convict.

Thursday September 25th 1862
Last night the 101st Ohio Regiment came in and quartered in our tents. Accommodated them as well as we could. Toward a soldier I feel as though he is my brother battling for the same cause, "our country." Though I am sorry to say that some of them I am ashamed to own as even being Union Soldiers. All kinds of wickedness are carried on. It would be idle for me to even attempt a description of the vices of camp life. As cleanliness is essential to good health, those of us who were left behind concluded to do up some clothes washing. Accordingly I was dispatched to the river after

water while another went after a wash tub and board. I need not add that it was done up in a neat and womanly style. At twilight I am seated on the trunk of an upturned oak beneath the banks of the placid Ohio, Away up the river I hear the soul enlivening strains of music issuing from the steamer "Florence" as she slowly and proudly approaches. Is there anything more calculated to drive away dull melancholy than music. 'Tis sweet at merry eventide, though absent from the dear music of home to catch the enlivening strains as they are wafted on the evening zephyrs across the unrippled waters to the shore. Wrote a letter to Lute Adair.

Friday September 26th 1862
Teams came over this morning to take the tents and baggage. After assisting to lead I walked down to the river landing crossed over in the steamer ferry boat "Isaac Bowman" walked up through the city of Louisville to the encampment of the 86th. Just as I arrived on the ground the regiment was on the point of leaving. I shouldered my gun and was off with them. After marching up Broadway for about two miles we came to a halt and laid down for the night on the pavement.

Saturday September 27th 1862
Went into camp. A little sprinkle of rain fell. Received seven letters from Indiana. Better believe I was glad.

Sunday September 28th 1862
I am sorry to say it yet I did forget that this morning was Sunday. I feel considerably under the weather. Why it is I cannot tell. Have not heard a sermon for two weeks. Wish I could again enter the church door at Thorntown. Today seems to be a day of general rejoicing among the boys of the old regiments. I saw many old friends.

Monday September 29th 1862
Today visited the encampment of the 10th. Saw John G. Davis and Elisha Little, old friends with whom I became intimately associated in other days. Elisha came over with me and remained all night. Hear Jesse Hill, chaplain of the 72nd preach a short discourse. Jesse Welch, E. Little and myself slept under a tree near the tent.

Tuesday September 30 1862
Went over to see Frank who has been left at the hospital. I found him better and glad to get away. After visiting the 10th and 15th we wended our way

slowly to camp.

Wednesday October 1st 1862
Truly, "The melancholy days have come the saddest of the year." "Marching orders!" Tents are struck and the "long roll" is called. Our regiment is out in line all ready to go. "Forward march" is the order and off we start. We start out the Bardstown Pike where we meet with a large force all going the same way. Buell's army moving after Bragg. I have to fall out of ranks and go it on my own hoof as I am almost "gone up". Through the kindness of Jim Cockram who had charge of the ordnance team I was permitted to ride a couple of miles. The army halted to camp for the night but I cannot find my regiment. I begin to think about lying down somewhere to rest during the night. Beneath the branches of a white walnut tree on the banks of a little brook in company with Jesse Welch I find myself resting for the night.

Thursday October 2nd 1862
The morning dawneth. Daylight peepeth over the eastern hills. I awoke from my slumbers and found myself all right. I started on with nothing to eat but hard crackers for my breakfast. I learned from the teamsters that the regiment was a couple of miles ahead. Through the kindness of a straggling Pennsylvania Cavalryman I was permitted to ride a mile which relieved me much. Overtook the regiment but was soon on the move again. Two of our pickets were shot last night by the enemy. I saw their graves. Heavy skirmishing in front. Marched about 4 miles when went into camp. A rainy night by the way which made it very disagreeable.

Friday October 3rd 1862
Breakfasted this morning on hard crackers and coffee. At about 11 o'clock we resumed our march. Crossed a little stream upon whose banks we encamped last night we wound around a circuitous route for about 18 miles when we halted in a field on the banks of Salt River. Again compelled to fall by the wayside. Rode a few miles in the ambulance. The country along the route is gently undulating though in some places it may be said to be hilly. It is a fine farming country and the grain produced is not surpassed anywhere, yet not withstanding all this the country is not well watered. I lay down for the night on a pile of straw.

Saturday October 4th 1862
As we encamped last night on the banks of Salt River I improved the opportunity of bathing in its waters which was quite refreshing to the outer

man. On the move at 8 o'clock. Soon after starting I saw a man tied to a tree labeled with the word "Thief". The country through which we pass today is beautiful. The soil is fertile producing grain equally with any country I have ever seen. Leave the main pike and took the Boonesboro road. After reaching a little town called Fairfield which is about 10 miles from last night's encampment struck off in the direction of Bardstown. I learn that a severe skirmish took place with our advance guard near Bardstown. Several prisoners taken. Our regiment was placed on picket duty. Twelve were detached from each company to stand at the outposts. I laid down supperless and very tired.

Sunday October 5th 1862

Again the Sabbath dawns but with it comes no churchgoing bell. The good do not meet to worship God as in other and happier days. Here the day is used as though it was not designed for any special use. The regiment is again on the move. Make our grand entrance into Bardstown where it is said the enemy a few hours before had possession of the place. I learned from citizens as I passed through that yesterday they were retreating toward Lexington with about 30,000 strong. The Union sentiment was not strong, yet in a few instances the ladies were out waving their handkerchiefs and the "Red White and Blue." Heaven bless the loyal ladies of Bardstown. Out we go on the Lexington Pike in hot pursuit of the enemy. Leave the main pike and take a by-road for the purpose of intercepting the rebels, who it is said are on their way back to Louisville. Halted in a field to rest. Went to a spring near by to replenish my canteen. Ben Compton spying a pig took a notion to have some fresh meat whereupon a bayonet was thrust into the heart of porky and life was extinct. Cut out a ham and put in my haversack to have a roast when we go into camp. Pass through a beautiful wood principally composed of poplar though it is interspersed with chestnut hickory and Lynn. The soil is fertile. Again I fell by the way. Reached the regiment about 10 o'clock which was encamped near a little town called Glennville 12 miles from Bardstown.

Monday October 6th 1862

On the march again this morning but I was quite unwell last night and therefore feel much unlike going, However, I start like the ballance of the boys. I am without rations. Very sick and compelled to stop in an old orchard where I lay the remainder of the afternoon. Frank was with me. Toward evening I succeeded in getting to a house a half a mile distant, and partook of the hospitalities of the inmates. I learned from the gentleman of the house whose name was Huntly(?) that he was reared in Illinois. He seemed to be a gentleman in every aspect a withal a good Union man notwithstanding he is the owner of 18 slaves. Country is rough and broken in travels today.

Tuesday October 7th 1862
I feel better this morning although I passed a very uncomfortable night. After breakfasting and paying off our bill started slowly along taking my own time. After traveling some miles we halted at the roadside where we met with some Union Ladies who had the kindness to present me an apple and a couple of peaches. Arriving within a mile of Springfield I met with some of the boys who informed me that the regiment was still on the move. Late in the evening I had the opportunity of a conversation with some "secesh" paroled prisoners. They conversed freely and was very affable in their manners. They said they were glad to get away and no money would induce them to go back to the secesh army. They report that two-thirds of their soldiers utter the same sentiments.

Wednesday October 8th 1862
Last night I lay down in the rear yard of a widow lady of whom the soldiers had taken everything. Went up to Springfield which was about a mile and called for breakfast at what is said to be a Union hotel. Paid 50 cents for a meal that oft times I would have turned away from. Springfield is 60 miles from Louisville. In company with Wells and Frank I started on with the intention of regaining the regiment but soon found that we were not able to go. Through the advice of a "darkey slave" we slowly wended our way to Judge Brooker's who I was informed by the "darkey" was a "strong Union man." We called for something to eat. In a husky tone he inquired why we did not receive our rations from the commissary. We told him the reason. He, however, gave us dinner but that then we must go on as fast as we could. Stung to the heart we ate our dinner and started on. We soon found we could not go and again inquired for a Union house. Again we were directed to what we supposed must be a good Union house. Our reception was much cooler than at Judge Brooker's. Hungry and tired and sick we lay down under a tree to rest for the night. Did not rest well.

Thursday October 9th 1862
Started again this morning without breakfast thinking perhaps I will find something by the way to eat. After traveling a couple of miles and finding nothing we came to a secesh hospital. As a matter of course we were turned away there. Not knowing what to do we chanced upon Dr. Voorhees who

advised us to go back to Springfield where Dr. Elliott was lying sick. We turned our faces thetherward but were so weak from hunger that we could not go. Happening upon a man who lived a quarter mile from the pike we laid our cases before him and begged him to give us a little of something to eat. He told us he was a very poor man and that the armies had taken everything from him, but he would do the best he could for us, having bought ten pounds of flour the evening before to keep his children from starvation. Accordingly we went with the man who conducted us into a dirty hovel where I partook of some unshortened bread and milk for which I paid 25 cents. This somewhat satisfied my hunger and I made my way back to Mr. Wharton's near Springfield. Through the kindness of Dr. Elliott who interceded for us we succeeded in getting permission to remain with him till we recruited our health. Mr. Wharton with whom we are stopping is a whole souled and generous man and does all in his power to render us comfortable. He is a good Union man and has two sons in the Federal Army. This part of Kentucky is broken and hilly though corn is raised to good advantage. As yet in all my travels in Kentucky I have not seen a school house. Public enterprise is on the decline. Why this is I cannot tell unless the cause be that of the institution of slavery. Couriers from Perryville say that a desperate battle is in progress at that place. Heavy loss on both sides.

86th Indiana Regiment Volunteer Infantry

"The Gilded Puddle"

Perhaps the pursuit of Bragg's army by that of Buell's, taken as a whole, was the hardest and most trying march any Union army was forced to endure during the entire war. The army was not then supplied with the light and convenient shelter tents which it afterward carried. The bulk and unhandiness of the Sibleys made them no better than no tents, for either the wagons were never up with them, or the men were too tired to handle them at night when they reached camp. Therefore, they slept constantly without tents, exposed to the night air, in good and bad weather, in rain and in snow, and felt the full force of all the changes of weather.

The great exertion during the day heated their bodies and the cool nights chilled and stiffened their joints and bound their muscles. These things with the inexperience and the extreme scarcity of water, together with the very bad quality of most of it that could be procured, rendered the march a continual struggle for existence, and epoch in one's life to be remembered. It was a very

common, almost daily, occurrence to find
- "the gilded puddle
Which beasts would cough at,"
the only supply of water to furnish drink and from which to procure enough
to make a pot of coffee. Those of delicate nervous systems and dainty
stomachs, with a thought of home, its healthy food and drink, and even
delicacies, would sicken at the sight of a putrefying mule, half submerged in
the pond of water where they were compelled to get their supply.

The thought of a good, cool drink from the pure water of the well at home
would cause them to turn with unutterable disgust from this festering filth with
its green scum. Such men were already more than half beaten without the
suspicion of the smell of gun powder. Others, however, of firmer fibre,
stauncher mold, and iron nerve, and a resolution that would never say "hold,
enough," parted the thick green scum, filled the canteen, shut their eyes and
drank deeply of the water as it washed back and over the festering animal
matter, set in motion as it was by the dipping of many canteens. Such material
makes invincible soldiers, as near, at least, as human beings can be called
invincible. Of such material was the Army of the Cumberland composed.

Father Abraham at Washington had no better, truer, soldiers than those of
this old army after the chaff was winnowed from it. All the Eighty-sixth now
lacked to complete the test was the baptism of fire - the battle's storm and
hail to finish in every particular its initiation. In looking back over this trip
through Kentucky after Bragg's army it is with horror that one thinks of the
abominable character of the drinking water, the scant rations and the general
treatment the men received. It is a wonder that so many endured it and
survived.

Friday October 10th 1862

Rested very well during the night but still feel weak. Saw Mr. Rosseau a
brother of the General. He seems to be gentleman of much information.
Today I have been perusing "Harper's Monthly Magazine." The house at
which I am stopping bears the impress of having seen better and happier
days. I learn that just a few short months ago the house was blessed with a
wife & mother. She was stricken by the hand of disease and was laid in the
cold earth. Soon after an only daughter said to be beautiful and
accomplished, too, passed away. Traces are left to show that she was
educated. Her books and magazines are left untouched. The piano that she
so oft has cheered the family circle with strains of sweetest music is now

heard no more. A young man aged about 16 is left to cheer the old man who is tottering for the grave. Like many others he has taken to the bowl to drown his sorrow. Wrote home. A sprinkle of rain fell which made glad the earth.

Saturday October 11th 1862
Truly   "The melancholy days have come
              The saddest of the year
          Of wailing winds and naked woods
              And meadows brown and sear."
Those beautiful lines of W. C. Bryant never before struck me more forcibly than today. What a melancholy day! Still at Mr. Wharton's. Write letters to Lide Gibson and Anna Cones.

Sunday October 12th 1862
This morning I took my departure from the house of Mr. Wharton where I had been hospitably entertained for a few days. While I take my gun on my shoulder the friends at home are preparing for the duties of this holy day. I long for the time to come when I shall mingle my voice again with those I most love. Today for the first time in all my travels in Kentucky which has been about 75 miles I see a school house. As I near Perryville I come on the field where a few days before a hard fought battle was contested. O the horrors of the battlefield. All the houses in and around Perryville are used as hospitals. I went to the door of a few of them. There I beheld the wounded and dying at the sight of which my heart sickens. A dead rebel was lying at the roadside as yet unburied. He had fallen away from home and among strangers. In an evil hour he had raised the arm of rebellion against the government which had protected him and he died the death of a rebel.
Passed through Perryville and stopped at a secession house to stay all night.

Monday October 13th 1862
Resumed my journey this morning, Passed through beautiful country, indeed the most beautiful I have seen in Kentucky. Regained the regiment about 3 o'clock. Glad to see the boys again. The usual routine of camp life commences which to me is very monotonous.

Tuesday October 14th 1862
Encamped last night on the lands of Gen. Boyle within a mile of Danville, by the way a beautiful camping ground. Again on the move. Pass through the beautiful town of Danville. Feel quite unwell as a consequence of which I am compelled to fall out of ranks. The country through which we pass is the

garden spot of Kentucky. The next town is Stanford the County Seat of Lincoln County. About sunset I, in company with Frank and Pitman, stop at a house in Stanford for the purpose of getting something to eat. It proved to be the residence of Dr. Huffman who was post surgeon at Stanford but now a Union refugee. Mrs. Huffman politely invited us to stay during the night at which request we acceded. In a few moments Dr. Huffman returned home after an absence of six weeks. Very sick during the night.

Wednesday October 15th 1862
After bidding Dr. Huffman and his family adieu feeling very grateful for their entertainment we resumed our march. Hear cannonading ahead. Supposed to be skirmishing at Crab Orchard. Soon after starting I come in contact with the rear guard which came very near raising old "nick" in me as big as a dog. Shoulder straps make men tyrants. Remove them and they have lost their patriotism. Deliver me from ever being a shoulder strapped tyrant.

Thursday October 16th 1862
I am more concerned that the war is prolonged on account of officers making a speculation, Hundreds are following the army for the mere purpose of making money. The officers have caught the mania and with many of them money is a greater incentive than patriotism. I am led to exclaim "How long O Lord, will this state of things continue?" The Prayer of every Christian heart should be "Cut us not off in our wickedness." Wood's division is remaining status quo and I go to the 40th to encamp.

Friday October 17th 1862
As we can hear nothing positive of the whereabouts of our regiment we go in search of Jesse Welch who is lying sick somewhere on the road. Going back the distance of perhaps four miles met with Rev. Mr. Harker who informed me that the regiment was 10 or 12 miles ahead. He advised us to go on. Lay down for the night under an oak tree.

Saturday October 18th 1862
This morning I am slowly wending my way toward the regiment. Before coming to Gen Buell's Headquarters I was advised to go around as he was arresting all stragglers. Accordingly we start around to avoid being arrested. Scaled some of the loftiest hills in Kentucky. From their summits methinks I could speak to the world of the debauchery, crime, corruption and misery connected with this war. I succeeded in getting around without being molested. Encamped for the night under a tree.

Sunday October 19th 1862
Early this beautiful Sabbath morning we resume our march. Pass through Mount Vernon the Co. seat of Rock Castle County. It contains 20 to 25 houses most of which are very much dilapidated. Pass over hill and dale for about 4 or 5 miles when I come to the teams of the 86th and where the regiment was encamped a day or two. Remained there during the night.

Chapter Three
The Wildcat Hills

Monday October 20th 1862
On the move again this morning in pursuit of the regiment. On the way I meet with Lieut. Thomas who is going home. I stop by the way and send a line home. In the evening we overtake the regiment which is encamped in the "Wildcat" battlefield. Here it was that the rebel Gen. Zolicoffer was repulsed by the federals one year ago.

Tuesday October 21st 1862
I feel better this morning. Today I came across a stray volume of the "Young Ladies' Magazine," a periodical of much merit published at Nashville Tenn. which did me much good to peruse its pages. Among the articles I read was "The Lone Grave." It was indeed touching. I could hardly refrain from weeping as I compared the circumstances of the stranger traveler and the stranger soldier. How many of our poor soldiers die by the way with no sympathetic hand of father mother sister brother or wife to soothe their dying pains. Another article which struck me forcibly was "Let me die among my kindred." Is not this the prayer of every soldier in the field today? How bitter the thought to think of dying away from home among strangers in a strange land where we are surrounded with none but the cold and heartless. On the other hand how cheering the thought to know that we will die "among our kindred." From the depths of my heart this is my prayer "Let me die among my kindred" It is announced that our company goes out on picket. Accordingly all things are ready and off we start. After going about a mile we come to a halt and half the company are placed at posts while the other half is held as reserve.

Wednesday October 22nd 1862
This morning the reserve relieved the first half. About noon I am placed at a picket post on the brow of one of the loftiest hills in Kentucky. The hill is studded with numerous pine trees. When the zephyrs of October breathe through their leafy boughs a melancholy music is poured forth on the air. Aerial hues & alternate lights and shades magically adorn their atmospheric heights and paint the declivities with charming hues and rainbow tints and conclusively the legends of the simple inhabitants of these hills all concur to excite our most exulting admiration, and form a rich inheritance for minds possessing the talents of deep and vivid imagination. Metaphorically speaking these hills are the monuments of eternity. I was soon relieved of

my post when in company with Frank and Lieut. Doster I went farther up & stood on a craggy cliff, fearfully projecting forward and glittering in the rays of the noonday sun. As far as the eye could reach is one continual range of hills rearing their cloud crested heads toward the throne of the Great Eternal. This scene presents an immutable picture, especially the beautifully sloping valleys which are surrounded by a transparent haze occasioned by the burning forest. Their peaceful dells and quiet halls are immersed in a flood of mellow light illumining their secret recesses with mystical beauty. As I quit the spot my mind involuntarily reverts to the Eastern Continental mountain ranges where they have been of inestimable benefit in preserving the liberties of countries. Such may be the case now. If it is the soldier volunteer and the Great Rebellion of 1861 and the mountains of Kentucky will stand intimately connected on the pages of history.

Thursday October 23rd 1862
Feel quite well this morning. About noon the army commences to retrace its steps. At double quick we start off. About 15 miles nearer home we encamped for the night. Stopped in Mount Vernon and got my supper.

Friday October 24th 1862
During the night I was very sick. The regiment starts off toward Somerset which is about 25 miles distant. Rode in the ambulance. Encamped in the woods after traveling over one of the roughest roads in Ky.

Saturday October 25th 1862
On the move again. Rode in a wagon and rode all day. Nothing worthy of note occurred on the route today. Commenced snowing after going into camp which is about half a mile west of Somerset. Slept in the hospital tent. The country in the vicinity of Somerset is very rough.

Sunday October 26th 1862
Arose this morning and found the ground covered with snow to the depth of about five inches. The woods are ringing with the click of the soldier's ax preparing shelters from the chilling blasts of a sudden winter. Passed the day very uncomfortable.

86th Regiment, Indiana Volunteer Infantry, abridged

Kentucky Applejack

Heading for Nashville in October, 1862, the regiment was in the mountainous region of Kentucky called the Wild Cat Hills. Having come from the flatlands of Indiana, the men were not used to the terrain. Added to this the lack of proper food, clothing and shelter, along with the long marches for only recently initiated men, many soldiers were straggling behind.

Unused to heavy loads, they would first stop to rearrange the items in the knapsacks, then to throw out some of the items, then some pitched knapsacks and all into the ditches. One morning after bivouac in the wood, the men awoke to tree limbs crashing about them, with some men being injured. Six inches of snow had fallen, weighting down the brittle limbs.

The men cut trees for fuel and shelter. But here bad weather caught them unawares, and the severe exposure increased the number of sick among those already greatly exhausted and worn out by the long continued marching, and its many privations and extreme hardships. A temporary hospital was established in Somerset to take care of the sick and wounded, but the command did not stay there, and resumed the march, reaching Columbia on the 31st.

The usual routine was somewhat altered due to the supply of applejack, and those who wanted it had a little more leisure to look for it, so those disposed to imbibe freely were sometime slow about reaching camp and were often inclined to be boisterous when they did reach it. Others were 'too full for utterance' and navigation, and tarried by the way-side until the mighty influence of the 'jack' had abated its control. Then they came to camp soberly and demurely. Poor fellows, they looked badly enough, and no doubt they felt even worse than they looked."

Monday October 27th 1862
The sun arose beautiful this morning. As it is rumored that we will stay in camp today I prepare to wash my only shirt. Dry it and put it on. Wrote a letter for Jesse Welch who came up to the regiment yesterday.

Tuesday October 28th 1862
Had orders to march at 1/2 past 6. On the move at the appointed time. After traveling perhaps six miles the regiment came to a stand still and remained in status quo till night. Came across I. R. Dean an old student of

Thorntown who is in the 21st Kentucky. Had a long and pleasant conversation with him about "old times" etc. Near Sunset the regiment again started. Passed over the battlefield of Mill Springs. This battle was fought on the 19th of Jan. last. Here is was that the rebel Gen. Zolicoffer was killed and the rebels generally routed. Encamped for the night near this place.

Wednesday October 29th 1862
Off again this morning at "double quick." Nothing of importance occurred along the way worthy of note. Stopped about the middle of the afternoon. Something uncommon.

Thursday October 30th 1862
Nothing occurred today to change the monotony of the tramp. The country through which we have been traveling for the past few days is very poor. The soil being of a yellow clay color. Scrubby timber is the prevailing production of the earth. Farms are few and far between.

Friday October 31st 1862
Columbia being only 5 miles distant from last night's encampment we soon reach this point. Drew overcoats and dress coats. Wrote letters this afternoon.

86th Regiment, Indiana Volunteer Infantry, abridged

Col. Hamilton Organizes the 86th

*T*he morning after reaching Columbia, clothing was issued to the Eighty-sixth. The simpletons, nearly to a man, drew overcoats and dress coats, and many of them other articles of clothing. These men already had a sufficient load to carry. Since leaving Louisville the men had thrown away fully one-half of their loads, and now were again loaded as fully as they had been previously.

Leaving Columbia early, the weather was cool and most of the men put on their dress coats and overcoats thinking that the easiest way to carry them. The heat increased with the march until it became quite warm. Soon the men were sweating at every pore, but there was no time given to adjust loads.

Hard marching at unabated speed caused many men to give out and fall behind. When the regiment halted about 3 o'clock, there were only 140 men to stack arms. Col. Hamilton looked at the men in blank amazement as they stood in ranks before him. Then he became angry, growing hotter and hotter until he was in a terrible rage.

He charged back on the incoming stragglers swearing that he would arrest and punish every one of them. He then ordered their arrest and all were collected under a large tree in an open space just to the rear of the regimental line where all could see and hear. He continued to rage and swear and tell them of the terrible punishment to come. It was a perfect volley of epithets and abuse.

It was fun for the boys who came in on time, and for some who were in the arrested squad, but quite a serious matter for others. Most of them knew the Colonel as a hot-headed but kindly natured man who would relent, and take it all back when his anger had cooled.

He soon had 200 men under the tree and would gallop his charger in a furious manner upon every new arrival. He fumed, fretted, chafed and frothed. One supposed he would have them all shot at sunrise. At length his anger began to cool and he gave up in disgust and told them to go to their companies, but threatened "the direst punishment" upon future stragglers.

The tirade of the Colonel against the boys occasioned much merriment for those who were watching the circus at a safe distance. The affair was known as "the organization of the Eighty-Sixth Regiment by Colonel Hamilton."

Saturday November 1st 1862
Continued our march. Passed through Edmondton the County Seat of Metcalf County. Encamped for the night on the banks of a stream which bore the name of Russel's Creek. Had mush for supper. Had my dress coat and haversack burned.

Sunday November 2nd 1862
On tramp again. Today I have thought much of home and its sweet associations. How I could enjoy a Sunday out of camp! O for the time to come when I shall be freed from living the life of a soldier and live as a Christian and a civilized man.

Monday November 3rd 1862
Passed through Glasgow and encamped on Beaver Creek about four miles from the town. Here the mail came to us. Received letters from Mattie, Mollie and Sallie also Lide. Glad to hear from them.. Writing letters.

Tuesday November 4th 1862
Remained in camp today washing clothes.. Wrote letters to Gustie Haworth sweet little girl and Lide Gibson. Dr. Elliott resigned. Goes home in the morning.. Frank is very sick.

Wednesday November 5th 1862
On march again. I am compelled to leave Frank who is very sick. He goes to the hospital. Dear friends must separate however closely they may be attached to each other. Marched fifteen miles today to the Gallatin Pike.

Thursday November 6th 1862
Encamped last night on Peter's Creek. A small sprinkle of rain fell last night but the morning is beautiful. Got meal and milk along the way and had mush and milk for supper.

Friday November 7th 1862
Encamped near Scottsville the Co. seat of Allen Co. Cool and cloudy. Snowing nearly all day. Crossed the Tennessee line. Couldn't perceive any peculiar emotions on entering a seceded State. The first school house I see in this state is an old log shanty. The whole length of a log is taken out on either side for the windows. As usual, no school. The country here is but little better than in Kentucky.

Saturday November 8th 1862
Started early this morning with the intention of going 25 miles. It wearied me much. My first day's travel in Tennessee produced no peculiar sensations. Passed through some beautiful country. Gallatin is the first town of importance. Everything bears the impress of decay. The white population has vamosed and nothing but darkies are left on the streets. The sidewalks are overgrown with grass, revealing at once the great evils of war, that of depopulating flourishing towns and cities. Encamped near the Cumberland River.

Sunday November 9th 1862
The morning is beautiful. Not a cloud to be seen. The haziness which pervades the atmosphere reminds me very much of an October morning at home. Thoughts of home and its dear associations - associations in the family, social and class circle run at random through my mind. Why am I deprived of them all? Simply in defence of Justice and Liberty.

Monday November 10 1862
On march again this morning. Moving in the direction of Lebanon
Tennessee. Crossed the Cumberland River. This is a beautiful stream. Its
waters are clear and swift. How loathe the soldier was to leave its liquid
wave, perhaps the next sip to be taken from a mud puddle. Halted at a little
village called Silver Springs.

Tuesday November 11th 1862
Remained in camp today. The day is a beautiful one. The sun shines
beautifully. All nature seems to have put on a smile, perhaps only to cheer
the weary soldier as the gloomy hours pass.

Wednesday November 12th 1862
Rainy morning. Nature seems to have changed her garb which so beautifully
adorned her person yesterday. The cold November rains are falling. Dull
melancholy pervades all nature. Today a soldier, a member of Company B,
died. A few short months ago he left home buoyant with the hope that he
would again mingle his voice with those he left behind. But he was stricken
by the hand of disease and his remains now lie "alone" on the gory soil of
Tennessee. Those beautiful lines of the poet can now be fully appreciated
commencing:
  "Soldier, rest, thy warfare o'er
    Sleep the sleep that knows no breaking."
Yes, "Wm. Rose, Co B, 86th Regiment Ind. Vol." is sleeping the sleep that
knows no breaking. He has gone to rest.

Thursday November 13th 1862
Again the sun sheds a brilliant lustre over the earth. Still in camp not
knowing when we will move. I have thought much today on the subject of
a "soldier's life" - the toils, hardships and privations connected therewith,
especially how little sympathy is manifested on the part of one soldier toward
another. Few are the words spoken to cheer the sick and toil worn soldier.
How often do we hear it from the lips of a fellow soldier in regard to some
poor fellow who can scarcely drag his weary body along that he is "playing
off" or some such language. My heart has been made to ache by such
remarks in regard to those whom I knew were really not able to be up. O
for a fellow-friend who can sympathize with the sufferings of a soldier.
Today another soldier went to rest. One by one as the leaves of the forest
they fall, yet no tears are shed to consecrate the spot where they lie. Near
our camp is situated the house of God. The good do not meet to worship

as in other days but instead one grand military encampment is seen. It seems that the Bible has been exchanged for the sword.

Friday November 14th 1862
Another beautiful morning dawns. Went out on company drill. Remained perhaps a couple of hours when we returned to camp. Soon after received orders to go out on picket which is a change in the monotony of the camp. Stationed at a post in charge of three men. Relieved at twilight, Passed the time in eating persimmons, cracking walnuts and perusing old letters from "dear ones at home." There is something in reading old letters which renders it a pleasant and agreeable task. Why it is I cannot tell.

Chapter Four
Silver Springs and Rural Hills

Saturday November 15th 1862
And still another bright and beautiful morning dawneth. Relieved from picket this morning and returned to camp. Soon after had marching order. Marched perhaps ten miles south of Silver Springs and halted on "Rural Hills." The country through which we pass is very rough being an almost unbroken forest of Cedar.

Sunday November 16th 1862
Another Sunday morning is here yet I hear no church-going bell. Near the encampment is an old camp meeting ground and in the same enclosure is the burying ground. Both are in a dilapidated condition. I visited them this afternoon. The stones that mark the spot where the dead lie is nothing but limestone rudely hewn out. It is a lonely spot and I did not linger long among the tombs. I next went to the campground where a spacious roofing is erected for the chapel It has the semblance of happier days, Years ago when the good met beneath this roof to worship God little did they there think that the picture would change and instead of bowing at the sacred alter they would with upraised arms strike at the best government to world has ever seen - the government that protected them to worship here according to the dictates of their own conscience no one daring to molest them. Yet the picture is changed. Instead of witnessing the assembled throng worshipping with Bible and hymn book they are using the sword and rifle, instead of witnessing fruitful fields and a peaceful people, the picture presents desolated fields watered by the blood of the inhabitants.

Monday November 17th 1862
A dull gloomy morning. A haziness pervades the atmosphere. All day long it seemed as though the funeral of the year was approaching. In the evening the mail came in. Each countenance was lighted up as in expectation to hear news from home. Anxiously they awaited the distribution of the letters and papers. Then might have been seen a half a dozen surrounding a small camp fire reading the "missives" from dear ones at home. Then came the comments thereon, etc. There is nothing that cheers the heart of the weary soldier so much as letters from home. It lifts the fainting spirits and brings new life to his drowsy hours. Wish I could get letters oftener.

Tuesday November 18th 1862
This morning we were suddenly aroused by whack, bang, whack bang in the direction of our pickets which soon brought us into line of battle. They were attacked by the enemy and the indications were good for a hot time. But as luck would have it at the point where they made the attack we had been reinforced the night before by the 8th Kentucky. They supposing it to be our whole division retreated. The "dogs of war were let loose upon them and they instantly vamoosed." The enemy lost fourteen killed wounded unknown. Our loss none though three prisoners were taken. I must confess that at first I felt somewhat streaked, but I soon became calm and collected and didn't care whether the lads came in or not.

Wednesday November 19th 1862
Rainy morning. Wrote a letter to Annie Cones and had just commenced to write Sallie and Mollie Fdwards when the brigade had marching orders. Not withstanding the heavy rain in progress we were soon in line awaiting the order "Forward march." Soon the tug of war came, Splash, splash, splash through the mud about shoe mouth deep for about 10 miles when we halted on the bank of Stone River 9 miles east of Nashville. Very tired when we went into camp. Had a mess of sweet potatoes for supper.

Thursday November 20th 1862
This morning our company was ordered on picket duty. Reserve stationed south of camp. At 11 o'clock I was placed at a post to be relieved every four hours. While there I mused upon the past. I reviewed my past life. Thought of the many "ups and downs" through which I have passed, together with the happy hours and pleasant scenes that have been intermingled. My next relief was the lone starry hour of midnight. O what a sacred hour is this. A spellbound silence reigns. I read in the volume of the past. I read of infancy then manhood. Of infancy's unclouded sky of manhood's stern realities. I opened the Great Volume of the future but I could not read. I tried again but its pages were written in characters that I could not understand. I closed the volume and concluded to wait for time to unfold its mystical pages.

Friday November 20th 1862
The weather is cool and cloudy. Relieved from picket duty by Co. G. Came to camp. Had orders to march. Struck tents. Loaded the wagons. Started them off guarded by Co. B. Fell into line. Marched a couple of hundred yards. "About faced." Marched back. Put on as "Corporal of the guard." Pitched tents. Cooked supper and concluded to remain over night. Received

a letter from Mattie Sayler. Wrote. Prof. Smith.

Saturday November 22nd 1862
The night was cool and clear with frost. Relieved from guard. Wrote Jo Foxworthy a letter. Quite an excitement was created in camp this morning by the 44th Ind. firing off their guns. The 86th supposed it to be the enemy upon. Such a jumping into line with gun in hand I have not witnessed since I have been in the war. The afternoon witnessed a flag presentation. It was presented to the 13th Ohio by the ladies at home for bravery and courage displayed on the fields of "Carnifex Ferry" and "Shiloh." The presentation address was short and appropriate and as the speaker unfolded its folds in the air a patriotic thrill pervaded the hearts of all the soldiers present. I thought of those lines of the poet:
    "Flag of the free heart's only home
    By angel hands to valor given
    The stars have lit the welkin dome
    And all thy hues were born in heaven."
When the clamorous trumpet of war is hushed and the soldiers of the 13th Ohio have retired from the clangor of arms and the drum rolls a peaceful hurra it will then be cheering to look on the old flag that has wreathed a garland of victory and placed it upon the brow of the soldier volunteer.

Sunday November 23rd 1862
The Holy Sabbath is again here. It is a lovely Sabbath morning. The sun sheds a brilliancy over the earth. Wrote a letter for Enoch Watkins to his family. Took dinner with him. In the afternoon heard a sermon by the Chaplain of the 11th Kentucky. How soul cheering were the hymns the soldiers sung on the occasion commencing.
    "How happy every child of grace
      Who knows his sins forgiven
    This earth he cries is not my place
      I seek my place in heaven"
Cheering thought to the Christians to know this weary earth is not his home but he has a place in heaven.

Monday November 24th 1862
Again ordered on picket. Wrote letters, For the first time since I entered the State of Tennessee I sat down and partook a meal cooked by a woman. She was strong for the Union as was manifested by their actions. I shall long remember Mrs. Wolford the first woman with whom I ate in Tennessee. Received a letter from Frank Cones and Jesse Welch. Glad to hear from

them. Sorry to hear of their continued ill health.

Tuesday November 25th 1862
Took breakfast at the house of Mr. Wolford. Relieved from picket by Co, H. Came back to camp. Received a letter from Annie Cones also a line from sweet little Ona. Writing letters. Put a pocket in my overcoat - a necessity by the way. Marching orders but I think I will stay till morning.

Wednesday November 26th 1862
Advanced today to within a couple of miles of Nashville. What the next movement will be I know not. Received a letter from Frank Cones and Jesse Welch in which I learn that they and Pitman will be discharged.

Thursday November 27th 1862
Wrote a letter for Dock Adair who is very sick. Received a letter from W. A. Haworth. It did me much good to hear from him. I learn from him that Rev. Mr. Warner is teaching school at Morrison's S.H. Wrote an answer.

Friday November 28th 1862
The country in the immediate vicinity of Nashville is delightful just such a one as I would like to live in were it not for the curse of human slavery. The climate is mild which makes it very pleasant indeed. "Marching orders." Traveled perhaps 4 miles when the brigade halted near the Lunatic Asylum on the Murfreesboro road. The country through which we pass is fine. In every direction in which the eye can turn are beautiful farms - presenting to the vision a scenery that poets and painters would delight to look upon. It seems as though that Rock and hill and brook and vale has charms for the imagination.

Saturday November 29th 1862
Nothing worthy of note occurred today to relieve the dull monotony of the camp. Night reading in the Bible. While reading I thought I could adopt the lines commencing:
"This book is all that's left me now
    Tears will unbidden start
With faltering lip and throbbing brow
    I press it to my heart."

Sunday November 30th 1862
Cloudy morning. Spent most of the day in reading the pages of Sacred Writ.

This day closes the season of Autumn. The old year is fast ebbing away.

Monday December 1st 1862
Grey haireth winter is here. He came last night. I did not know when he came but when I arose this morning he introduced himself. It was a cool reception but think in all probability we will become tolerably well acquainted before three months shall pass away. Last night a heavy rain storm visited our encampment. Occasionally a soldier meets with "actions" and "orders" that are a great bore. All ordered out for general inspection but returned without the glimpse of an inspector.

Tuesday December 2nd 1862
Yesterday the 86th was ordered on picket. My company was stationed about two miles from camp on the banks of a little meandering stream which ran through a beautiful wood. It was gently undulating which made it a pleasant situation. A melancholy silence pervades, yet for all this I love such a day in winter. Wrote letters to Annie Cones. Many are the vices incident to camp life & prominent among them is card playing. Since I entered the army I have been indeed surprised to see so much of it carried on. Men too, professing to be followers of Him whose Divine injunction is against all such engage in it & when reproved the devil whispers in their ear "there's no harm in it." O for men who have the stamina to resist the temptations incident to camp life - who have the principles of Christianity so instilled in their souls that the world the flesh and the devil cannot prevail against them.

Wednesday December 3rd 1862
The morning is clear but cool. Ordered out on general inspection. Inspected army accoutrements and knapsacks. Received letter from home. Wrote letters to Jas H. Smith and home.

Thursday December 4th 1862
Ordered on picket after marching about 5 miles on circuitous route was stationed about 3 1/2 miles from camp.

Friday December 5th 1862
Commenced snowing this morning which makes it look very much like winter. Relieved from picket by the 19th Ohio.

Saturday December 6th 1862
Early this morning the 14th Brigade was ordered to accompany the forage

train as convoys. Went perhaps the distance of 8 miles without seeing nary a rebel. While the train was being loaded I went to a house near by which had been evacuated by the white population. A few Negroes were left. They hadn't "moved dere tings to massa's parlor." The consequence was when the Lincum soldiers came they "cornfiscated" all the movable property. The house left traces that its inmates had been somewhat literary as papers magazines and books lay strewn from garret to cellar. I succeeded in getting a couple of titles of which are "Ruth Hall" by Fanny Fern and "Course of Composition and Rhetoric" by Quackenbus, Besides quite a number of New York Ledgers. As I started away I picked up an old hand trunk which contained some spicy correspondence. I have not the space here to insert.

Sunday December 7th 1862
Another bright Sabbath morning dawns clear and cool yet the day reminds me very much of home. I do not hear the tones of the Sabbath bell reminding that "another six days work is done another Sabbath is begun."

Monday December 8th 1862
Last night just as we were retiring for the night an order came in to have three days rations prepared and in haversacks. The consequence was a great many wry faces. To be disturbed when one is just preparing for a good snooze is of all things most provoking, but the soldier learns to take such things patiently as they know they cannot be avoided. Much to their surprise they heard the order "Get ready for picket." A change was noticed in such countenances as a change from a surly to a pleasing one, because there is nothing that a soldier dislikes more than a march and nothing he likes better than to go on picket, especially when they go in the neighborhood of turkeys, geese, hogs, sheep and anything they can get in the eating line. The day is a beautiful one and I spend it reading "Ruth Hall" a story written by Fanny Fern. Fanny is a good writer and the characters she brings forward is a true delineation of nature.

Tuesday December 9th 1862
This is a beautiful winter morning unlike a winter morning in Indiana. Wrote a letter to Jesse Welch. Finished reading "Ruth Hall." Relieved from picket by the 9th Indiana.

Wednesday December 10th 1862
The sun shines. Ordered to march. Struck tents. Waited patiently an hour after which the order was given "forward" and all moved off keeping step to

the music of "Yankee Doodle" our national air. The time was when there was an inspiration in this old tune but the manner in which it is played here is almost an intolerable boor. The regiment moved back toward Nashville a couple of miles and encamped in a beautiful wood. Received a letter from J.N. Adair and answered the same.

Thursday December 11th 1862
Beautiful morn. Did up some washing. Wrote letter to Annie Cones. Went out on Battalion drill this afternoon. The drill ground is an open field farm which on the left is presented a beautiful landscape. As far as the eye can reach is one continual wave of hills while on the right can be seen the tented city of Smith's Division. The scenery here presented to the eyes is grand almost bordering on the sublime. Here we behold the wondrous works of an Almighty hand beautified by the genius of man.

Friday December 12th 1862
"I have prayed - God knows how often
    That I might but live to see
For a moment all the loved ones
    That are very dear to me."
"Live to see my darling mother
    Lay my head upon her breast
As I used to in my childhood
    When she cradled me to rest."
"Live to see my brothers, sisters,
    Once again before I die,
Oh! it would not seem so fearful
    If I knew that they were nigh."

Yes, I want to "die among my kindred" I often think of them. I think of my childhood's happy home and almost wish I was a child again. The morning is a beautiful one, and finds me in the dingy smoky shabby and dilapidated city of Nashville having arrived there about daylight guarding 2000 paroled prisoners who were taken by Morgan at Nashville. Started this morning about one o'clock and returned to camp at 11 having traveled during the time 20 miles. Then I was very sick during the afternoon. Received a letter from my dear old friend Jas J. Smith. Glad to hear from him.

Saturday December 13th 1862
Being very much wearied from the previous night's tramp remained in camp

this forenoon. On drill in the afternoon. Wrote a letter to Jas. H. Smith. Soldiers are "hard up" sometimes as such was my case when I wrote the letter on scraps of an old envelope.

Sunday. December 14, 1862
Instead of preparing for the duties of the sacred day the regiment is ordered to go as convoys with the forage train. I was detailed to remain with the wagons. Went perhaps the distance of eight miles where we found forage in abundance on the banks of the Cumberland. Some beautiful farms are to be seen here, as well as stately villas which occupy them.

Monday December 15th 1862
Cloudy and windy this morning. "Get ready to go on picket" is the order. All is confusion getting ready for duty. After being stationed which was about three miles from camp it commenced raining and continued during the day which made it very disagreeable to the pickets. At the post where I was stationed were four men whom I had in charge. Built a rail pen, covered it with oil cloth, blankets, made a booming fire of rails and huddled around it with the capes of our great coats thrown over our heads to protect us from the chilling blasts of a Tennessee storm. Relieved about twilight - Came to the reserve where we found nothing but wet, wet, wet, wet. Built up another shanty made a fire in front. Ate our frugal meal which consisted of crackers and fat meat - went to bed without a murmur, showing that the army is a good place to learn patience if nothing else.

Tuesday December 16th 1862
Arose this morning and found the sun shining brilliantly. Relieved from picket by the 79th Indiana. Came to camp and found a letter from Lide Gibson and home. Together with a pair of mittens. Answered the letters. The wind is blowing fiercely reminding one of an Autumn day at home. Another soldier has gone to rest. John Miller of Co. F is now beneath a little mound of earth "alone." Away from loved ones has he fallen. "Oh! mocking earth with Thy skies blue and placid silver streams" snatching from the frenzied grasp the treasure of loved ones at home. A few days before his father too passed away. A heavy stroke on the family to part with father and son in so short a time.

Wednesday December 17th 1862
Commenced early this morning to do up some washing which I dispatched in a neat and womanly style. At times I dote on "good old days gone by." I

muse upon them and sometimes wish that my lot had been cast in a different age. Sometime I say it with old Hessiod:
"O would that nature had denied me birth
  Midst this late race: This iron age of earth."
But I know this is a wicked thought. I should be content with the lot which has fallen to me. Contentment insures happiness. Dick came in while writing and dropped me a bunch of mistletoe with which the forest trees in the south seem to abound. The stem, branch, leaf, and the little white berry shows with what exquisite beauty the Divine Hand displayed in its formation. Lieut. Doster came up this evening after an absence of about a month. Glad indeed were the boys to see him.

Thursday December 18th 1862
The night was cold. The ground froze very hard. Went on company drill in the forenoon. On Battalion drill in the afternoon. Wrote letters.

Friday Dec. 19th 1862
Regiment ordered on inspection. Came back about 2 o'clock. Wrote to Frank Cones. This eventide I sit on a log writing in my journal. I have just finished my supper which consisted of a small piece of light bread & a cup of tea. A rarity by the way. Near me is seated Jim Darrow eating beef broth and crackers with a knife. In front to me is Dock do. 'Tis a beautiful evening. The stars are just making their appearance. 'Tis a lovely hour.

Saturday December 20th 1862
This morning our brigade was ordered as convoys to the forage train. Went the distance of 8 miles.

Sunday December 21st 1862
On picket again this morning. Stationed on the reserve. Felt quite unwell.. Reading in Parley Universal History. The news is not very flattering for a peace. If there is anything more that the soldier desires more than anything else it is a return of a lasting and honorable peace. Haste the day when the wreath of peace shall again encircle this once happy land.

Monday December 22nd 1862
Relieved from picket this morning by the 19th Indiana. Quite unwell. Received a letter from Frank and Annie Cones. Immediately answered them. Wrote home.

Tuesday December 23rd 1862
Moved this morning. Went perhaps a quarter of a mile where we encamped on the side of a hill which faces the east. Still unwell.

Wednesday December 24th 1862
The regiment went on picket this morning, but I was unable to go. Reported to the surgeon who gave me enough medicine to either kill or cure. Visited the hospital where John Mikesell is lying very sick. I tried to talk with him to cheer him.

86th Indiana Regiment, Volunteer Infantry

Fire!

Never will it be forgotten by the members of the Eighty-sixth so long as life and memory shall last. After being permitted to retire to rest the men slept undisturbed for some time when one of the tents of Company H caught fire. This aroused the inmates who at once raised an alarm which awakened others of the company and regiment.

The spirit of Christmas, of fun and frolic, took hold of all for a short time, and the camp of the Eighty-sixth became a perfect bedlam beyond all description. Cat-calls, yells and camp slang made it an uproarious time for the space of fifteen or twenty minutes when nature again asserted herself and all returned to bed to secure the much needed rest.

Thursday December 25th 1862
Today is Christmas. While friends at home are enjoying the festivities of the occasion we are here upon the tented field. Unwell. Only able for light camp duty. Witnessed a flag presentation in the 59th Ohio, It was presented by the citizens of Clermont O. and in their behalf Col. Fife of the 59th O. made the presentation speech. On its folds were inscribed "Shiloh, Corinth, Ivy Creek, Perryville and Crab Orchard" the names of the fields upon which the 59th had displayed their valor and courage. Said Col. Fife "On our left is the hermitage the home of the revered and honored Gen. Jackson. On our right are the pickets of the enemy in array against the Union and ever the grave of the honored Gen. Andrew Jackson." Christmas evening was spent in listening to speakers from Col. Hamilton, Capt. Sheath and Capt. Lambert, interspersed with music by the 59th Ohio Band and The "Hoosier Glee Club."

Chapter Five
Murfreesboro and Stones River

Friday December 26th 1862
This morning the "Army of the Cumberland" moved in three columns in the direction of Murfreesboro. The right commanded by McCook, the center by Crittenden and the left by Thomas. Our regiment had orders to move at 8 o'clock. Eight o'clock came and with it came rain! rain! rain! Nine o'clock came. Ten o'clock and still we were huddled in the rain like so many chickens. Eleven and twelve came. By this time the boys began to get hungry and preparations are made the satisfy their hunger. One or two came and we began to move. Slowly we march out the Murfreesboro pike and halt in a wood to camp for the night. Although it is dark and wet yet cheerily the boys begin to make preparations for supper. Some go in search of water while others bring up some rails to make a fire. Supper over we fix ourselves down as comfortably as we can considering the good prospect for rain. Jim Darrow, Jake Bozzle and myself put up some rails and made a tent of our oilcloth blankets in which we slept as comfortably as though we were in the most commodious tents of Gen. Rosecrans.

Saturday December 27th 1862
The morning is cloudy indicating rain. "Fall in" is the order. March a couple of hundred yards and come to a halt. Soon it commenced raining and oil cloths are in good demand. The rain came in torrents but still standing waiting further orders. Night comes and we begin to move. On we go splash-it-a-splash through the mud about 6 miles when we come to a halt and encamp for the night. Fortune favors the soldier sometimes. Near by was a barn full of corn blades. The boys were not long in discovering the fact. They were soon scattered over the regiment upon which we reclined our weary bodies. On the plantation where we encamped are about a hundred slaves. I went to their quarters for the purpose of getting some bread. I succeeded in getting a couple of dollars worth for which I paid Confederate script. To a person unacquainted with the ways and customs of the darkies, there are some things very amusing. They all have the idea of freedom in their heads. My opinion is let the war terminate as it will, slavery is doomed and the "institution" that the Southern people so much idolize will be wiped from existence. Of these darkies I inquired if their "Missus" was secesh. "Yas sah" was the answer. "Well" says I, "You will all be free the first of Jan." was the unanimous exclamation of all of them. Many other things of an amusing character took place but I cannot here state.

Sunday December 28th 1862

A beautiful morning after the storm. Heavy firing is heard on our right. We are marched out a half a mile to the south and formed in line of battle. "Tis the Holy Sabbath. Instead of listening to the preaching of peace and good will on earth toward men we are listening to the command to fire low. What a strange but striking contrast between the blessings of peace and the horrors of war! Slowly but steadily the sun comes his way through the dim blue ether above, yet no signs of an advancing foe. The boys begin to get hungry. Fires are kindled and meat placed on the ends of sticks are soon over the fire broiling to satisfy their hunger. Later in the day I visited a church nearby. It proved to be a Presbyterian church and bore the name of "Smyrna Church". From appearances it looked as though it had been some time since Christians had met there to worship there. The leaves had fallen and were still unmoved. The tread of worshipers was heard no more. Where are they? Yes where are they? Are they not arranged in arms against their own government that protected them in their worship here.

Monday December 29th 1862

Another clear morning. Expecting every moment to receive marching orders. Remained in camp till perhaps one o'clock when we were again on the move. The country through which we pass is good. Beautiful farms are seen in every direction. We advance to within about 4 miles of Murfreesboro where we go in camp. Thousands and thousands of camp fires are lighting up and shedding a halo which magically adorn the earth. Perhaps by morning the ball will be opened and one of the bloodiest battles of the war will be the result.

Tuesday December 30 1862

The morning dawns and with it is heard heavy picket firing in front. Rained during the night and the day is a cool and cloudy one. Soon we are drawn in line of battle not knowing when we will be in the thickest of the fight. Both on our right and left as far as the eye can search are seen long lines of men with bayonets glittering in the air ready for the approaching conflict. Gen. Rosecrans reviewed our men. Waited patiently all day but as yet I have learned nothing particular of the heavy firing on the right. Encamped on the same ground. It is expected that by tomorrow the ball will be opened. May God in his mercy avert the coming storm. Into his hands I commit myself.

[Penciled in here is "Battle of Stones River or Murfreesboro p-530."]

Indiana's Roll of Honor, Volume II

The Death of Corporal Rosbrough

*C*orporal William Rosbrough, of Company B, one of the color guard, at the battle of Stones river was shot through the breast and fell. His comrade, in the rear rank, stepped promptly into his place. Rosbrough crawled out of the line. As his comrade raised his gun a rebel bullet struck the barrel, bending it, and rendering the gun useless. Rosbrough seeing this, and very much exhausted, said, "Here is my gun; there's a load in it, but no cap," at the same time shoving it along the ground. His comrade caught up the gun, capped it, fired, and, casting his eye towards Rosbrough, saw that he was lying in a uncomfortable position. Placing his hand on Rosbrough's head, he discovered that he was dead. A few moments after, a soldier, searching his cartridge box for ammunition, found but one cartridge. Rosbrough had fired thirty-eight rounds!

Go For Him!

*P*rivate Twomey, of Company A, 30th Regiment, was a good representative of the Irish race. Brave to rashness, he never looked for consequences, but "went for the cursed ribbles" whenever there was a chance. During the battle of Stone's river, there was a point in our lines opposite which the enemy's works were formed at almost right angles. One day a rebel officer was seen riding along the line, and advancing beyond the intersection of their lines. Twomey and a comrade noticed it, and concluded to "go for him." One was to fire at the man, the other at the horse. Both fired. Horse and rider fell.

Twomey started like a deer for the officer. His comrade's courage failed. Over the four hundred yards in front Twomey ran with great speed. The rebels were puzzled by the strange movement. Reaching the horse, Twomey fell flat alongside, pulled a waterproof overcoat from the dead officer, took a watch from his pocket, and a flask of whiskey from his saddle bags.

Springing suddenly up, he ran swiftly toward the Union lines, reaching them without a wound, although a heavy volley was fired at him. Twomey was afterwards accidentally shot by a comrade, and disabled for life.

Story from the 51st Regiment
Indiana's Roll of Honor, adapted

The Mule's Revenge

As the 51st was moving from Murfreesboro to Nashville, Col. Abel D. Streight ordered that all the men who could be furnish with animals should be mounted and that these, with three companies on foot, should scour the country between Palmyra and Fort Henry, collecting all horses and mules which could be found.

The foray across the country was attended with many amusing incidents. Most of the mules were young and unbroken, and the efforts of the men to ride them was attended with strange gymnastics.

The animals, though lean and scraggy, so soon as saddled, went off on what the men called a "sheep gallop." Running about a hundred yards, some planted their fore feet firmly in the loose soil, and kicking up their hind feet, sent their riders flying into the air as if shot from a bow. Others, in the exhibition of their mulish nature, reversed the order of locomotion, and running backwards, threw their saddles forward on their necks, and dropping their heads and elevating their heels, dumped their riders like sacks on the ground. The road was strewn for miles with mule-demoralized soldiers, making their mark upon mother earth.

Mike O'Conner, a real "broth of a boy," declared, "be jabers, me mule kicked me hat af me head and the very buttons off me coat, and threw me forty fut above its head, and then, divil that he is, he shot at me with his heels while I was in the air!"

Wednesday Dec 31 1862

The wind was heavy last night. Flying clouds in the morning. The ball is opened on our right wing. The distant roar of artillery and musketry sounds like the rumbling of distant thunder. An order is read by Col. Fife from Gen. Rosecrans in which the General praises the men very highly for the conduct in yesterday's fight together cautioning the men to fire low and stand like men. It seems that our brigade was ordered on the extreme left. We marched perhaps a mile in that direction when the order was countermanded and we were turned toward the rear as it was said that the rebel cavalry were cutting off our train. In fact they had captured the train. We started back on "double quick" to intercept them. On the way knapsacks, blankets, coffee pots and other things not really necessary on the battlefield were thrown in every direction. We formed in line of battle in a cornfield after having "double quicked" about two miles. Our cavalry were in front who fired upon them two or three rounds which took effect & we had the pleasure of witnessing the "reb" scatter. They left us in possession of the train which they had captured a few moments before. We were then ordered to take our original position on the right center. The enemy were making heavy inroads on McCook's Corps they slowly massed their whole force on our right. Back we "double quicked" in line of battle over stones and through cedar thickets to support McCook who was rapidly falling back hotly pursued by the enemy. We marched out through an open field. Occasional shots from the woods revealed to us that the enemy was near. Slowly advanced during the time had orders to fall down several times. We succeeded in getting to the fence which enclosed the field. We were ordered to "fall down". "Fire" was the next command which was executed with promptness. A volley of musketry from the enemy came rattling like hail which greatly reduced our ranks. By this time they were flanking us both on the right and left, being exposed to a heavy crossfire the brigade was ordered to retreat. I did not hear the order and consequently was considerably in the rear when I observed that the regiment were falling back. They fled precipitately and seemed perfectly panic stricken. In short they ran like a flock of scared sheep. I ran after them until completely exhausted when I fell in a fence corner thinking perhaps that here I might find a shield from the volleys of musketry from the enemy. Nearly every step I took across that field I saw a man, a comrade, fall near me. An exclamation of "Oh! I'm killed" and all would be over with those who had come in contact with the fatal shot. Many were wounded whose sufferings were intense. Their groans and shrieks are still ringing in my ears. Such a scene I never before witnessed I hope never again to witness a similar one. I can only attribute my escape to the intervening mercy of the Almighty God who answered not only my own prayer but the prayer of friends at home. The enemy advanced and I was taken as a prisoner of war. I was taken back over the battlefield which extended about three miles. Taken to Murfreesboro. Passed over the field where the dead lay strewn everywhere. To say which side lost the most I could not but as near as I could judge I supposed the number to be equal. I conversed with Confederate officers who told me that they had been upon the fields of Bull Run and Shiloh but they had never seen the equal number slain before. Night closed the bloody contest. As yet I do not know the true result - but - I have fears that we have not been successful. Whether the fight will be renewed tomorrow or not I do not know. About 2700 prisoners were taken during the day who were placed in the Murfreesboro Court Yard, without fire, without anything to eat. Thus the old year closed! It closed witnessing one of the bloodiest battles of the war! I trust the year 1863 will close in peace. [Penciled in, "Taken prisoner - Stones River."]

86th Indiana Regiment, Volunteer Infantry, abridged

Orville S. Hamilton

*I*n chapters of this history, in the account of the organization, the fact was mentioned that Orville S. Hamilton was commissioned as Colonel. There were those, however, as a matter of fact, who were commissioned as officers and sent to the field, who should never have been selected for the positions which they were not able to fill.

The story of the displacement of Colonel Hamilton in command of the regiment has never been told or printed. The special matters that led to the relievement of Colonel Hamilton at Stone's River and placing Colonel Dick in command were then unknown and unsuspected by either. It is not believed that Colonel Hamilton up to the day of his death knew of the manner in which it was brought about.

There were a number of line officers present that morning who were not taken by surprise when the change came. There are but a very few of the number alive today who were in the secret, but time has removed the need for absolute secrecy.

There was no mutiny, nor conspiracy to do a wrong, but the belief that the time to demand a change in the commandership of the regiment had crystallized into quiet action on the part of quite a number of the officers who felt convinced that a great battle was at hand. Bragg had been driven down from the Ohio river through Kentucky and into Tennessee, and had taken his position on ground of his own choosing to give Rosecrans battle. It did not require a great military genius to realize this fact, and that the battle would be hotly contested. Colonel Hamilton could not handle the regiment. It was believed that Colonel Dick could.

The name of the regiment and the lives of the men were at stake. But little was known of the articles of war, although all realized that care must be taken.

It was secretly decided to go to General VanCleve, who was then commanding the division, lay the facts before him, ask him to remove Colonel Hamilton in some way, and place Colonel Dick in command.

Before daylight of the morning of the opening of the battle, these officers quietly assembled just outside the bivouac of the regiment, and started for General VanCleve's headquarters not far distant. On the way, for some reason best known to the older heads, the youngest officer in years and as an officer, was selected to present the case to the General.

On arrival at the General's tent it was found that he was already up and dressed. The sentinel challenged as they approached. The countersign was given, and as they reached the tent the old General stepped out, and in his kindly manner asked the cause of the visitation.

The officer selected to speak stepped forward and began his statement, but he only succeeded in uttering the first sentence which sufficiently disclosed the purport of the visit, when he interrupted and stopped any further words by saying, "Not another word, gentlemen, not another word. You certainly do not realize the dangerous position in which you are placing yourselves. Go back to your regiment, go at once."

Crestfallen and sick at heart these officers started to return. After they had gone but a few steps an orderly came hurrying up and said the General wished to see the spokesman of the party. This officer on returning was told by the General that he would look after the interest of the regiment, that all would turn out for the best, and that he would be along the line at daylight.

At day break the entire army was formed in line of battle, and so stood in line until after daylight, when it was discovered that General VanCleve, with his Assistant Adjutant General, were coming down the line and stopping at the different regiments when some command would be given, the movement executed and then resume its position in line as before.

As it came nearer it could be better understood. The Colonel of each regiment was directed to give some certain command, with an explanation of the movement before the men were permitted to attempt the execution.

General VanCleve and the brigade commander, Colonel Fyffe, finally reached the Eighty-sixth Indiana, when he stated to Colonel Hamilton that he was testing his regiment so that he might be satisfied that the officers and men could change their formation, if it should be necessary, in action.

He then said: "Colonel, you will 'Change front forward on first company.' Give the commands. But first, explain it fully so that there can be no mistake. Now give the command."

Colonel Hamilton gave the command as directed, but there he stopped. Then was heard the voice of the old General: "Instruct your regiment, Colonel.

They are new men. Instruct them, Colonel."

Again the Colonel gave the command, "Change front forward on first company." And again he stopped, more confused than before. Again came the words of the General. "Instruct your men; instruct your men."

The third time the Colonel gave the command, but this time he was excited and confused beyond measure, and the sharp tones struck his ears: "Colonel, you must obey my orders; instruct your men how to execute the movement."

The Colonel broke down completely, called in a confused and utterly dazed manner for the Lieutenant Colonel, and unbuckling his sword belt turned on his horse, gave the sword to the Assistant Adjutant General, dismounted, and the command of the regiment then by order of the General devolved upon the then Lieutenant Colonel Dick.

In what has been said of the Eighty-sixth Indiana regiment and its first Colonel, all intention to cast any reflection upon the bravery of honesty of purpose of Colonel Orville S. Hamilton is most emphatically disavowed. No one who knew Colonel Hamilton ever doubted either his bravery or his earnest desire to do all within his power both as a man and an officer, to make his regiment all that it should have been.

More than this, the writer, from personal intercourse with him, was led to believe, and now believes, that Colonel Hamilton was of that proud disposition that led him to wish for the very highest position for the regiment that it was possible for any body of troops to attain. The only trouble with him was that there was no military genius of any kind in his make-up. He was a man of good strong mind, and reputed to be a good lawyer, but not one particle of that strength of mind was in a military direction, He could not understand why a military command was given in a set form, nor could he realize that there was a reason for every movement in the tactics, and therefore could not put any of his memorized tactics into practical use.

But when relieved and entirely free to withdraw from the terrible battle that was then opening, and which so soon afterward struck his regiment with such terrible and deadly effect, instead of leaving the field, dismounted from his horse, sent the horse to the rear, and then securing a gun and cartridge box took a place with the men of his regiment and remained through the whole of the battle doing duty in the ranks as if he were an enlisted man.

It is due to the honor of Colonel Hamilton; it is due to the honor and magnificent record of the Eighty-sixth Regiment of Indiana in the War of the Rebellion, that the bravery of Colonel Orville S. Hamilton should be chronicled with the history of the regiment.

Chapter Six
Captured!

1863

Thursday January 1st 1863
"Happy New Year!" No, did I say "happy new year?" I only quoted the greeting of loved ones at home. Another year is begun. The morning dawns finding me in the Murfreesboro Court Yard having passed a very uncomfortable night - having passed it without fire and with but one blanket though many of the men had none. About 5 o'clock we are taken out and put in an old mill. Here it is no better as we are not allowed fire. All day long we remained there with nothing to eat. Wearily the hours passed by awaiting either to draw rations or leave. Sundown came and we were removed to an old school house lot to encamp for the night. Here we are as thick as bees some without blankets or overcoats and all without anything to eat. About 9 o'clock we draw a pint of flour to the man. Here arose another difficulty. After getting the flour had nothing to cook it with. But "Yankees" are not always at their wits ends as was witnessed here. The flour was mixed on a board after which they put it on the end of a stick and held before the fire to cook. Time came for sleep but not much sleeping was done so destitute of clothing were they. Thus New Year's was spent in a Southern prison.

86th Regiment, Indiana Volunteer Infantry, abridged

The "Tour of the Confederacy"

*F*our months before the battle of Stones River, the Eighty-sixth had entered the field with a thousand men. Disability, disease and death had decimated its ranks until that morning it numbered 368, including officers. The aggregate loss on that bloody day was 194, ten more than half. When the roll was called on New Year's morning, 1863, but one hundred and seventy-four officers and men answered to their names. Ninety-nine men and two officers were captured.

The prisoners were marched double-quick in the direction of Murfreesboro. Upon arriving in the city they were placed in the court house yard surrounded with a stone fence. Having been relieved of their ponchos, blankets and overcoats by rebel officers who had quarters in the court house, and with neither fire nor food, there was much suffering from cold and hunger.

They were moved to a schoolhouse lot and there provided with flour, which was mixed with water to make a dough which was wound around sticks and held before the fire to bake.

The next morning they were loaded aboard platform cars headed toward Chattanooga. Exposed and cold, without protection of blankets or ponchos, they suffered much, especially when it began to rain. Arriving in Chattanooga they were marched to the banks of the Tennessee River under the shadow of Lookout Mountain.

The next day they were provided with axes to cut down trees for firewood. They went without food until evening, when they were provided with corn meal, sugar and metal skillets to bake it in. At 3 a.m. lines were formed and they started for the Atlanta depot in box cars meant for freight and cattle, packed so close they could neither sit nor stand with any comfort.

From Atlanta they were taken to West Point, to Montgomery, Alabama and back to Atlanta. They were loaded again and taken to Dalton, Georgia, then to Knoxville, Tennessee. From there they were taken to Richmond, Virginia and Libby Prison.

The days were passed getting acquainted with fleas, having prayer meetings, reading and re-reading any scrap of paper.

The enlisted men were taken to City Point to be paroled. They were kept in a parole camp and then transferred to Camp Chase, near Columbus, Ohio, After two weeks they were taken to Camp Carrington in Indianapolis and given eight days furlough.

Friday January 2nd 1863

At 6 o'clock this morning the prisoners were ordered in line as cars were awaiting to take us further south. They did not start however until about 8 o'clock when off we start bound for the unknown regions of the Southern Confederacy. Placed on platform cars on the Chattanooga and Nashville R.R. Passed through Tullahoma a town the Federal soldiers will long remember. The country along the route is barren and unfruitful, quite unlike the immediate vicinity of Nashville. Arrived at Chattanooga and marched to camp near town Distance 13 miles. No rations yet.

Saturday January 3rd 1863
Our encampment is on the banks of the Tennessee River where we get water sufficient to wash our faces and hands the first time since we were captured. Anxiously we await the expected rations. Toward evening they come consisting of corn meal, bacon, rice, sugar and salt. Preparations are made for cooking and it commences to rain which it unceasingly continues till we are again ordered to "fall in" and march to the train. We are put in box cars and start toward Atlanta, Georgia on the Chattanooga and Georgia R.R.

Sunday January 4th 1863
We are soon in the State of Georgia but being after night I could not see much of the country. What I did see after daylight is very poor. The soil being generally sandy or of a red clay, and very unproductive. Reached Atlanta about 5 o'clock where we were marched to a vacant lot and encamped for the night. Distance traveled today 130 miles. The city of Atlanta contains 15,000 or 20,000 and is one of the most beautiful cities I have seen in the south. Drew a piece of bread and meat.

Monday January 5th 1863
Left Atlanta this morning at 8 o'clock bound for West Point on the A & W Pt. R.R. Arrived at West Point at sunset having traveled today 86 miles. The country along the route is rather inferior. I have not seen a farm or a plantation in the State of Georgia that I would have. At West Point is the Tallahatchie river a stream about the size of the Wabash. At this place is the State line between Georgia and Alabama. Went to rest on a cotton bale which lay in the R.R. depot. Rested well until it commenced raining when I went into a box car and slept till morning.

Tuesday January 6th 1863
Awoke this morning and found it raining "tremenjus" but it soon cleared off. I went to a house near by and procured some biscuit corn bread and meat. Had a short conversation with the man of the house. He was originally a Union man but was forced into the secession camp by the force of circumstances. He said that this was the sentiment of a majority of the citizens but that now they were the most rampant in the mania of secession. We started to Montgomery the Capital of Alabama. Nothing occurred along the route worthy of note. The country is no better than in Georgia. The slaves were busy plowing, unusual to me especially this time in the year. The weather is cool though not unpleasant. Arrived at Montgomery at about 11 o'clock at night. Distance from W.P. 86 miles.

Wednesday Jan 7th 1863
A depression of spirits was caused this morning among the prisoners this morning when they got aboard the train backward bound. The cause no one can tell though various are the conjectures as to our destination point. It is the opinion of some that we will be sent through our lines at Murfreesboro & others think that we will be held as prisoners of war. At any rate we go backward toward Atlanta.

Thursday Jan 8th 1863
Reached Atlanta about daylight after traveling all night. Go to a camp near Atlanta where we draw rations and cooking utensils. The rumor is current that we will be retained by the Confederate Government as prisoners which casts a shade over the countenances of the prisoners. All hopes of seeing home which but a few hours ago flitted across their minds now suddenly vanish. Physicians are going through the camp looking after the wounded and sick. The current rumor afloat is now countermanded and the report is going the rounds that we will start at 8 o'clock which is quite reviving. Truly I am sick of the Southern Confederacy, yet I believe they have treated the prisoners as well as they could under the circumstances! At 8 o'clock we are ordered to "fall in". We take the Chattanooga R.R. bound somewhere unknown to me.

Friday Jan 9th 1863
After traveling all night I find myself at a station on the C.R.R. 100 miles from Atlanta called Dalton. All day long we await the train to take us to Knoxville in East Tennessee. Wearily the hours pass but no trains come and we are compelled to remain till morning.

Saturday Jan 10th 1863
Awoke this morning and found the rain coming in torrents. Ate the last crumb of bread I have. I know not when or where the next will come from. At 11 o'clock the train starts which is quite a relief to the worn out prisoners. The East Tennessee R.R. is rough. East Tennessee is a beautiful country, the finest I have seen and as Parson Brownlow has said it is the Switzerland of America.

Sunday Jan 11th 1863
This beautiful Sabbath morning I find myself in the beautiful city of Knoxville, the home of renowned patriot and exile Parson Brownlow. Here it was that he suffered in the cause of the Union - here it was that he was imprisoned and here in this portion of the State many patriots have sacrificed their homes

- yea have been driven from them because of their devotion to the Union - and here this morning I find myself held as a prisoner of war guarded by a strong force, not even permitted to get water to slack my thirst. Have nothing to eat today. The day passed and yet no rations are on hand. Toward evening some ladies hearing that the prisoners were without rations brought their baskets well laden with provisions. They announced that it was not for sale. 'Tis true that it was but a mouthful for but a few yet it was an evidence that Parson Brownlow's fruits of loyalty still survives his exile. They wished to talk with the prisoners but were not permitted by the guards. One of them did ask where Parson Brownlow was, notwithstanding the orders she had received from the guard and then added that she would like to see him and hear him make a speech once more. She was not permitted to say more but looked as though a tear might fall because of the order. However her heart was brave! As she turned away she said she was afraid of no bayonet and defiantly shook her delicate arm at the guard. After dark we received a loaf of bread and a small piece of meat. That there is loyalty in Knoxville is no doubt. Though the sentiment is suppressed. Brave hearts are they who can still stand up and say they love the old Union in preference to the bogus one instituted by Jeff Davis and his herd of petty tyrants. May the loyalty that exists in Knoxville still live and grow and burn in the hearts of the people. May the day soon come when they shall be released from their thralldom and the Infernal hordes of Usurpers be driven from the soil of E. Tennessee and the "Stars and Stripes" again wave in triumph over every house top and the music of the Union be wafted on every breeze until the hills and dales would reverberate with the echoing accents of "Union forever, Freedom to all".

Monday Jan 12th 1863
Having passed the Sunday in Knoxville, we start this morning in the direction of Bristol on the E.T. & Va. R.R. O what a delightful country we pass through. No wonder Parson Brownlow loves his home. No wonder he calls it the "Switzerland of America". In the afternoon we come to Greenville 15 miles from Knoxville - the home of Andy Johnson whose name is familiar to all Union loving people. Nightfall comes and we come to the Wautauga River. The bridge across this river was burnt a few weeks ago by Col. Carter commanding a Federal force of cavalry. He also burnt the bridge across the Holston river 9 miles distant. Camp for the night on the Wautauga river and in the little village of Owensboro. Made a fire of the remains of the old bridge.

Tuesday Jan 13th 1863

Took breakfast at a Union house in Owensboro. The man of the house informed me that in the village then was not a single secessionist living - that it was Union from post to pillar. He said that many Union people had fled from there because of the conscript. There were forty conscripts in the county and they had only succeeded in getting three - the remainder having run away and joined the Union Army! A small flat boat was at the river but this was not sufficient to take the prisoners over the river. They were ordered to wade. I was among the latter number. After wading across the prisoners were compelled to walk the nine miles intervening the rivers. All along the way through E. Tennessee we were met with demonstrations which was conclusive evidence that the people still loved the old Union. Such expressions as "Hurrah for the Union!" "Hurrah for the Union Soldiers!" "Hurrah for Uncle Abe's boys!" showed that they were for the Union from choice not because of compulsion. Crossed Holstein [Holston] River and after waiting perhaps a couple of hours again got aboard the train bound for Bristol 11 miles distant from the river and 130 miles from Knoxville.

Wednesday Jan 14th 1863

At Bristol is the Va & Tenn State line. Here we took the train on the E.T. & Va. R.R. which runs from Bristol to Lynchburg. The country through which we travel today is very broken. Stock raising seems to be the principal employment of the citizens of this portion of Virginia. If they had to live on the products of the soil it would be slim living.

Thursday Jan 15th 1863

After traveling all night arrived in Lynchburg. Distant from Bristol 220 miles. Remained here but a few moments when we were again on the way bound for Richmond. Where ever I go in the South I find a suppressed Union sentiment. At Lynchburg I met with a man who was a strong Union man but dared not utter his sentiments. He wanted to get away. I put him on a plan which pleased him very much. I told him that he could go to Richmond with the prisoners and stand his chances with them of getting a parole as a Union prisoner. He started off with a smile saying that he would go and bid his wife "goodbye" and go with us. Rougher and rougher the country gets. O what a Confederacy they will have should they be so unfortunate as to gain their independence.

Friday Jan 16th 1863

This morning arrived in Richmond the Capital of the Confederate States. The long expected city we are now in. Marched across the James River and up through the city to our prison. As we marched up through the streets we were everywhere met with taunts and jeers and derisions - some calling us one thing others another, at which we "Yankees" as we are generally termed could do or say nothing but silently pass by without a resenting word. We are confined in the celebrated "Libby prison" - the veritable "tobacco houses." The room in which I am confined is, I should think, about 50 by 30 feet and 250 men placed there. It is a general inquiry of the guards and of every person whom the prisoners think ought to know. "When are we going to leave here?" "Where are we going?" Sometimes their answer would be "We intend to keep you and hang you!" at which answers I concluded they know nothing about it.

Saturday Jan 17th 1863
Clear and cool this morning. Passed a very uncomfortable night being very sick. Feel quite unwell. But, here I am in prison not knowing when we will get away. It may be soon and it may be some time. On each countenance may be seen an anxious look. This can be easily accounted for. Each prisoner is anxious to know when he will be released from this wearisome place. A general uneasiness is perceived on the minds of all as may be witnessed by a continual walking to and fro by most of them, while others are variously engaged. Squads may be seen together discussing the probable result of our getting away. Some are card playing, some are at checkers while I notice one in the 250 reading God's Holy Word. I had a dream last night I dreamed of being in the Sabbath School once more. There were seven classes of little girls and boys. They looked so sweet - so much like angels and when they sang that beautiful hymn commencing:
    "I want to be an angel
    And with the angels stand."
my soul seemed stirred within me and I felt as though I was not in prison but was standing at the portals of glory. When will the time come when I shall again assemble with those I love in the Sabbath School? Sometimes I think I can hardly wait, but again I think "My suffering time will soon be o'er."

Sunday Jan 18th 1863
Bright and beautiful is this holy day, yet I am not permitted to enjoy the pure air and sunshine of heaven. I am confined in prison! It is now rumored that we will remain here some time. I however hope for the better. Today my mind reverts back to the better and happier days - days when I spent the Sabbath in the Sanctuary of the Lord instead of a cold and dreary prison -

days when I had congenial companions instead of being surrounded with none but the wicked, but I am in the midst of adverse circumstances. Though my lot may be hard, though there is nothing seemingly to cheer the heart in the dreary place, yet my trust is in God. I feel that he is my preserver, Benefactor and Friend. I spent a good part of the day in perusing the pages of His Holy Word, and in singing the songs of Zion.

Monday Jan 19th 1863
The morning is clear and beautiful. Not a cloud obscures the sky above, yet the thought of being confined in this dreary prison is a cloud on the sky of my mind. The day passed with nothing to change the monotony of prison life. Reading the New Testament.

Tuesday Jan 20th 1863
O how wearily the hours lag by! It seems as though the time of our release never will come. I am weary and tired of prison life. Perhaps if my health was good I could pass the time more pleasantly. Have slept but little since I came here on account of cold.

Wednesday Jan 21st 1863
Rainy morning. Still in close confinement. I spent a good part of the day in reading the Bible. Read 52 chapters in the New Testament.

Thursday Jan 22nd 1863
Dreary day! Prison hours are very long! When will the time come that I can again say in the language of a true American Citizen "I am a free man?" Bound down as it were I am here confined for daring to take up arms in defense of my country! God hasten the hour when I shall be released and feel that I am free! Perusing the pages of Sacred Writ.

Friday Jan 23rd 1863
And still another dreary prison day. Cloudy without the prison and cloudy within. Anxiously each prisoner awaits the hour when he shall be released! I find that the most profitable use of my time is in the perusal of the pages of God's Holy Word.

Saturday Jan 24th 1863
Today is my birthday! I am now 24 years old. In reviewing my life I see many, very many errors that I have committed for which as I grow older I hope to make amends and pray God to assist me by His grace. Still within

the walls of a dreary prison. Gloomy place! My thoughts often wander back to my native home. I think of father, mother, brothers and sisters. I think of many other dear friends who are very precious to me. When shall I again see them? Sometimes I think I cannot wait but then again I think patience and prayer are the best things to make me happy. Continued reading the scriptures and meditating thereon. The weather without continues cloudy and gloomy. It is amusing to see the prisoners - to see how they while away the hours. Some pass it away in repining, Some keep up a continual walking to and fro with eyes fixed on the floor. Some are playing cards - some checkers. Old letters - dear missives from loved ones are brought forth and read and read and re-read. Odd scraps of newspapers are well used. Stray leaves from old books we perused and more than one I now see today perusing the pages of the Bible. But the whole theme of conversation is in regard to getting out of prison and seeing home. They talk of home. They dream of home and "home, home, sweet home" seems to be the uppermost in their thoughts Home! How full of meaning it comprehends all that is dear to the poor hardship-enduring soldier. Sweet and endearing are the associations connected with the good "Home!"

[In the margin of this page are the words, "Happy Birthday! - in Libby Prison." An arrow points to January 24.]

Sunday Jan 25th 1863
Another six days are gone, another Sabbath dawns! It dawns not as I have seen it in other days, yet for all this it seems a holy time. The day was spent in reading the Psalms of David. At night, the prisoners held a prayer meeting - the first I have attended since leaving Louisville. The prison seemed as though it was a palace as the petitions ascended the Throne of the Great I Am.

Monday, Jan 26th 1863
This morning we exchange rooms. Worse than ever. O horrid place can I think of remaining here long! But the prospect is that we will get away soon. At last they tell us that we will be sent away tomorrow.

Chapter Seven
Repatriation and Home

Tuesday Jan 27th 1863
Am ready this morning about 2 o'clock to take our final departure from Richmond. No trouble to make the move as they are all anxious to leave. Without anything to eat, we take the Petersburg train which is 32 miles distant from Richmond. Arrived at Petersburg and take the train for City Point 9 miles distant.
On the way across the canal at Richmond the bridge broke down and several were drowned, the number I did not learn. At Petersburg I sold my mittens for a couple of light biscuits. As we neared City Point the flag of truce boats came in view. Again I saw the "Stars and Stripes" floating in the breeze of heaven. A joyful thrill came over me as I again beheld the beloved emblem of our national existence. I could then appreciate how dear it was to the American patriot heart. I felt as though I was under the protection of friends instead of foes. Poets may sing and Orators may declaim of the benefits and beauties of the "old flag" yet until a person is deprived of them and know that he is from under their protection he cannot tell how dear they are to his heart. I got aboard the "Metamora." Soon it was plowing the main down the James River toward Fortress Monroe. The river at City Point is about 4 miles wide. The river widens as its mouth is neared until it becomes quite a sea pass Newport News which is ten miles from Fortress Monroe. Here we begin to see the blockading squadron. Grand sight to see the "Linkum gunboats." Fortress Monroe next come in view.
Cast anchor to remain for the night. Lay down to sleep on the waters of the Chesapeake bay.

Wednesday Jan 28th 1863
This morning about 8 o'clock the proud ship is in motion bound for Annapolis. Leave Fortress Monroe and soon are out of sight of land and the boisterous waters of the Chesapeake. Here is displayed the wonderful works and power of the Almighty. I feel like saying with the poet:
> "We are out on an ocean sailing
> To a home beyond the tide."

Toward night the waters become so rough by the storm which is raging that we are compelled to cast anchor. I trust however, that -
> "All the storms will soon be o'er
> Then we'll anchor in the harbor."

Thursday Jan 29th 1863
The morning dawns and the bay is still ruffled. Remain til nearly night when the storm subsides and we are again in motion. Arrived at Annapolis at 9 1/2 o'clock. Draw rations and remain on board during the night.

Friday Jan 30th 1863
Remained aboard the Metamora till about noon when we are taken off and quartered in an old United States store house. In the evening, draw blankets.

Saturday Jan 31st 1863
Another beautiful morning. I find that we are quartered in the United States Navy Yard. Here is located the U. S. Navy School, but the buildings are now used as the U. S. General Hospital. This morning I visited the monuments erected to the memory of those who have fallen in some of the naval engagements. Here is the monument of the five brave officers who fell in the battle of Tripoli in 1804. At the base of the shaft of this splendid structure on the west is the inscription:
"Erected to the memory of Capt. Richard Somers, Lieutenants Jas. Caldwell, James Decatur, Henry Wadsworth, Joseph Israel and John Jorsey who fell in the different attacks that were made on the City of Tripoli in the year of our Lord 1804 and in the 28th year of the Independence of the United States" On the East is an engraving of the engagement. Near the center of the Navy Yard is the monument of Commodore Herndon. The inscription is simple being simply:
"Commodore Herndon"
Connected with the Hospitals which occupy the Navy School building is a reading room where the convalescent officers and soldiers may find anything in the way of books, magazines and all the late papers of the day free of charge. I visited the room and spent a pleasant hour in perusing the papers of the last month. I wrote a letter home informing them of my whereabouts. Having no money I had it franked by the surgeon of the hospital.

Sunday Feb 1st 1863
This beautiful Sabbath morning finds me on the land of the free. I cannot find language to express my feelings. I can only say that I am happy. Again visited the reading room where I spent a pleasant hour. At two o'clock a minister, of what denomination or his name I did not learn preached to the prisoners. Suffice it to say that he was a whole souled Christian as was manifested by his preaching. His text was 1st Kings 2nd Chapter and 2nd verse. His sermon was particularly addressed to young men. He said the

army was the place to show what a man was - in short to bring out the gold. How true!

Monday, Feb 2nd 1863
The morning is clear with a strong breeze from the lake. Again visited the reading room. Reading in Zions Advocate and Journal.

Tuesday, Feb 3d 1863
Not having a pencil I neglected to record the incidents of today, though I doubt not they are recorded in the Diary kept by my Heavenly Master. Every word, thought and deed are recorded. In the great day - the day when I shall see my heavenly home, may I not blush to read in that Great Diary the incidents of today recorded for me.

Wednesday Feb 4th 1863
O how cold it is this morning. Still at Annapolis not knowing when we will be sent away. Spent the day in the reading room.

Thursday Feb 5th 1863
The weather grows colder. Drew a full suit of clothes. Bathed and put them on and felt like a new man. My comrade J. North went to the College Hospital. I felt so lonely! Thoughts of home usher into my mind. A tear is wiped away and yet another comes until at length I have to sob aloud. But then I am comforted with the thought that God will wipe away the tears of them that weep. "Blessed are they that mourn for they shall be comforted." Comforting thought!

Friday Feb 6th 1863
Wet and dreary morning after the snow storm of yesterday. There seems to be quite an uneasiness manifested among the boys on account of several cases of small pox having occurred among the prisoners just arrived from Richmond. I do not feel quite so lonely yet I long for congenial companions - companions in whom I can confide but I cannot find them. In the evening took a stroll over the city of Annapolis. Mailed a letter to Melvina. Went to the barber shop and had a shave and hair cut.

Saturday Feb 7th 1863
The morning is a beautiful one after the wet and dreary day of yesterday. Went "down town" again this morning. Visited the printing offices of the "Republican" and "Gazette" They are both small and "weekly" not hardly sufficient patronage to keep them alive.

Sunday Feb 8th 1863
Bright and beautiful is this another holy Sabbath day. A sacred brightness gilds the horizon. I went to the M.E. Sabbath School this morning. It reminded me of other days - days when I was permitted to meet and mingle with those I love in the Sabbath School. This is the first time I have been in the Sabbath School for six months. Remained for church. Heard Rev. Mr. Riley preach from the words "What will it profit a man if he shall gain the whole world and lose his own soul? Or what will a man give in exchange for his soul?" Great and powerful was the manner in which this man of God expounded the words of his text. In the evening he continued his subject.

Monday Feb 9th 1863
The sun shines beautifully. We were removed from the barracks near Annapolis to the "Parole camp" about two miles from the city. After reaching camp we found no tents or anything for sleeping accommodations but the cold wet sand consequently there was considerable dissatisfaction among the boys. Through the kindness of W. Hirsh a Co C boy I was taken in and cared for. Saw John Bayer and learned that Lieut Gillinan was wounded.

Tuesday Feb 10th 1863
Clear morning. The day feels like a warm day in spring. Wrote Annie a letter. I feel today as though I would like to be any where besides where I am. Received a Testament from the agent of the Baltimore Bible Society who was gratuitously distributing them to the paroled prisoners.

Wednesday Feb 11th 1863
A snow storm occurred today which reminded me of a winter day at home. Feel quite unwell. Visited the reading room connected with "Camp Parole Hospital." Did not remain long on account of feeling unwell.

Thursday Feb 12th 1863
Nothing of very much importance occurred today. Still unwell. Wrote a letter to Capt. Lambert. Spent a few moments of the evening in the reading room.

Friday Feb 13th 1863
Cool. Wrote W.A. Haworth. Heard a sermon of Henry Ward Beecher's.

Saturday Feb 14th 1863
Today is a blank. Nothing occurred worthy of note.

Sunday Feb 15th 1863
The Sabbath is again here. Rainy morning. Remained in camp all day. Reading in the Testament.

Monday Feb 16th 1863
Took a jaunt out through the country today. The country is rough and hilly. As yet I have received no word from home. Why it is I cannot tell.

Tuesday Feb 17th 1863
Received a letter from T.A.H. Cones. A deep snow fell. Concluded to start home afoot. Got five miles in the country where I put up for the night.

Wednesday Feb 18th 1863
Traveled all day and turned in for the night at a Mr. Anderson's. Very tired and sick. The soil is very sandy over the country we passed today.

Thursday Feb 19th 1863
Came to the Baltimore & Washington R.R. where I was intercepted by the guard and arrested. Put in the guard house to remain until sent away.

Friday Feb 20th 1863
Remained in guard house all day.

Saturday Feb 21st 1863
Still no tidings come of our release. Dreamily the hours pass.

Sunday Feb 22nd 1863
Washington's Birthday! Today one year ago I was in the full enjoyment of life. Snow storm.

Monday Feb 23rd 1863
The sun shines brilliantly. Still confined in the guard house. Tonight about 9 o'clock we succeeded in getting out. Left the guard watching an empty guard house. Good joke on the guard. Made tracks for Annapolis.

Tuesday Feb 24th 1863
Arrived at "Camp Parole" today about 12 o'clock after having rested at a guard station till this morning. Received a letter from home. Feel glad, gladder, gladdest.

86th Indiana Regiment, Volunteer Infantry, abridged

The Story of John Gilliland

*D*uring the earlier months of 1863, especially January and February, the official mortality rate throughout the army was great. Shoulder straps fell like the leaves of autumn after a hoar frost. General Rosecrans made use of every means to promote efficiency. He was lavish of praise to the meritorious, and utterly ruthless toward the undeserving. By General Orders, No. 30, dated February 24, he dishonorably dismissed fifty-two officers of all grades from Colonel down to Second Lieutenant, for various offenses, such as absence without leave, cowardice in the face of the enemy, drunkenness, disobedience of orders, gross neglect of duty, incompetency and other peccadilloes detrimental to military discipline, two of whom were from the 86th, Colonel O. S. Hamilton and First Lieutenant John S. Armitage, of Company B, the former for incompetency, and the latter for abandoning his company in the face of the enemy. The fault for which Colonel Hamilton was publicly disgraced was expiated in the front line at Stone's River, and though his own officers and men could not refuse their admiration for his heroic conduct, yet General Rosecrans was inexorable. In July Captain Nelson R. Smith, of Company G. was cashiered by order of court martial on a charge of drunkenness, while Captain William C. Lambert, of Company I, met a like fate by a similar process, on a charge or cowardice. First Lieutenant John Gilliland, of Company I, was arrested and tried by court martial, charged with being a deserter from the Fifty-first Illinois Regiment.

The story of Lieutenant Gilliland has in it all the elements of somber romance and is of thrilling interest. He was born in the northeastern part of Montgomery county, Indiana, where he grew to manhood with absolutely no education. Though he could neither read nor write, yet he was a magnificent specimen of the physical man, naturally intelligent, industrious, and of kindly temper. It so happened that in 1861 business took him to Illinois, and to the town in which the Fifty-first regiment of that State was being organized. Being an intensely loyal man, he enlisted.

The Fifty-first went at once to the front, and Gilliland saw active service in the first year of the war, proving himself a brave and true soldier. In 1862 he was allowed to come home on a furlough. While home the Eighty-sixth was organizing at LaFayette. Gilliland went up to that city with the boys from his neighborhood, and having some knowledge of drill his services were called into requisition. Not knowing the enormity of the offense of desertion he made the proposition to the members of Company I that if they would elect him First Lieutenant he would enlist with them. Ignorant of the fact that he was still in the service they accepted his proposition.

As First Lieutenant of Company I he commanded the respect of his men and the confidence of his superior officers. His ability and bravery were repeatedly demonstrated, and but for his illiteracy would have made an officer of marked distinction. All went well with him until the battle of Stone's River. Just before this memorable engagement Captain Lambert of the same company, was taken sick quite suddenly and was unable to enter the action. The command of the company, therefore, devolved upon Gilliland and he led the men through the battle with distinguished bravery.

Just here Gilliland made a great mistake. After the battle he very foolishly preferred charges of cowardice against Lambert, alleging that he had feigned illness in order to avoid the dangers of shot and shell. If Gilliland had not been living is a glass house himself his action might have been reasonable, but as it was it proved his ruin. Captain Lambert, who was cognizant of Gilliland's military record, promptly retaliated by preferring charges of desertion against his accuser. He was placed in arrest, and tried by court martial at Chattanooga during the latter part of 1863. In the meantime Gilliland was permitted to march in the rear of the regiment nominally under guard. The President of the court was Lieutenant Colonel Brown, of the Sixty-fourth Ohio. The court arraigned "Private John I. Gilliland, Company E, Fifty-first Illinois Volunteers," on two charges, the first of which was desertion, and the second was violation of the 22d Article of War in that he enlisted and accepted a commission in the Eighty-sixth Indiana Infantry, he being at the time a deserter from the Fifty-first Illinois Infantry. To the charges and specifications Gilliland pleaded "not guilty." The finding of the court was in both charges and in all the specifications, "guilty." Then followed this awful sentence: "And therefore the court does therefore sentence him, Private John I. Gilliland, Company E, Fifty-first Illinois Volunteers, 'to be shot to death with musketry at such time and place as the Commanding General may direct, two-thirds of the court concurring therein.'"

Before the finding of the court martial could be promulgated it must necessarily be transmitted to the War Department for approval or modification. June 4, 1864, more than a year after he had been arrested and eight months after he had been arraigned, the Secretary of War modified the sentence, upon the recommendation of his commanding officer to executive clemency, on account of his good conduct in battle, so as to restore him to duty in Company E, Fifty-first Illinois Volunteers. Finally, the order reached the Eighty-sixth while the army was in Northern Georgia. Gilliland did not wait to hear the modification of the sentence. There being no strict watch over him he experienced little difficulty in escaping from the army that very night. From that time on nothing was heard from him by his comrades-in-arms or by his family for more than a quarter of a century.

One summer evening, along about 1890, many years after the war had passed into history, Tilghman Bailey, of Company I, was standing in front of his farm house, a few miles from Clark's Hill, and watching his cattle feeding in the adjoining fields. As he rested there content with his prosperity, he was approached by an old decrepit, stooping and travel-stained stranger, who was evidently suffering from consumption. He was poorly clad, but when he spoke, addressing to Bailey some commonplace remark, his voice and something in his manner brought up a flood of half-forgotten recollections. Sometime, somewhere he had seen this strange man before. Conversation was continued on timely topics, and suddenly to Bailey as they talked, came the identity of the man, causing him to exclaim involuntarily: "Isn't your name John Gilliland?" The old man's face lighted up at the recognition. Bailey, of course bade him stay and he shared with him the hospitalities of his home. Here the story of the wanderer was told. When he left the regiment he made for the mountains, away from the railroad and from any thoroughfare. Stopping at the house of an old mountaineer he told him his true story. The rustic of the forest and hills gave him shelter and assured him that he should be protected from both armies. And there he remained for twenty-five years. At last, overtaken by ill health and becoming weary of his voluntary exile, and stirred by the recollections of his youth and the memories of kindred and friends, he ventured a visit to his old home, hoping that he would, unmolested, be permitted to die in the land of his birth. The fruition of his hopes were realized, for in less than a year afterward, John Gilliland was "honorably discharged" by the Great Commander. Verily, truth is sometimes stranger than fiction.

Wednesday Feb 25th 1863
Clear morning. Unwell. Wrote T.A.H. Cones a letter.

Thursday Feb 26th 1863
Rainy day which makes it a dreary one. Nothing occurred to change the monotony of the camp.

Friday Feb 27th 1863
Received a letter from Annie & Frank. Glad to hear from them.

Saturday Feb 28th 1863
Writing for the Company Sergeant filling out the muster rolls. 'Tis Saturday night yet the week closes not as it does at home. No preparations are being made for the Sabbath. No thought of the morrow for once enters the minds of the many soldiers in this vast encampment.

Sunday March 1st 1863
Spring time has again come yet I am away from home among strangers and as it were on a foreign shore. I wonder if they miss me at home when the shadows of evening gather around the family circle and they are seated around the cheerful hearth. Do they still set me a chair at the table at the accustomed place where so often I have sat and feasted on the good things prepared by mother's hand? How well do I remember the many times she saved for me the fat limbs of a fried chicken. I wonder if loved ones there watch for my approaching footsteps. Yes, I believe they still think of me. But here I am, this Holy Sabbath, not surrounded with any of the benign influences of home, but am surrounded with none but the low, vicious and wicked. Gladly would I see home were it possible but I must rest content.

Monday March 2nd 1863
Nothing going on in camp to change the monotony thereof. Borrowed $5.00 from A.R. Crafton. Spent an hour in the reading room.

Tuesday March 3rd 1863
Wrote home. A storm in the afternoon. In the reading room where I spent a pleasant hour in perusing Harper's old magazines etc..

Wednesday March 4th 1863
A cold day. Wrote a letter for the "Indiana American." Nothing more worthy of note occurred today. Received a letter from W.A. Haworth.

Thursday March 5th 1863
Wrote W.A. Haworth a letter. Also wrote Emma. The day was spent with

but little calculated to advance or improve my intellectual or moral facilities.

Friday March 6th 1863
Spent a good part of the day in the reading room perusing "Harper's Monthly."

Saturday March 7th 1863
Rainy and dreary day. In the reading room. 'Tis again Saturday night. What a different picture is presented in the preparations made for the duties of tomorrow as compared with home. Wonder what they are doing at home. I expect they are thinking of me.

Sunday March 8th 1863
Again the Sabbath dawns. In company with some of my fellow soldiers I attend church at Annapolis. On entering the church door my ear is greeted with the sweet songs of Zion uttered by infant lips. What a delightful picture to look upon. How it reminds me of the words of Our Saviour when he said "Suffer little children to come unto me and forbid them not for of such is the kingdom of heaven." I am reminded of other and happier days - days when my youthful feet trod in the path that led to the old frame church which stood on the village lawn. Can I forget the impressions that were then instilled into my young and tender mind. Sabbath School over I remain seated for church. While seated there awaiting services to commence I mused upon the past. I thought of the many times I had met with friends to worship. I cannot but love the scene that we daily witness or rather what we weekly witness in a land of peace. The assembly of the good to worship God. How lovely is the sight to see children, the lambs of the flock meeting in the Sanctuary. Then the youth and middle aged. Then by lovelier far the aged sire whose head is silvered o'er with the frosts of many winters and the aged matron leaning on her staff to stay her trembling limbs. The preacher took his text. His sermon was the teaching of earnest practical Christianity. As I left the church I felt as though I had been much benefitted.

Monday March 9th 1863
Received a letter from my friend Howard Cones. Preparations are being made to leave on the morrow in accordance with the order from the War Department. Did up some washing.

Tuesday March 10th 1863
This is the fixed day for our departure from "Camp Parole." The men were

stirring early making the necessary preparations. Anxiously they awaited orders all day to move. At length the expected orders came. Soon we were all in motion like so many sheep. Had not gone far when the order was countermanded on account of there being no boat to take us away. Got nearly back to camp when word came that the boat had arrived. Boarded the boat & remained till morning.

Wednesday March 11th 1863
The boat moved out this morning in the direction of Baltimore. Arrived at Baltimore at about 11 o'clock, but did not get off the boat. Waiting patiently all day. Slept on the hurricane deck.

Thursday March 12th 1863
Early this morning we landed and were taken to the "Union Reliefs Association" where we breakfasted. After marching almost all over the City of Baltimore were taken to the B & H R.R. where we got aboard the train bound for Pittsburg via Harrisburg.

Friday March 13th 1863
Still on the go this morning. Here we go up the "Blue Inniatta" over snow crested mountains, through forests, over bridges, through tunnels winding our way over the Alleghanies till we come in view of the "Iron City." Arrived in Pittsburg where I partook of the hospitalities of the citizens in the way of a splendidly gotten up supper at the "City Hall."

Saturday March 14th 1863
This morning took the P.W. & C.R.R. Passed through northern Ohio as far as Crestline the country is gently undulating presenting to the eye beautiful scenery. From Crestline to Columbus the soil is of a rich quality though the country is level. At any rate everything has a different appearance to that of the Southern Confederacy. It bears the aspect of thrift and enterprise. Arrived at Columbus about 4 o'clock. Marched up through the city and out to "Camp Chase" 4 miles from the city.

Sunday March 15th 1863
Took a stroll around camp this beautiful Sabbath morning. It is a large encampment and has the appearance of a young and thriving city. The soldiers are all quartered in whitewashed barracks. There are about 1100 secesh prisoners. The day closed with nothing particularly interesting.

Monday, March 16th 1863
Wrote to my friend Howard Cones. Told him to send me $10.

Tuesday March 17th 1863
The day is a beautiful one! reminding me of other spring days- days when war was not known - when peace was the requiem that was sung around the fireside circle - when the "soldier volunteer" was surrounded with friends of childshoods years.

Wednesday March 18th 1862
The morning is cool. Acted in the office as clerk. I have often thought what a pleasant thing it would be were there less profanity among the soldiers. A writer in the "Atlantic Monthly" says. "One of the greatest discomforts of a soldier who desires to remain a gentleman in the camp is the perpetual reiteration of language which no decent lips would dare to utter in a sisters presence."

Thursday March 19th 1863
The morning is cloudy and cool. Took a stroll down the pike toward the bridge across the Sciota river. This soil in the Sciota bottom is on the richest quality. Returned and reading in the "Cincinnati Commercial." Saw that the French had captured the City of Mexico.

Friday March 20th 1863
A genuine March day. Snowy and stormy. Went to the city of Columbus.

Saturday March 21st 1863
Cloudy morning. In company with P. Pery went to the library connected with "Camp Chase" where I got a book, the "Four Pillars of Christianity."

Sunday March 22nd 1863
A beautiful morning in spring. All nature has put on a smile. The birds are warbling their sweetest notes. The Spring time has again come yet the loved ones are far away. I often think of the "absent." Heard a short discourse from a minister whose name I could not learn. His remarks were very applicable to the soldier.

Monday March 23rd 1863
Today took a stroll through a beautiful wood near camp through which flows a beautiful little streamlet. I sat me down on the grass grown banks to muse. The gentle murmuring of the water as it flowed over its pebly bottom

reminded me of a little stream upon whose banks I have so often sat in days gone by but like the bubbles of that little stream I have been born down the current upon the stream of Time. A few years ago I was at the source of this stream but each day brings me nearer the mouth or perhaps I, like many of the bubbles I saw, will be broken and my name forgotten.

Tuesday March 24th 1863
Still no tidings from home. Writing letters home to Frank Cones & Melina and W.A. Haworth.

Wednesday March 25th 1863
Weather changeable. Sometimes raining, sometimes snowing and withal very disagreeable.

Thursday March 26th 1863
Weather continues changeable. It is amusing to go the Post Office. Anxiously and patiently each one awaits his turn to "inquire." Each one expects to get a missive from loved ones at home. Some get the expected missives and some do not. A perceivable difference can be seen in their countenances. While the one can scarcely wait to open the envelope and read the lines penned by some loved friend the other goes away with disappointment stamped on his physique. I have to note myself among the latter number.

Friday March 27th 1863
Clear and beautiful after the storm of yesterday. It is just such a day as I love in spring. A couple of the softer sex visited the camp today. It is so seldom that soldiers have the pleasure of beholding rareties that they gazed with admiration upon them. They seemed like angel visits.

Saturday March 28th 1863
Beautiful morning. Preparations are being made for our departure on the morrow for Indianapolis. Anxiously awaiting a letter but none comes.

Sunday March 29th 1863
Early this morning we were "Homeward Bound." Took the cars for Indianapolis on the C.P. & I. R.R. The country through which we pass is a beautiful one. Though level yet it presents the appearance of being cultivated by a white man. On entering my native State a peculiar sensation came over me, though had I not known that it was "old Indiana again"

perhaps it would not have been so. As I neared the "Railroad City" I felt that I was "almost home." Arrived in the city at dusk, and quartered at Camp Carrington the identical ground on which the 86th Regiment encamped seven months ago.

Monday March 30th 1863
Early this morning I went "down town." Met with old friends among whom was J.H. Smith whose memory I shall always cherish. Also met Dr. Boyd from Thorntown. Strange to say he could not recognize me. Though it was from the fact of my having so much changed in health.

Tuesday March 31st 1863
"Snowy and Blowy" as we children used to say. Went to town saw Col. Maxwell who went with me to see Adj. Gen. Noble in regard to a furlough. Met with Mr. Goodwin in the Book Store who invited me to accompany him home. I willingly accepted the invitation. Glad to see Mrs. Goodwin.

Wednesday April 1st 1863
Came to town but returned to Mrs. Goodwin's where I remained overnight.

Thursday April 2nd 1863
Came to town. Reported at camp. Obtained a furlough for ten days. Went up to Thorntown. "Home again." Glad to see many of my old and tried friends, who gave me a cordial reception. Being solicited to address them on what I saw in Dixie I complied with the request. Went home and met mother, sisters and brothers.

Friday April 3rd 1863
Spent the day in making calls. In the evening went out to W.A. Haworth's with whom I was glad to meet. Glad to see Sophia and "Gustie."

Saturday April 4th 1863
Spent the night. Got a haircut. Good discussion on war, holy scripture and such. Went home. Reading God's Word.

Sunday April 5th 1863
This bright and beautiful Sabbath morning I can but thank my Heavenly Master that through many changes I am permitted to meet in the class room, in the old church and in the Sabbath School. Heard Prof. Smith lecture. Subject "The Human Tongue."

Monday April 6th 1863
Went to the election. Called at Mr. Higgins'. Addressed the citizens in the vicinity of Hills School House.

Tuesday April 7th 1863
At home. Took tea with S. Green. Addressed the citizens in the vicinity of Morrison's School House. Went home with W.W. Haworth.

Wednesday April 8th 1863
At town. At home. At Jamison's School House.

Thursday April 9th 1863
At Uncle Robert's & Uncle John More's S. House.

Friday April 10th 1863
Home again. Bade them all farewell. Came to Thorntown at the Union Society. Went serenading.

Saturday April 11th 1863
Spent the forenoon in making calls. In the afternoon bade Thorntown farewell. Came to the city and reported at Camp Carrington.

Sunday April 12th 1863
At class at Robert's Chapel. Heard a even sermon there.

Monday April 13th 1863
The day passed with nothing of importance. Feel quite lonely.

Tuesday April 14th 1863
Copying my journal. Received a note from Mert Saylor. Answered same.

Wednesday April 15th 1863
Writing in this journal. This part of my life is blank.

Thursday April 16th 1863
Writing in this journal. This part of my life is blank.

Friday April 17th 1863
Plucked the first flower of spring. Hail radiant spring. Thou hast come and the cold and dreary winter is gone. Hail, Spring!

Saturday April 18th 1863
Went up to Thorntown. Glad to get back again. Went out to W.A. Haworth's. Came back to town early this morning. Quarterly meeting. Heard Rev. Mr. Birgner preach. At Sabbath School and Sacrament of the Lord's Supper. Heard Rev. Mr. Cunningham preach at night.

Monday April 19th 1863
Went out home this morning. Father sold his farm today. Remained overnight.

Tuesday April 20th 1863
Went with father to Darlington at G. M. Kinsey's. Stayed all night at John Hutchings. Saw Lou who has been married since I saw her.

Wednesday April 21st 1863
Came to Thorntown with the intention of going to Indianapolis but was too late for the train. Rainy day.

Thursday April 22nd 1863
Came to the city and reported at camp. From April 22nd 1863 until May 31st 1863 I was at home and at Indianapolis. The transactions were so monotonous that I did not keep a record of the events. Suffice it to say that I enjoyed myself hugely . After remaining there in full felicity till the above date I succeeded in getting transportation to the regiment having been duly and regularly exchanged. All prisoners are exchanged up to April 1st.

Chapter Eight
Bound for Dixie

Friday May 29th
Stayed last night with my dear friend James H. Smith, a noble fellow. I went to work and succeeded in getting transportation. I made some calls after which I took the Jeffersonville train at 6 o'clock bound for Dixie. Arrived in Jeffersonville crossed the Ohio and went to Barracks No 1 Louisville where I remained till morning.

Saturday May 30th 1863
Early this morning to the _____ and after traveling all day passing through _____ Kentucky arrive in Nashville at six o'clock.

Sunday May 31st 1863
Took the train for Murfreesboro. The ever memorable battlefield of Stone River. Again met the 86th after an absence of just five months this day. Glad to see the boys again. Met with a cordial reception. In the afternoon visited the 40th where I met many old friends.

Monday June 1st 1863
Morning pleasant. In company with Jim Darrow and Dock. I visited the 72nd. Saw many Thorntown boys.

Tuesday June 2nd 1863
Nothing of importance occurred to change the usual routine of camp life. Wrote letters to home.

Wednesday June 3rd 1863
In company with Jim Darrow I went to see the fortifications which are very formidable and which I think would frustrate the enemy no matter what his force might be.

Thursday June 4th 1863
Beautiful morning. Stayed around camp. Wrote a letter to Frank Cones and James H. Smith. Visited Capt. Lambert who is sick at the officers hospital in Murfreesboro.

Friday June 5th 1863
Clear day. On drill today. Drilling goes the same. Wearied me much.

Saturday June 6th 1863
Today set apart as wash day. Consequently we are exempt from all military duty except that of cleaning up, etc..

Sunday June 7th 1863
Tis the Sabbath, the time of rest. Gladly does the soldier welcome this day. Heard no religious services of any kind yet it seems much like the Sabbath because of the stillness which pervades.

Monday June 8th 1863
Chilled all night. Burning fever all day. Not able to sit up at all during the day.

Tuesday June 9th 1863
Reported to the surgeon this morning. Without examining me or even casting his eyes towards me he reported me to the company for duty. When will such men get their just dues?

Wednesday June 10th 1863
Showery all day. Feel quite unwell. Wrote home. Commenced the study of rhetoric and geometry. With what success the future only can tell.

Thursday June 11th 1863
Still continues showery. Studying my lessons in geometry and rhetoric.

Friday June 12th 1863
On drill both forenoon and afternoon. Clear day.

Saturday June 13th 1863
In the afternoon went to Stone River to bathe. Suffering with a severe headache.

Sunday June 14th 1863
This beautiful Sabbath morning I took a stroll in company with Darrow to a beautiful wood near camp. It bore the mark of once having been a beautiful lawn to the rear of which stood a stately villa occupied no doubt by a rich rebel. But lo all now is desolation and ruin.

Monday June 15th 1863
Wrote a letter this morning to my friend Jo Foxworthy. Witnessed a flag presentation by the citizens of Fountain and Warren Counties to the 86th

Reg. Ind. Vol. The presentation speech was made by a Mr. Poole of Attica. Col. Dick replied in a short and I presume an appropriate speech. The tone was so low I could not hear it.

Tuesday June 16th 1863
Today witnessed the execution of a deserter in the 9th Ky. The scene was such that I have no desire to witness again.

86th Regiment, Indiana Volunteer Infantry, abridged

The Execution

Desertions from the army had grown to alarming proportions. When caught the deserters were usually given a trial and a light sentence imposed. They were seldom executed, and even when a court martial imposed a sentence of death the kindhearted President would interpose with a pardon. The most usual sentence was that the deserter should return to the army and serve out all of his original time of enlistment which had not been served, without pay.

An instance of this kind occurred in the Ninth Kentucky. A soldier named Minnick had deserted for the third time. With each recurrence he was caught and returned to the regiment. The last time he was tried by a court martial and sentenced to be shot. This occasion the President declined to interpose.

The execution of Minnick took place on the 16th of June (1863), about a mile north of the encampment of the Eighty-sixth. A detail of one man from each company of the Eighty-sixth was made to do the shooting. The convicted soldier was placed in an ambulance, seated on his coffin, a rough box, and taken to the place of execution, accompanied by the entire Twenty-first corps.

When the corps arrived at the chosen place it was formed into a hollow square, with the fourth side left open, to witness the sad affair. It was used on this occasion for an imposing display, and to intimidate and prevent other soldiers from committing a like crime. All who witnessed it seemed to feel the solemn presence of death.

The coffin was placed in the open part of the square. Minnick took a seat on the rough casket. The Adjutant General in a clear but tremulous voice read the finding of the court martial to the troops. When the Adjutant finished reading, the guards, detailed to do the firing, were ordered forward, and their muskets, which had been loaded by other soldiers, were handed to them.

Half of them contained blank cartridges, so that none of them knew whose shot killed the prisoner.

The condemned soldier was blindfolded, and the final order: "Ready - Aim - Fire!" was given and the doomed man fell over dead. The troops then formed company front and marched in review by the coffin to view the body of their late comrade. This was the only execution that the Eighty-sixth was ever called out to witness.

Indiana's Roll of Honor, Volume I, abridged

The Chaplain and the Deserter

Father Cooney, chaplain of the 35th Regiment, was loved by the men of his regiment. In the discharge of his duties, he did not conform himself to his own regiment, but whenever and wherever his service were required, they were freely bestowed.

Michael Nash, a private in the Sixty-fifth regiment Ohio Volunteers, was sentenced to be shot to death at Nashville, on the fifteenth of June, 1863. The sentence was to have taken effect between the hours of 2 and 4 p.m. Father Cooney, hearing of the affair, started for Nashville, to be present at the execution, and administer the rites of his church to the condemned man.

Having prepared the unfortunate soldier for his final march, the Chaplain made inquiries respecting his case. The facts were these: On the morning of the thirty-first of December, when Johnson's division was surprised, and McCook hurled from his position by a superior force, the Sixty-fifth was thrown into momentary confusion. Nash, being separated from his command, fell into the tide of fugitives who were retreating towards Nashville.

By the irresistible current of panic-stricken soldiers, he was carried back to Lavergne. Here he was arrested. From the evidence it appeared that Nash did not intend to desert. He might have been brave as those, who stood the galling fire; but having been caught by the rushing current of a panic, he was swept from the field.

It was now half past twelve p.m. on execution day. If the unfortunate man was to be saved, no time must be lost in communicating with the General. Without making known his intentions to anyone, Father Cooney telegraphed General Rosecrans, at Murfreesboro, the facts of the case, and the circumstances supporting them, and concluded by saying:

> "Were I under the impression that he intentionally deserted, I would not say a word in his behalf; the good of the service would require his death. But I am convinced of the contrary. I respectfully beg, therefore, for him some other punishment than death.
>
> P. P. Cooney
> Chaplain, 35th Ind. Vols.
>
> Two o'clock arrived, but brought no answer to the dispatch. The detail to fire upon Nash assembled; their guns were loaded; the ground for his execution was selected, and about three thousand persons were assembled to witness the tragedy.
>
> The open coffin awaited its victim, and an artisan unfastens the heavy shackles from the culprit's limbs, that he may take his last march on the great highway which leads from Time to Eternity. A messenger enters the cell and hands to the jailer one of those "yellow-covered" communications. "His death warrant," whispered someone, and all was still as death. The jailer broke the seal and read aloud:
>
> "Michael Nash, sentenced to be shot today, is reprieved.
> "By order of Maj. Gen. Rosecrans."

Wednesday June 17th 1863
Received a letter from Melvina. Unable _____

Thursday June 18th 1863
Answered the letter I received yesterday though hardly able to write.

Friday June 19th 1863
Still unwell. Keep my bed most of the time.

Saturday June 20th 1863
The boys went across the river today to clean off a camp to which we move.

Sunday June 21st 1863
Tis a lovely Sabbath morning. Feel better today. Walked over to where the 40th is encamped.

Monday June 22nd 1863
Today we changed camps. Moved across Stone River on the west side near the fortifications. Not able to sit up.

Tuesday June 23rd 1863
Fixing up camp, cleaning streets etc. Received a letter from F.M. Cones.

Wednesday June 24th 1863
Today the army of the Cumberland commanded by Gen. Rosecrans moved from Murfreesboro in the direction of Shelbyville, at which point it is said the enemy has concentrated his forces. It may be that a hard fought battle may take place and it may be that the enemy may fall back to Chattanooga. The future is looked forward to with interest. Simultaneously almost with the movement of the army a heavy rain commenced and continued all day coming in torrents. Almost such a day when Rosecrans moved from Nashville the 26th of December.

Thursday June 25th 1863
Continues to rain. Notwithstanding the heavy rain the bustle and confusion of an army in motion continues unabated. This afternoon appearances are that the rain is over.

Friday June 26th 1863
Received letters from my friends Ollie Higgins and James H. Smith. Wrote to Annie Cones and J.H. Smith. Still rainy and wet.

Saturday June 27th 1863
Detailed today at Brigade Headquarters as orderly.

Sunday June 28th 1863
Reported for duty at headquarters. It seems very little like Sunday today. I wish I could enjoy a Sabbath again.

Monday June 29th 1863
On duty today. Riding considerable among the regiments of the brigade.

Tuesday June 30th 1863
Went to Murfreesboro after a box of provisions sent from home. With it I received some Ladies Repositories and letters from my friends Foxworthy, Frank and Annie Cones.

Wednesday July 1st 1863
Reading in the Repositories does me much good, does me more good because they come from home.

Thursday July 2nd 1863
On duty again today. The leisure time I spent in reading.

Friday July 3rd 1863
Wrote to Ollie Higgins. Took a stroll with Belknap over to convalescent camp. Had a pleasant conversation with Col. Blake who has command of the camp now.

Saturday July 4th 1863
Tis Independence Day. The glorious 4th. While friends no doubt are celebrating this day at home, soldiers are celebrating it in the field. Would that the soldiers too could celebrate this day at home.

Sunday July 5th 1863
Started this morning about six o'clock on march. As I had a horse to ride it was much easier than on former marches. Marched today 23 miles over a country most of which was rather barren. Halted at Woodbury for the night.

Monday July 6th 1863
Started early this morning again. Did not march so hard as yesterday. Came within six miles of McMinnville and camped for the night. The country about the same as yesterday.

Tuesday July 7th 1863
Entered McMinnville about 10 o'clock. Encamped close to town where it is supposed we will remain sometime.

Wednesday July 8th 1863
On duty today. Nothing worthy of note occurred . The same drill monotony prevails as usual.

Thursday July 9th 1863
Went to the river this morning which runs near our encampment. Barren Fork is a swift silvery stream winding its way through the rugged recesses of the hills which border the Cumberland mountains. I bathed in its waters and felt much refreshed. In the evening good news, glorious news came in. Vicksburg has Fallen! Lee's army completely annihilated! Gen. Meade garnered a great victory etc. Important if true. If this be correct, Gen. Meade is the right man in the right place, just such a man as has long been needed in the army of the Potomac. Inquiry for the elements which work together

in our country for or against the consummations of the utter soul of Lee may be as needful, if not as exciting, as the study of events which led to recent conquests or defeats, or which, keeping the allied armies of England, France and Turkey before Sebastapol disturbed the political relations and threatened to whelm all the nations in wars, confusions distresses and uncertainties. The want of the right man in the right place has been pronounced by the leading organs of opinion in England to have been the chief cause of the long siege in the Crimea. With the woeful waste of life and treasure which the history of its camps and trenches, its stratagems and marches and fights exposes. Similar is our care today in America consequently for the right man in the right place war's triumphs must wait, it may be at perilous sacrifices..

Friday July 10th 1863
The day is cloudy, ominous of rain. Went out to escort the 13th and 59th Ohio in who have been to Manchester. I thought while the boys were wading the river that it would be a good sketch for Frank Leslie. Many amusing incidents occurred while crossing.

Saturday July 11th 1863
The morning is hazy. Very warm and sultry. It may be that I will some day experience what one of England's truest said
  "Sleep after toil, port after stormy seas
  Ease after war, death after life, does greatly please"
The rest of heaven would be less inviting to the Christian but for the toils of earth.

Sunday July 12th 1863
The Holy Sabbath dawneth. Another six days are gone and unremembered with the buried past. This holy day dawns not as bright and beautiful as I have seen it in other and happier days - when I mingled my voice with the loving ones at home. Hearing that there were to be religious services in the village church I accordingly made preparations to go. I went and took a seat in the back part of the house. The preacher, an aged man, whose locks were silvered o'er with the frosts of many winters had taken his text - but - from the run of his subject, he was on justification by faith. I left with the impression that the picture is changed in the McMinnville Baptist church from that of two years ago. Then it was a congregation of citizens worshiping under their own vine and fig tree. Now it is mostly comprised of soldiers who had left their homes in the free north to crush a rebellion which was conceived in sin, brought forth in iniquity as a child of satan, and will go as

Babylon went. In the afternoon the dreary hours gave scarce a sound save the continued beat of ceaseless, countless, drizzly drops of rain. Silently I sit and listen to the rain while two are sleeping - sleeping when all the rain falls now unhindered. But while I listen to the gentle patter of the soft rain overhead I think of those lines of Luella Clark:
"Beyond these stormy skies lies realms of calm
Then, surging, soar
Larklike above thy pains."
Yes, on the still shore of hope we can pluck leaves of palm to strew along the paths on our onward, upward flight to the bright mansions where the weary are at rest."

Monday July 13th 1863
Still cloudy portending rain. Went to a blackberry patch for the purpose of getting some blackberries. In the afternoon a sprinkle of rain fell. I neglected to say yesterday that I wrote letters to my friends Foxworthy, Prof. Smith and Miss. Burton.

Tuesday 14th 1863
Eleven months today since I volunteered in my country's defense. Spent a good portion of the time today in reading.

Wednesday July 15th 1863
Received letters today from home. Abbie Waring, Nate Hargon and Annie Cones. Glad to hear from them.

Thursday July 16th 1863
Assisted Lieut. Sells to make out the pay rolls in Co. J, 59th Ohio. Signed the pay rolls in my own company. Wrote a letter for Andrew Rash.

Friday July 17th 1863
On duty today. Reading the "Lady of the Lake". Writing for Lieut. Sells.

Saturday July 18th 1863
Received four month's pay, $52.00. Sent $40.00 home by the allotment plan. Heard of the fall of Port Hudson as also the fall of Charleston.

Sunday July 19th 1863
Somewhat cloudy this Holy Sabbath morning. Went to church. Heard the pastor a Baptist minister.

Monday July 20th 1863
On duty today. Nothing of very much importance occurred.

Tuesday July 21st 1863
At the river washing. Had blankets washed up. Wrote a letter to Lide.

Wednesday July 22nd 1863
Received a letter from home. Glad to hear from those I most love.

Thursday July 23rd 1863
On duty. Had considerable riding to do. Wrote letters home and Frank
Cones.

Friday July 24th 1863
"The world is _____ for a _____ garden
You are to be a seed not a _____ you will sprout
        yourself and you will decay"
"Thus spoke Gail Hamilton.

Saturday July 25th 1863
We can only realize the glory of coming time by considering the grandeur of
the present. The present speaks with eloquence and sublimity of the distant
future. Not a year, scarcely a day, but records some improvement but the
day that I have just spent is passed with no observed improvement.

Sunday July 26th 1863
Again on duty. Wrote letter to my friend Mate Harryman. Tis the Sabbath
day. I hear the church bells calling the good to the house of God. They
assemble but I am not permitted to join them.

Monday July 27th 1863
Today I was detailed as clerk for the Reg. on Col. Dick's staff. Wrote a letter
to Lida Gibson.

Tuesday July 28th 1863
Writing in the office. Sent letter to Mate and Annie Cones.

Saturday August 16th 1863
The days that have intervened nothing has occurred to change the monotony
of the daily routine of duties. Some day I have been busy writing, others any
thing to do. I like my present position and will endeavor to discharge my

duties to the best of my ability. Yesterday I received a letter from my friend Mate Hargrave. I was very glad to hear from her. This morning I received a missive from Lida Gibson. She is a whole souled girl and a good friend. Would that all my friends were as true. The morning is a lovely one. All nature smiles. Everything looks fresh and gay since the refreshing showers of yesterday. The prospects at present are favorable for a speedy close of this cruel war. The surrender of Vicksburg and Port Hudson and the victory of Meade at Gettysburg are casting a gloom over the minds of the rebels and begin to talk like dictating terms of peace -- over the left.

Indiana's Roll of Honor, Volume I, abridged

Paddy and Billy

In the 35th Regiment, Indiana Volunteers, called the Irish Regiment, there were two inseparable friends, Paddy Smith and Billy Lyon. Paddy was a soldier of fortune; Billy called himself "a very unfortunate sojer". They had been in the service some months without receiving any pay. The Paymaster had not yet put in his appearance, and everything was to be done "as soon as I gets me pay." Paddy, who was over 50 years of age, was taken sick with "camp-typhus" and after medical arts failed to help, the chaplain, Father Peter Cooney, was called.

As Father Cooney prepared the dying man for his journey, Billy, sobbing like a heartbroken girl, came to stay with Paddy and "watch the sands of life run out."

"Well, Paddy," said his friend, "an y're goin' ta lave us?"

"Indade I suppose I am," said Paddy, "An glad I am to lave this dirty world."

"You may well say that Paddy, but faith you've had your own fun out iv it," retorted Billy.

"Oh, Billy, ain't you ashamed to use such levity," said Father Cooney. "When will you be ready to leave it?"

"Be jabers," said Billy, as the tent shook with merriment, "as soon as I gets me pay."

Indiana's Roll of Honor, Volume II, abridged

Irishmen and Ribbles

*P*rivate McMann, of Company A, was another Irish genius. Soon after he joined the Thirtieth, a charge was made by the regiment on the enemy's works. The assault was peculiarly dangerous, and the old soldiers screened themselves much as possible, taking advantage of the protection the ground afforded.

McMann rushed on, paying no attention to cover or danger, and was the first man to enter the rebel works, using his gun as a shillelagh and making a terrible noise. After the fight was over, his clothes were found pierced with bullets, but he was not wounded. The old soldiers cautioned him about exposing himself so recklessly, and told him how to accomplish his objective without so much exposure. Mac's answer, after hearing their counsel, was, "And now, will some iv yees be after telling a poor divil how to kill ribbles and watch stumps at the same time."

Chapter Nine
The Chickamauga Campaign

Thursday Sept 3rd 1863
Since last writing in my journal a few doings have occurred. During the time General Monotony had commenced. The same routine of business occurred daily. The time has now come that I must bid McMinnville adieu. My stay has been a pleasant one indeed. I almost hate to leave here as bad as when I left home. At two o'clock we started going in the direction of Dunlap. Over a very rough country we marched about 12 miles. Laid down to rest in an open field.

Friday Sept 4th 1863
At the sound of reveille this morning at three o'clock we were making preparations for the days march. The mules commenced braying, the drums commenced playing, rails were laid and fires were made, the men were all astir which made a continual whir. Such is the confusion in such a profusion that no one knows how soon his toes may get a crouch which brings an ouch and may perhaps if his corn cracks get a smash in the crash bringing an oath which has its groth. And thus this tumult is kept up until the word "forward" is given, when a yell is heard which resounds till the echo is lost in the sinking swelling forests. Ascended the Cumberland Mountain which is something near three miles at an angle of 45 degrees. Encamped on the mountain top.

Saturday Sept 5th 1863
Descended the mountain into the Sequatchie Valley. The scenery is indeed beautiful. As far as the eye can reach away down the valley is girted on either side one continual range of mountains lifting their tops heavenward as if seeking a place among the celestial spheres where the toils of earth below are not known. It is just such scenery as poets and painters delighted to look upon. We encamp in the valley at a little village called Dunlap the county seat of Sequatchie county. The county has but lately been laid out and consequently the town is of little import.

Sunday Sept 6th 1863
On the march again this morning by 4 o'clock down the valley. The scenery as we advance grows more beautiful. Encamped on a beautiful spot of ground near a large spring.

Monday Sept 7th 1863
Again on march. The country we pass through is very indifferent. Pass through Jasper, a dilapidated town near the Tennessee River. Pass Battle Creek a place many of the soldiers will long remember. Came to Bridgeport and crossed the Tennessee River where we encamped for the night.

Tuesday Sept 8th 1863
The morning was introduced by a plunge head foremost into the Tennessee River. Passed over a country that has been forsaken by anything like civilization. Marched 15 miles. The weather is very dry and warm. Dust is about six inches deep which makes it very disagreeable traveling.

Wednesday Sept 9th 1863
This morning we started from Whitesides, 15 miles from Chattanooga. Soon after starting we heard to our joy that the rebels had evacuated their last stronghold. Our forces entered the city at ll:50. The stars and stripes now float over a place that it never has before since the breaking out of the rebellion. Bragg is in full retreat. We have orders to pursue him. Accordingly preparations are made and we light out.

Thursday Sept 10th 1863
We encamped last night 11 miles from Chattanooga. It is useless for me to give even the plans of our attack. Came to Chattanooga, lightened the baggage and started in rapid pursuit. Whether or no we will overtake the enemy the future will reveal. Went into camp about two o'clock.

Friday Sept 11th 1863
Rejoined our division after an absence of several weeks. Close on the heels of the enemy after a march of perhaps eight or ten miles. We occupied Ringgold, a small village on the R.R. 23 miles from Chattanooga. A rebel mail was captured here which was just ready to be sent off. Latest southern papers and many amusing letters though all breathing a tone of despondency were captured. Halted a few moments. Crossed the Chickamauga river at which place the rebels burned the R.R. bridge. Encamped about 5 miles from Ringgold.

Saturday Sept 12th 1863
About faced and came to Ringgold from whence we came across a very poor country to a place near Gordon's Mills at which place we found the corps and went into camp.

Sunday Sept 13th 1863
This beautiful Sabbath morning instead of listening to the chiming of the Sabbath bell calling the good to the house of God I am listening to the sharp crack of the rifle on the picket lines between ours and that of the enemy. Orders have come that an advance must be made. Already we begin to feel our way out. Listen "It is, it is the cannon's opening roar". A battle seems to be imminent. The shells now buzz over head. From the sound of their cannon they are rapidly retreating. Our force with Gen. Beatty in front followed by Col. Dick's brigade are driving the enemy. Who can tell the effect or express the feelings on such an occasion as this.
Safely have I been delivered out of one battle. May the good Lord spare me once more. Returned to camp.

Monday Sept 14th 1863
Moved out early this morning in a westerly direction. After marching perhaps four miles we came to a halt while two brigades were sent on a reconnoitering expedition. Went into camp about night.

Tuesday Sept 15th 1863
Retraced our steps this morning. Came to a place called Crawfish Springs, Geo. The springs are indeed beautiful. The water gushes from under the rocks in a stream equal to a river and in fact is the source of the Chickamauga river. Went into camp here.

Wednesday Sept 16th 1863
Remained in camp today, wrote a letter home.

Thursday Sept 17th 1863
Wrote Frank Cones. Laying around camp.

Friday Sept 18th 1863
Cloudy morning. Feels much like an autumnal morning. Reading in the Louisville Journal. Speaking of the occupation of E. Tennessee by our forces. Prentice beautifully says, "It was a scene for the printers noblest effort. Aged men with silvered locks, matrons who for two years had been condemned to a hated espionage, and persons of every size and age joined the glad acclaim, and with faltering accents and tear streaming eyes hailed the deliverers. They saw the glorious emblem of their country's honor, the flag of the free hearts only home once more dancing proudly to the music of the wild huzzas and playing with the breezes that came from the mountain fastnesses of the

"Switzerland of America" where the river Holston has its fountain heads amid the crags of the Cumberland range and -- the eagle and the stork on cliffs and cedar tops their eyries build." It is indeed a beautiful picture of the welcoming of their dear ones to their own firesides once more. Orders came about noon that our brigade must move immediately. Moved to the left about two miles when the 13th was stationed on the crest of a hill to support a battery. The 59th Ohio and 44th Ind. were ordered farther to the left to support Col. Wilder who it was said was getting worsted. They moved rapidly to their position when it was ascertained that the enemy was near. They formed in line and waited for their approach. The enemy came in force and opened fire. The 59th held them at bay till they were flanked by the enemy both on the right and left - when they fell back perhaps 200 yards in good order. The casualties in the engagement were one man wounded and two missing. The firing was terrific and reminded me very much of the ever memorable Stone River. Tomorrow the ball will be opened and perhaps one of the bloodiest battles of the war be fought. It may be a reenactment of the bloody scenes of Stone River. Into the hands of Him who ruleth for the best I commit myself. My prayer is that I may be safely delivered from the firey darts of the enemy both physically and spiritually. I lay down to rest well on account of its being so very cool. Overcoats have been in good demand all day and as a matter of course it was a severe night - especially when it had to be passed without fire.

Saturday Sept 19th 1863
The morning dawned clear and tranquil. Would that the nation today was as pure and as bright and could shed such a halo of happiness as do the sunbeams that gild the eastern horizon. But, alas, it is not the case. Friend and brother in mortal combat. How many have this morning beheld the rising of the sun for the last time, and how many, how very many will sleep the sleep that knows no waking unprepared. The sun has gone to rest. The day has been a bloody one. Many fallen heroes are sleeping upon the field. They have gone to that country from whose bounds no traveler ere returns. About noon our division was ordered into a thick woods where the grounds so hotly contested ever since the battle began. About three o'clock were repulsed and driven back. Among our losses is Lieut. Wood brigade inspector. He was indeed an amiable and noble young man. Received letters from Annie and home.

Sunday Sept 20th 1863
How brightly the morning dawns. The boom of artillery and the roar of

musketry is again heard. Again our division is ordered in. Hotter and hotter grows the fight. Anxiously every heart is beating. It goes, now comes. At last we are driven, routed. Our brigade is scattered to the four winds. Fall back. We know not where the men are. It may be they are among the killed, wounded and prisoners. The remnant of the division is ordered back to Chattanooga. The day has been indeed a bloody one. I don't wish to again witness such another scene as was witnessed today. These lines of Walter Scott are indeed now applicable to the many brave ones who lie on the long to be remembered battlefield of Crawford Springs.

   Soldier, now thy warfare o'er
Sleep the sleep that knows no waking
   Dream of battlefields no more
Days of danger, nights of waking
xxxxxxxxxxxxxxxxxxxxxxxxxxxxxxxx
   No rude sound shall reach their ear,
Armors clang or war steed champing,
   Trump or pibroch summon here,
Now bring clan or squadron tramping"

Monday Sept 21st 1863
Our division is encamped at Chattanooga. What the program is I know not. Wrote home.

Tuesday Sept 22nd 1863
This morning we mounted our horses in obedience to orders and went out the Harrison road a couple of miles. Stationed the men in a line of skirmishers preparatory to the reception of the enemy. We had not to wait long before they made their appearance against some of our forces at Mission Ridge three miles distant. - Our forces repulsed them when through fear of the enemy flanking them they fell back to our line. Again they came driving our men into fortifications which had been thrown up during the day. The men are hard at work. Soon they will have formidable intrenchments.

Wednesday Sept 23rd 1863
The works have grown up as if by magic. The ax and pick and spade were used faithfully all night by our men. We will soon be prepared to give the enemy a warm reception. Today I feel much depressed in spirits. The causes I cannot tell unless it be the reverse our army has met with in the recent engagements at Crawfish Springs. All mail communication has ceased and I can neither hear from home nor write.

Thursday Sept 24th 1863
Awakened early this morning expecting an attack by the enemy. The
cannon's opening roar betokened that the enemy was not far off. It is said
that they have massed their forces on the left wing four corps strong.
Remained in camp all day awaiting future developments. Rode down to
Chattanooga and found it a desolate looking place. I would like so much to
hear from home. A letter would cheer me considerably.

Friday Sept 25th 1863
Went across the river to the teams. Found nearly all Head Qrs over there.
The weather is very dry and dusty. One continual cloud of dust pervades the
atmosphere which renders it very disagreeable both to man and beast.
Wrote a letter in the afternoon to my dear friend Lide Gibson. In the evening
I am sitting on the parapet of Ft. Bragg. In the distance I can see the enemy's
camp fires. No doubt they too see ours. It has been unusually quiet along
the lines today. What the next move is I know not.

Saturday Sept 26th 1863
Early this morning I started across the river. Put on some clean duds and now
feel like a new man. Came back and commenced making out reports. Saw
an account of the recent battle in the dailies from Cin. N. & L.

Sunday Sept 27th 1863
The sun shines brilliantly this holy Sabbath morning. Thoughts and memories
of other Sabbaths usher into my mind. I have seated myself beneath the
branches of a spreading oak within the fortifications perusing the pages of a
stray volume of Harpers. Reading an account of the battle of Antietam which
was fought Sept 17th 1862. How truthful is the picture when he calls the
battlefield a hell of smoke. After the work of the day has been accomplished
and he bivouacs for the night he says "there was no tree over our heads to
shut out the stars and as I lay looking up at these orbs moving so calmly on
their appointed way I felt as never so strongly before how utterly abased in
the face of high Heaven is this whole game of war relieved - relieved only
from contempt and ridicule by its tragic accompaniments and by the sublime
illustrations of man's nobler qualities incidentally called forth in its service.
Sent to occupy this little planet one among ten thousand worlds revolving
through infinite space how worse than foolish these mighty efforts to make
our tennancy unhappy or to drive each other out of it" In the afternoon we
cleaned our quarters among the tombs. How strange it seems that I should
take up my abode in such a place 'ere soul and body are separated. Not ten

paces from my quarters three graves are being made to deposit the bodies of some soldiers. Their history is not known by the grave diggers. All that is known of one of them is that he was found in an old tenantless house dead. He evidently had been wounded as shown by his mangled condition when found. They have fallen away from home. No hand of a beloved friend to soothe or comfort as they lay on their couch dying. They have fallen in a noble cause. May they rest in peace.

Monday Sept 28th 1863
Busy writing on the official reports of the brigade in the late engagements. The aggregate of losses and casualties foot up as follows:

	Killed	Wounded	and Missing
Com. Of.	5	15	2
E. Men	11	161	71
Total	16	176	73
Grand Total			365

The above includes the time commencing 18th, inst. and ending the 22nd.

Tuesday Sept 29th 1863
Still writing on the reports and making out the trimonthly returns. The day is clear, dry and dusty. What the enemy will do in front no one can tell.

Wednesday Sept 30 1863
The day is cloudy, ominous of rain. Still very busy on the monthly reports. Received letter from my friend Frank Cones.

Thursday Oct 1st 1863
A rain has made glad this earth our habitation and still continues to come in torrents. This makes it disagreeable sojourning among the tombs. In speaking of the tombs I am reminded of what Fannie Fern says in one of her books. Speaking of a funeral procession after it had entered the cemetery she said "all about on either side were graves, some freshly sodded some green with the verdure of many summers, all containing sacred ashes". How applicable to my present location. In another place she continues "O Earth, Earth with thy mocking skies of blue, thy myriad memory haunting odorous flowers, thy silver placid streams. Thy wheels of triumph ever rolling - rolling on over maimed, crushed but not destroyed bodies. Snatching from our frenzied grasp the life long coveted treasure."
Received letters this morning from Flora Welch, Ollie Higgins and wrote Annie P. Brown.

Friday Oct 2nd 1863
The sun shines brilliantly this morning. Not a cloud obscures the blue sky above. Been very busy all day making out the monthly returns.

Saturday Oct 3rd 1863
Clear morning. Picked up the Nashville Courier and saw the definition of the Indian name Chickamauga to be "River of Death". How memorable in history will this stream be as upon whose banks many a patriot has shed his blood that the country might be saved. Chickamauga! The name will live in the memory of the soldier. One of the most hotly contested and sanguinary battles of the war was fought on its oak bestudded and thickly overgrown banks.

Indiana's Roll of Honor, Volume II , abridged

Jacob Liveringhouse, company K, 30th Regiment, Indiana Volunteers, a lad of seventeen years, was captured at Chickamauga. He was then acting as orderly for General Johnson commanding the division to which the Thirtieth was attached. He was taken to Richmond, and there imprisoned, and subsequently sent to Danville. On the twenty-sixth of January he made his escape from the rebel prison, and reached our lines at Suffolk, on the seventh of February. On the twenty-seventh of June, when the Thirtieth made the charge on the enemy's works at Kenesaw mountain, Liveringhouse was orderly at regimental headquarters, and, therefore, not obliged to take place in the ranks. He, however, volunteered, and in the charge captured a rebel lieutenant and private, and brought them in as prisoners.

Perington Small, company D, 30th Regiment, Indiana Volunteers, was captured on the twenty-third of June, and sent to that hell upon earth, Andersonville, Georgia. He escaped from the prison five times, and was recaptured - once with bloodhounds. At last he was successful, and reached our lines at Atlanta on the fifteenth of August.

Colonel Dodge, of the Thirtieth, was taken prisoner at Chickamauga, while commanding the brigade. He was placed under guard of a rebel lieutenant and sergeant. By using strategy he succeeded in not only escaping, but also in bringing in the rebel lieutenant and sergeant prisoners.

Sunday Oct 4th 1863
The morning clear yet how unlike Sabbath it seems, perhaps on account of being very busy in the office. Copying Gen. Rosecrans address to the Army of the Cumberland. He congratulated the army for the brilliant and successful campaign in driving the enemy from middle Tennessee and occupying the point for which they had set out - Chattanooga. He deplores the loss in the recent engagements and of the Army's being compelled to fall back but consoles the men by saying that the enemy's force far outnumbered our own, and that the men fought bravely and fell back in the face of a fresh arrival of hostile troops. He begs the officers and soldiers to unite with him in thanking Almighty God for his kindness and goodness toward us.

Monday Oct 5th 1863
The day has been unusually cool though clear. Wrote a letter to the Lebanon Patriot. The _____ has changed hands as well as name. Wrote also to my friend Ollie Higgins. The enemy was occasionally throwing shells today which interrupted our repose considerably.

Tuesday Oct 6th 1863
The day has been clear but cool. Wrote a letter home. Copying the official report of the battle. Witnessed the interment of Sergt. Major of the 11th Mich. Vols. The ceremonies were sad and impressive. The minister who officiated on the occasion reminded the living present that they too were on their funeral march, that they too were hastening to the grave as fast as each revolving sun sped his onward course. He has fallen among strangers in a strange land while discharging the duties which devolved upon him as a soldier. The wound he received proved fatal and tonight while his friends, no doubt, are thinking of him as still living and wish that they could hear his footsteps upon the threshold of the old "homestead" he sleeps in the Chattanooga graveyard. Death! How solemn the thought! Especially solemn when the thought gently steals over one that perhaps he may fall away from the "loved at home". How often have I breathed the prayer "Let me die among my kindred". Deep buried now in the silent earth he is left alone. A little mound only marks the spot or tells of a form that is cold and still. Yes,
    "Strangers may pass with a careless air,
     Nor dream of the hopes that are buried there".
Wednesday Oct 7th 1863
The day indeed has been a gloomy one. Everything bears a melancholy aspect. Nature seems to have robed herself in the habilaments of mourning

at the reverses with which our army has met. Or it may be that it is because the funeral of the year is approaching.

Thursday Oct 8th 1863
Clear today. Nature has somewhat changed since yesterday. A more pleasing countenance is seen on her physique. Each day witnesses a burial of one of more soldiers. Today a captain of the 10th Ohio was deposited in his last resting place. Received a letter from Nellie.

Friday Oct 9th 1863
Pleasant day though a heavy fog obscured the surrounding objects this morning. Making out an ordnance report. Suffered much from the headache today. Another and still another falls. A captain in the 35th O.V.I. was buried this evening. The funeral rites were performed by an Episcopal clergyman of which church it seems the captain was a member. The ceremonies were very impressive especially the prayer of the gray haired preacher. He prayed for our country, the army of the Cumberland, its beloved Rosecrans, officers and men. Thus the high and low will fall.

Saturday Oct 10th 1863
Today Col. Dick was relieved of his command of the brigade. A change is going on all over the army. Gen. Beatty assumes command of the brigade and Gen. Wood of the division. The staff of Col. Dick go to their regiments. During the time I have acted clerk for the adjutant I have endeavored to do my duty. Visited the 40th Ind.

Sunday Oct 11th 1863
A holy calmness pervades. I feel lonely this morning. It seems almost like leaving home to bid adieu to the officers and soldiers at headquarters. "I feel like one who treads alone" "some banquet hall deserted". I do wish that I could attend church today but I cannot and therefore must rest content. Removed our quarters to the regiment. Took up my quarters with the Colonel.

Monday Oct 12th 1863
Cool and cloudy day. Indications of rain. Busy all day making our reports of ordnances and ordnance stores.

Tuesday Oct 13th 1863
Awoke this morning and the patter of the soft rain on my canvased roof made

me feel as though it was a joy to press the pillow which consisted of my coat doubled up and listen to the patter of the soft rain overhead. Continued raining all day which made it indeed dismal and gloomy. Dreary October.

Wednesday Oct 14th 1863
Wet, wet, wet! Raining all day. Received letters from Annie, Mary and Frank. Wrote Frank and Nellie. In the evening in company with my friend Billings I took a field glass to get an obsquint at the Mr. Reb.

Thursday Oct 15th 1863
Last night was an uncomfortable one on the soldier. All night long the rain came in torrents and the wind blew fiercely. It still continues to rain this morning. Wrote to my friend Mary.

Friday Oct 16th 1863
Still continues cloudy and damp. Visited the boys at brigade headquarters. Reading the debate of Parson Brownlow and Rev. Pryne on the slavery question.

Saturday Oct 17th 1863
Clear this morning after the few cloudy days which have glided by. In company with John Cast I went to the river to bathe. "Tis Saturday night."

Sunday Oct 18th 1863
Again the Sabbath dawns. Cloudy again this morning. Indications of rain. In the afternoon my old friend Elisha Little of the 10th Inc. visited me. Our chaplain held religious exercises in the regiment.

Monday Oct 19th 1863
Clear again this morning. The day is indeed beautiful. Building a chimney to our tent. The chaplain is acting as mason while I act as tender. Fire feels comfortable tonight.

Tuesday Oct 20th 1863
Finished making out the ordnance report. Commenced reading Story on Promissory Notes.

Wednesday Oct 21st 1863
Commenced writing a sketch of the regiment to be published in a book which is now ready for the press by David Stevenson of Indianapolis entitled Indiana's Roll of Honor.

Thursday Oct 22nd 1863
Still writing on the sketch. Suffering with the toothache.

Friday Oct 23rd 1863
Rainy and wet. Received the Indianapolis Journal, the compliments of my friend J.H. Smith.

Saturday Oct 24th 1863
Cloudy day. Finished writing the sketch of the regiment. Preparing for the duties of the morrow.

Sunday Oct 25th 1863
Calm, still Sabbath - no not calm and still. The busy hum is heard in every camp fire, preparing for the approach of stern winter. Work and business continues as though the day had not been set apart for rest. My quarters are still among the tombs - the place
> "Where servants, masters, small and great,
> Partake the same repose
> And here in peace the ashes mix
> Of those who once were foes."

How true these lines are, and how well they apply to the present..

Monday Oct 26th 1863
Bright and beautiful has been this day. Wrote a letter home. Heard James E. Murdock Esq. of Cincinnati recite some readings. Among them were "The Sleeping Sentinel" "On Board the Cumberland" "Our Fathers" and the beautiful poem "The American Flag".

Tuesday Oct 27th 1863
Nothing going on in camp more than usual. The same routine of duty each day is kept up. Wrote a letter home.

Wednesday Oct 28th 1863
Reading history today which is very interesting. Learned that the war of the crusades of the 12th and 13th centuries was a war waged by the Christians against infidels.

Thursday Oct 29th 1863
Cloudy and windy today. The signs indicate that the funeral of the year is approaching. An order came today authorizing the commanding officer of the regiment to send one man from each company home to recruit for his

respective company. This elates some of the boys considerably.

Friday Oct 30th 1863
Arose this morning and found it raining. Made out the list of names of those who are to go home. The day has been a bleak wet one. Another October will soon be gone. Another November will soon be here.

Saturday Oct 31st 1863
'Tis the last of dreary October! The leaves are falling. Flying through the air. O what a lonely time. Writing for the adjutant.

Sunday Nov. 1st 1863
The morning is beautiful. I am not permitted to enjoy the day as I am very busy. Would that I could be free once more.

Monday Nov 2nd 1863
The day has been cloudy indicating rain. Wrote letter in answer to the one I received yesterday..

Tuesday Nov 3rd 1863
Clear and pleasant. Rec'd letters from home and from my friends Ollie and Nellie. Glad to hear from them.

Wednesday Nov 4th 1863
Received the appointment today as Sergeant Major of the regiment.

Thursday Nov 5th 1863
Cloudy and rainy. Dreary, dreary autumn day. Languidly the hours pass by.

Friday Nov 6th 1863
Clear and beautiful this morning. Instead of dreary and autumn one is reminded of a beautiful spring morning with all its invigorating influences. Saw somewhere that the waves of trouble like the waves of the sea, seemingly engulphing if let alone would (drop) harmless at your feet. Wrote letters home and to the Indianapolis Gazette.

Saturday Nov 7th 1863
Clear, Not a cloud obscures the sky. Rec'd a letter from Frank.

Sunday Nov 8th 1863
Early this morning the regiment started on picket. The day is cool and clear.

Reading. Passed the day rather unpleasantly. Night came and I saw that I was not much a better man.

Monday Nov 9th 1863
Relieved early this morning by the 19th Ohio. Came to camp and assisted in making out the trimonthly returns. Received several Indianapolis Gazettes.

Tuesday Nov 10th 1863
Wrote a letter to Frank Cones. Cold day.

Wednesday Nov 11th 1863
Clear and beautiful. Dress parade for the first time in my new position. Felt somewhat awkward but think I will make myself at home by and by.

Thursday Nov 12th 1863
Received Gazettes from Indianapolis. Reading "Fletcher's Appeal to Matter of Fact." The day has been pleasant. The same dull monotony pervades the "camp, the court, the inn."

Friday Nov 13th 1863
Pleasant day. In fact, nature smiles almost an outright laugh. Wrote letters home to Annie Cones, Annie Cramer and James H. Smith and will send them by John M. Cast who is going home to recruit. Busily engaged attending to my official duties. A sunset scene here is truly sublime as Walter Scott says in his Lady of the Lake.
   "The western waves of ebbing day
     Roll o'er the glen their level way.
   Each purple peak, each fluity spire
     Is bathed in floods of living fire."

Saturday Nov 14th 1863
Rainy morning but cleared off beautifully during the day. Reading Walter Scott's "Tales of a Grandfather".

Sunday Nov 15th 1863
At 5 1/2 o'clock this morning our regiment relieved the 59th Ohio on picket. The day is pleasant. I feel as though I should like to be at home where I could enjoy the privileges of this day. Rebel pickets stand in full view and not more than three hundred yards from ours.

Monday Nov 16th 1863
Relieved on picket this morning by the 19th Ohio. Came to camp and passed the day unpleasantly being quite unwell. Received the Gazette.

Tuesday Nov 17th 1863
Wrote a letter to the Gazette on the subject of enforcing the conscription. A meeting of the Indiana officers was held last night at the headquarters of Gen. Wagner, taking into consideration this question. A committee was appointed to prepare an address to the Governor petitioning him to fill up old regiments and drop the new organizations. Col. Hunter was chairman of the committee. The address will be adopted tomorrow evening, when they propose to hold another "Social".

Wednesday Nov 18th 1863
Very foggy morning. In fact the foggiest morning I ever saw. It was near two o'clock before it cleared away. The picket lines were advanced this morning. It created but little excitement though occasional shots were fired doing little or no damage. Answered a letter received from Annie Cones yesterday. Reading "Fletchers Matter of Fact".

Thursday Nov 19th 1863
Beautiful day. Indeed it feels , as some _____ said, that it is the years twilight. The sear and yellow leaf is falling from the surrounding forest trees.

Chapter Ten
The Battle of Chattanooga

Friday Nov 20th 1863

Still the weather continues beautiful yet there is a kind of melancholy pervading. "I'm pleased and yet I'm sad" expresses my feelings more fully than I can in my own language. Orders came today that tomorrow morning ere the sun dawns the regiment must be on the move. We go forth to again meet the enemy.

My prayer is that our arms may be successful, that the enemy may be put to flight, and victory crown our efforts. While I am writing the sweet strains of "Hail Columbia" from a neighboring band is wafted on the soft evening breeze to my ear. Oh! how sweet, how soul stirring and heart reviving come those welcome strains. What a sweet chorus when all join and sing

"Firm, united let us be
  Rallying round our liberty
As a band of brothers joined
  Peace and safety we shall find."

Would that we as a nation were united and all rallying round our birthright - Liberty. Truly there we would be as a band of brothers and peace and safety would be our resting haven.

Our marching orders have been countermanded. The clouds indicate rain. The chaplain held religious services in the regiment. Left or put $35.00 in his hands.

Saturday Nov 21st 1863

The rain came in torrents last night. Reading in the history of Scotland the working of the feudal system. Still continues to rain. Received a letter from friends at home. Wrote to sister Mellie at Wesley.

Sunday Nov 22 1863

Early this morning our regiment went on picket. The day is a beautiful one. The sun shines brilliantly. Would that I could enjoy this day at home. Spent the forenoon in reading. In the afternoon I exchanged papers with a rebel. I met him half way between the lines, shook hands as friends would do, sat down and had a pleasant chat. He told me he was a member of the 12th ____ that he was tired of the war and intended to quit the army at the expiration of his term of service which would be in the spring. After talking over some other things I extended my hand and bade him good bye, hoping that the next time we met we would meet on terms of friendship and peace.

I received the Knoxville Register published at Atlanta Georgia. It contained an editorial on the Ohio election, the import of which was that great frauds had been perpetrated in order to defeat - Vallandingham - that the people should not submit to them but rise in their strength and hurl the oppressors from their thrones.

Received orders to be ready to move on the enemy at 4 o'clock. Preparations were made for the movement but they again were countermanded. Slept but very little during the night. Read the Gazette.

Monday Nov 23rd 1863
Cloudy and cool. Relieved and came to camp. Went through a thorough ablution of my physical frame, but had scarcely got through when orders came to fall in. According to previous arrangements our regiment was consolidated with the 79th Ind. ours forming the left wing, the 79th the right and commanded by Col. Fred Kneffler of the 79th, he being the senior Col. Col. Dick was second in command. The word was given and we in company with the brigade and Division moved out. Outside the fortifications we formed in close column by Division. Pickets commenced firing driving the enemy before them. We advanced under cover of the guns
of Ft. Wood. We soon gained the roads and penetrated perhaps half a mile and deployed in line of battle. Skirmishing still continued the enemy fleeing like a flock of scared sheep. Our forces gained a knoll upon which a battery was planted from which we shelled the enemy's retreating columns. Night came on and we still occupied the same position. I lay down but I could not sleep for sometime. We lay crouched thinking that perhaps by morning we would be engaging the enemy in deadly conflict. I dozed and while I dozed I dreamed. It was a sweet dream but lo, when I awoke I found the living reality. Though I could hardly realize that we still occupied the same position, so changed were things.
Entrenchments were thrown up and a deep abbattis made by falling the timber which abounds the soil. I felt much more secure when I discovered this - felt as though I did not care whether reb. came or not. The day has been a cloudy one, all the time indicating rain, but fortunately it did not rain.

Tuesday Nov 24th 1863
Morning dawned, not clear and beautiful but with a cloud though not a moral cloud obscures. Everything indicates rain. In the extreme right the ball is opened. News by courier is that Hooker is engaging the enemy on Lookout Mountain, and is driving him taking many prisoners and pieces of artillery. On our left Sherman with two corps has formed a junction with

Howard's corps which is immediately upon our left. The day continues drizzly, rainy and wet. I took a stroll back from our entrenchments and went upon a knoll commanding a view of the whole field of operations. The sight is indeed grand beyond description.

86th Indiana Regiment, Volunteer Infantry, abridged

"First Up"
86th and 79th Indiana at Missionary Ridge

*T*he night of November 24 was not promising, and it more than fulfilled the unfavorable weather signs. As the night advanced it grew extremely chilly, and the soldiery unprepared for cold weather suffered much. Many were forced to rise at 1 or 2 o'clock, build fires and thaw out their benumbed extremities. On account of the cold it was a night of extreme discomfort. It was now the 25th of November, historic day. The Eighty-sixth was up betimes. Colonel Dick at no time allowed it to be napping when duty called for watchfulness. The orders of the previous day, to be ready to move at a moment's notice, were again published.

During the night, the enemy had withdrawn from Lookout Mountain and from Chattanooga valley, and on the morning of the 25th was massing his entire force on Missionary Ridge. The night of the 24th Sherman had succeeded in crossing all of his army over the river, had captured the Confederate outposts, and had secured a firm footing at the north end of Missionary Ridge near the railroad tunnel.

Early in the morning of the 25th, Sherman opened the battle and the sounds of the conflict were borne to the Army of the Cumberland as it lay awaiting its final orders to move. Throughout the forenoon the troops of the Fourth and Fourteenth corps listened to the din and roar of Sherman's army as the battle grew stronger and stronger from the addition of new troops.

From where Thomas' troops lay the reinforcements that were being sent by General Bragg against Sherman could be seen as they hurried along the crest of Missionary Ridge to the assistance of their Confederate comrades. As the morning wore on the impatience and anxiety of the Army of the Cumberland grew stronger and stronger. The Army of the Cumberland could not move, however, until Hooker could bring his troops across the valley and his line could be joined with Thomas' right. The rebels when they moved from

Lookout had destroyed the bridges across the creek, and these had to be rebuilt before Hooker could cross. This was done as speedily as possible, and by 3 o'clock of the 25th Hooker was in position.

At this time Sherman was holding his position by stubborn fighting, but was unable to make any headway, as the enemy had massed too heavily against him, and the fighting at the north end of the Ridge was most intense.

The brave Hardee, with Cleburne, Cheatham and Stevenson's divisions were on the right of the Confederate lines in front of Sherman, and wherever Hardee was, there was sure to be a vigorous defense or a fierce attack. Resolute of purpose, with splendid soldiers, he could be depended on to hold his ground to the last.

But Sherman, with the gallant Fifteenth corps, was equal to the emergency, and was holding his ground and fighting stubbornly to hold his position. The battle on the Union left - the rebel right - grew hotter, fierce, deadlier. The rattle of musketry was unceasing and frightful.

During all the forenoon and on into the afternoon the troops in front of the Army of the Cumberland had kept up an incessant and terrific fire. The enemy's skirmishers, almost equal to a line of battle in strength, had poured out a most frightful volume of musketry, while the batteries along the summit of Missionary Ridge kept up a vigorous cannonading. The casualties in this portion of the Union line were, however, not very great when considered with relation to the amount of firing that was done by the enemy.

General Howard, with the Eleventh corps, now came into line of the left of the Fourth corps, but moved off to the support of Sherman, and Baird's division of the Fourteenth corps moved in and took Howard's place. It did not, however, remain long; it too moved off to the left to the support of Sherman, and the left of the Fourth corps was uncovered. The shifting of so many troops to the left showed that that point was Grant's objective, and that he desired to carry the north end of the Ridge before he made the attack upon the rebel left with Hooker's forces. All orders show that he desired Sherman to carry the Ridge as far south as the tunnel before the combined attack should be made.

Sherman's battle grew more severe as the afternoon drew on. By 12:45 p.m. it had grown so hot that Sherman dispatched Grant: "Where is Thomas?" Thomas himself replied from Orchard Knob at 1 o'clock p.m. "I am here; my right is closing in from Lookout Mountain toward Missionary Ridge."

Now, artillery, cavalry, and infantry could all be seen passing on the crest to support and assist Hardee and engage Sherman's forces. These heavy reinforcements for Bragg's right indicated that he had divined Grant's plan of battle, of capturing the north end of the Ridge, and sweeping down its crest to the south with troops which were to be supported upon both flanks.

Sherman was meeting severer opposition than had been anticipated, and the time had now come for earnest work on the part of the Union right and center in order to relieve him and hold what had already been acquired. To do this it was necessary to throw forward the center and right so that Bragg would not be able to send forward any further reinforcements, and if possible force him to withdraw some of his troops from Sherman's front in order to protect his lines on Missionary Ridge.

The Fourth corps was selected as the first to make "the demonstration on the enemy's works." By this demonstration it was intended that the Fourth corps should capture the enemy's picket or skirmish line and take and occupy Bragg's line of works at the foot of the Ridge. To that end the orders were issued to the division commanders to move their troops outside their works, reform their lines, and that six guns from Orchard Knob fired in quick succession should be the signal for the attack. By this order it was not intended or expected to pass beyond the first line of the enemy's works, and they were all at the foot of the Ridge.

The order was communicated to each of the brigade commanders, and they at once put their commands in motion, crossed their works, reformed their lines, and awaited the signal from Orchard Knob. Each brigade was formed in two lines. The Third brigade of Wood's division, of which the Eighty-sixth Indiana was a part, was formed with the Seventy-ninth and Eighty-sixth Indiana in the first, or charging line, and the Thirteenth and Fifty-ninth Ohio, the Nineteenth Ohio and the Seventeenth Kentucky in the second line as supports. The Ninth Kentucky held the skirmish line, but some distance to the left of the brigade front.

While awaiting for the signal for the charge it may be well to look at the situation as it then confronted the front or charging line. The line of works at the foot of the Ridge was known to be very strong and most favorably situated for defense, as a sweeping fire of musketry could cover every foot of ground in its immediate front for several hundred yards. All along the foot of the Ridge there was open ground in which was left no shelter from the fire of the batteries on the Ridge, or from the fire of the infantry in the strong line of intrenchments at its foot. In fact, at the time the order was delivered it looked to be a fair chance for just such a slaughter of the Union troops as was afterwards made of the Confederates at Franklin.

Finally at 3:40 p.m. everything was believed to be properly arranged and in order, every emergency likely to arise carefully provided for. But it is the unexpected that happened in battle as elsewhere. All things being in readiness, boom! boom! boom! went the great guns from the crest of Orchard Knob, and roared and thundered out the signal that all might hear.

From where stood the ranks of the Eighty-sixth could be plainly seen the flame and smoke shoot from the mouths of the guns as if they would blow with their mighty breaths of flame the enemy from the Ridge. "One!" spoke an iron throat of Bridges' battery, and with the sound each man grasped his gun with a firm grasp, and stood with contracted muscles and compressed lips. "Two!" "Three!" "Four!" "Five!" "Six!"

Hardly had the last gun sent its messenger of death as a herald of the attack when the troops - Willich's - on Orchard Knob leaped up, out and over their works, and started for the enemy. They had not yet cleared their parapet when in trumpet tones Colonels Knefler and Dick gave the command, "Forward, march!" and the men of the two regiments, the Eighty-sixth and Seventy-ninth Indiana, at the same instant sprang forward with a cheer on that charge that ended in the most brilliant victory in the annals of war. And now that battle for the Army of the Cumberland was again begun. Now was the time for action - heroic action, Once fairly in motion the tremor of the muscles was over - was a thing of the past.

The Eighty-sixth and Seventy-ninth Indiana had a narrow strip of open woods through which to pass before coming to the opening in the immediate front of the enemy's works at the foot of the Ridge. Through this strip of standing timber the men pressed forward as in good line as was possible. However, as they drew near the farther side of this woods, which was rather more open, the men formed into a better line, and so the two regiments came out into the open ground in a fairly good line of battle.

As they cleared this timber they came into a full and perfect view of the enemy's works at the foot of the Ridge, as well as those on its crest, and about eight or nine hundred yards distant from the former, the objective point of the attack.

The sight of the enemy in his intrenchments seemed to act as an electrifier. The yell was given over and over again as away went the two regiments on the full run for the enemy, determined to have that line of works at all hazards.

Whether either Colonel Knefler or Colonel Dick gave the order to "double-quick," or "charge bayonet," on clearing the woods, no one can say, but it is presumed they did. At any rate the general shout of the line was sufficient to set every man going at his very best pace.

As the Union line cleared the standing timber and came out into the open ground the long line of Confederate batteries on the crest of the Ridge opened a terrific fire. There were Dent's, Cobb's, Mebane's, and Slocomb's batteries, and others, vomiting death and destruction upon the valley. The boom of the many guns, the shriek of flying shells, the roar of their explosions, the whir of the flying fragments were positively appalling, The Union batteries on Orchard Knob, Fort Wood, and other points added their volcanic roar to the unearthly noise of the rebel batteries.

The men who cast their eyes to the front, and then to the right, and then up the valley along the Union line and over the ground where it was advancing, could see in front a battery worked with fiery energy, and on the crest to the right a long line of rebel batteries with drifting clouds of sulfurous smoke above them. Here, there, everywhere the bursting shells and the smoke drifting lazily off could be seen. Some few burst on the ground, others five, ten, twenty, thirty, fifty, and some perhaps a hundred feet of more in the air above. Some burst far in front, others overhead far to the rear toward the reserve. It was truly a grand and magnificent sight. It was a scene to be witnessed but once in a lifetime, and no one cares to look upon its like again under similar circumstances.

There in front rose the great Ridge as a natural barrier, and on its crest the long row of rebel guns. Here below a long thin line of Union "blue-coats," a line of battle to be swallowed up, as it seemed, in the volcanic eruption, rushing grandly and heroically on in the very face of death, and above the heads of those heroic men the curling smoke from hundreds of exploding shells, which they apparently did not notice more than the drifting down of thistles blown by idle winds of autumn.

All this was grand and heroic, but this was not the battle. The two regiments passed resolutely and fearlessly forward - on toward the goal. All along the valley to the right, following the lead of these two superb regiments, the blue line swept steadily and grandly on, no faltering, no hesitation, but ever forward.

The Eighty-sixth and Seventy-ninth rushed forward through the fire and shot, and onto and over this line of intrenchments. So strong was this rush upon the enemy that he became panic stricken and abandoned them, and all who escaped capture fled precipitately up the rugged mountain side. The Union cheers of victory and exultation added to his fright and hastened his flight, as he hurried rapidly toward the works on the crest of the Ridge.

The men of the Union line arrived at these works almost exhausted in the effort made to reach the line in as short time as possible. Those who reached this line first, most of them, made a brief halt until some others began to arrive, for it must be understood where a line of men start out on a run some will be left, and consequently the line will become more or less disordered at the finish in an advance of eight hundred or nine hundred yards at the highest rate of speed that each was capable of attaining.

By this time the veteran rebel gunners had recovered from the frenzy of their first excitement caused by the sudden discovery of the audacious movement against their first line of intrenchments directly beneath them. The tremor of their muscles had given place to steely steadiness and they settled down to soldierly work, as their fire now clearly proved.

They were carefully depressing their guns with perfect range and were accurately delivering with terrific effect a plunging fire of shot and shell which no troops on earth could face and remain quiet and inactive in line.

It was but as the twinkling of an eye until the victors at this line of works saw and realized the situation. Even before half their comrades reached the works the leaders of the line saw that no safe lodgment for a line of battle could be made here. No thought of retreat was entertained. It was not so ordered. Every fiery blast of the batteries on the Ridge made their old line of intrenchments at its foot quake and tremble.

The command, "Forward!" "Forward!" was given and repeated. The command was received by the two regiments with a shout as if victory was already won. Granger's message, "Take the Ridge if you can!" passed along the bleeding line, but it was already advancing.

Then began the real battle of Chattanooga, the storming and capture of the heights of Missionary Ridge! At once the privates and officers of the Eighty-sixth and Seventy-ninth Indiana, inaugurated a movement that was to result in a grander victory than Grant had ever dreamed of even in his brightest dream of victories. The Army of the Cumberland was to show here its magnificent fighting qualities. Even now its advance, the Eighty-sixth and Seventy-ninth Indiana, were ahead of Grant's orders and expectations. In fact neither General Grant nor Thomas intended it.

From this point and upward the two regiments, like mountain goats, were advancing up the rugged face of a ridge four hundred feet high, exposed to a volcanic fire of the enemy entrenched on its summit. In the movement up the Ridge the gallant Colonels Knefler and Dick, quick to see its supreme importance, gave it the impetus of their commands and example and encouraged the brave men every step of the way up the steep acclivity. Instead of a mere "diversion" in favor of Sherman it was to be the culminating and deciding event of this great three days' battle.

Wood's division of the Fourth corps opened the battle on the 23d, and now the victorious assault of Wood's and Sheridan's divisions of that corps, with two divisions of the Fourteenth corps - the Army of the Cumberland still - decided the battle in a marvelously wonderful manner greatly to the surprise of General Grant.

This was truly the hurly burly of battle when "fearful scouring doth choke the air with dust and laden it with death." Onward, and yet onward, and upward, and yet higher, pressed that charging line, through the enemy's pitiless fire. The two regiments pressed undauntedly up the ridge. There was no halting, only to breathe and rest, for the climbing was extremely fatiguing. Only the hardiest could proceed steadily on even at a slow pace without halting to rest. As the two regiments advanced the enemy's fire grew hotter, fiercer, deadlier. Shot, shell, shrapnel, and as the disordered line drew nearer the crest, grape and canister were poured into the ranks of those faithful men at an appalling rate.

Beatty's brigade, of which these regiments formed the front line, had struck the Ridge at a place where there was a more prominent elevation - Signal Hill - and from where a point projected to the west from the general line of the Ridge. This conformation of the Ridge at the place of ascent of the Eighty-sixth Indiana gave the enemy's artillery to the right and left, as well as the battery on the elevation itself, a better sweep to the approaches to the heights, and a crossfire upon the assaulting forces now coming up, which opportunity they did not fail to improve. As the two regiments were so far in advance of the lines of the right and left they invited the fire of the whole of the enemy's line within striking distance.

But as this line climbed the Ridge, the infantry on the crest opened a hot and malicious fire of musketry upon the two Indiana regiments. Now the deadly zip, zip, zip of the minnie balls added this minor but more fearful strain to the heavier notes of the batteries, and the latter apparently redoubled their fierce activity.

The men of the Eighty-sixth and Seventy-ninth were now almost exhausted, and were creeping slowly up the Ridge turning to practical account trees, logs, stumps, and rocks as cover, returned the fire in a most valorous and effective manner, constantly encouraged in the advance by the officers of both regiments. Many were killed on both sides.

As the two regiments approached nearer the enemy's works the battle grew, if possible, fiercer. The mettle of both armies was here to be thoroughly tested. The enemy was stubborn, and tenaciously held his ground - clinging to his works, rallied by officers of high rank who exhorted the men to stand firm and hold their position.

As the assaulting line still crept nearer and nearer the works on the crest, occasionally the "swish" of a ramrod fired by some of the more excitable, added another variation to the already tumultuous roar of battle - to the shriek of shot and shell, the rattle of grape and canister and the zip of the minnie ball on the rough and stony mountain side.

The two regiments had kept well together as one regiment, and were far in advance of the rest of the line. They were now full nine-tenths of the way up the Ridge on the breast of Signal Hill and laid down there, waited and rested. To push out at this stage appeared suicidal for this mere handful of men, if they had not already got themselves into a veritable deathtrap

The lines at the foot of the Ridge had looked with wonder and surprise at the two regiments toiling toward the summit, until finally they together with their supports were ordered forward to join that small assaulting column which is now immediately under the guns of the enemy almost at the very summit of the Ridge.

But all things must have an end, and now the line of regiments completing the division's battle line have almost joined these two regiments that have so gallantly led the van. Looking to the right and down the slope of the Ridge could be seen the long line, scattered somewhat and broken in places by the enemy's fire, pushing and fighting its way up the Ridge, their regimental standards and the stars and stripes held aloft and floating in the breeze -

"The flags of war like storm birds fly,
The charging trumpets blow."

As this line of brave "blue coats," undaunted, unappalled by what they have witnessed, approached the brow of the Ridge the battle roar increased, and fighting was intensely furious and desperate along the entire line. This was the Battle of Chattanooga - the Assault of Missionary Ridge!

But as the whole battle front of the division approached the brow of the Ridge, followed by their supports, Colonels Dick and Knefler gathered their men for another desperate attack, determined to win the victory which they had striven so hard to gain and gave the command, "Fix - bayonets!"

They were soon ready and when the order, "Charge - bayonets!" was given, the brave men of these two regiments went forward with a rush.

Oh! It was a thrilling sight! Shot and shell were doing their murderous work. Nothing short of annihilation could stop these noble battalions.

Higher, and still higher, they crept, until at last, just as the sun was sinking in the west, they reached the summit, and then as the gathered billow thunders and foams along and over the sunken ledges of the sea, they, with one wild shout and burst, swept over these deadly batteries.

The Confederates saw and heard the preparation of the two regiments for the final dash and when it came they stood their ground, fighting desperately and hand to hand, but the assault was too grandly ferocious, and they broke and fled down the opposite declivity of the mountain, utterly dismayed and panic stricken.

As these two regiments swept over the works and on, they were followed closely by the battle line of Willich's brigade, and those fighting to the right and left soon had Signal Hill and the Ridge for some distance to the right of it, cleared. Thus was the Ridge and battle won as never before was won.

The next moment cheer after cheer went up all along the smoking crest and rolled down the crimson steep, till to the right and left and far below the air trembled with glad echoes.

Missionary Ridge was no General's battle. It was the battle of the soldiers themselves, who went, like an unchained whirlwind, without command, up to the crest, and to what, up to that time, was the most complete victory of the war.

Editor's Note: Of the Eighty-sixth Indiana Volunteer Infantry, six were killed in the battle, seven mortally wounded, twelve severely wounded, twenty-one slightly wounded. The losses greatly exceeded that of any other regiment of Beatty's brigade and was nearly double that of the Seventy-ninth. The small loss is explained by the steepness of the western slope of Missionary Ridge.

Headquarters 3rd Division, 4th A.C.
Chattanooga, Tenn., Nov. 27th, 1863
OFFICERS AND SOLDIERS OF THE THIRD DIVISION, FOURTH ARMY
CORPS - ARMY OF THE CUMBERLAND:

A Glorious Victory, under the providence of God, has crowned our arms. In producing this great result, your valor has been most signally displayed.

Ordered on Monday afternoon to make a reconnoissance of the enemy's position, you converted a reconnoissance into a substantial attack, most gallantly carrying a position strong by nature and intrenched. - But your crowning glory was achieved on Wednesday afternoon. You were ordered to carry the line of intrenchments at the foot of Missionary Ridge, for the purpose of making a diversion in favor of our troops engaged on the left. This you did, but you were not content to stop at the base of the Ridge. Your enthusiasm bore you on in splendid style, carrying the rifle pits which crowned the summit - capturing many pieces of Artillery, small arms and prisoners. The enemy began to retire in disorder.

Your achievement in carrying the rugged, fortified heights of Missionary Ridge, displayed a gallantry and steadiness under fire, and produced results unparalleled in the annals of warfare.

Your conduct was witnessed by many officers distinguished on other battlefields. Their admiration and appreciation of your services are unbounded.

I return you my most heartfelt thanks.

Th. J. Wood
Brig. Gen. Vols. - Commanding

Wednesday, November 25th 1863

After having spent a pleasant night in sleep I awoke and found that the clouds had cleared away and the morning beautiful. The general movement thus far has been a success. How it will ultimately terminate remains to be seen but the prevalent opinion seems to be that victory will perch upon our banners. From the firing it seems as though the skirmish lines were being advanced. The ball is opened on the left. Sherman's seems to be engaging the enemy. Hotter and hotter grows the contest. As yet I have not heard the result of the fight yesterday, though it is rumored that our forces were victorious. It is to be hoped that such is the case. We remained in the entrenchments until about 3 o'clock when the word "forward" was given. Formed in line with Willich's brigade. When the signal was given which was six guns again we started on double quick and with a yell. The rebel guns on Missionary Ridge opened on our advancing columns and made the air hideous with howling screeches. It seemed as though the thunder of the infernal regions was bellowing forth. But we heeded it not. On we went. We were ordered to "charge" the mountain. Up the men scaled in the face of the deadly volleys of the enemy. Through fire and smoke and hail of musketry the summit was reached and the "stars and stripes" was planted on the rebel works. The 86th and 79th Indiana were the foremost up. All honor to those noble men. Although many of our brave comrades have fallen yet the victory is complete.

Our division captured 36 pieces of artillery, 11 of which was captured by our brigade, and it is said that 50 were taken in the charge. The rebel colors were taken by Col. Dick. Gen. Wood passing by our regiment at dusk enquired what regiment, and upon being told that they were the 79th and 86th his answer was "The first regiment up" and immediately proposed three cheers which were given. Our colors received over 70 musket shots besides the staff being broken but they were nobly borne aloft by the color bearer Steven Broukhite until he received a wound when they were taken up by Sergeant Tom Graves. The history of this war does not furnish a parallel to the bravery and courage displayed by our men on the taking of "Missionary Ridge".

The annals of no other battlefield will furnish any such daring as was displayed by the brave heroes who planted the American flag - the glorious "stars and stripes" on the highest peak of what has been termed the monument of eternity. To him who ruleth the destiny of nations be the honor and glory. I write on the Ridge. It is night. Each mellowed shaft of the rays of the moon's pale beams seems to weep at the ghastly sight of mangled corpses strewn around.

"E're nature seems to shed a tear
  While death still held his revels near
  The blood stained corpse-decked battlefield"
Yes, the stoutest heart would pause and weep could they but gaze on the crimson flood. In one dark heap they all lie side by side, both friend and foe. On the hilltop's verdured crest while gallantly leading his men fell the brave and much loved Captain Southard. The graceful form of Paris(?) H. Peterson also fell in peaceful rest. A soul of youth -gentle boy - the pride of perhaps a mother's heart fell in the great and glorious cause of Liberty. Many others too fell who were buoyant with hope but they are with the gallant slain and sleep with those whose stars of life have set in blood.

Thursday Nov 26th 1863
Arose from my stony couch this morning and found the sun shining brightly. I looked around but the fog obscured the scenery. I took a stroll over the field and the ghastly sights were indeed horrible. It enshrouds the heart in mournful night where the bloody hours of yesterday is called to mind. At noon the fog cleared away and in every direction as far as the eye could reach was a continuous range of hills. The scenery is indeed grand beyond description. In the afternoon I received a letter from my friend Lide. I was so glad to hear from her and now especially as today feel lonely. At 8 o'clock orders were received to return to camp. Which were complied with, arriving about 10 o'clock.

Friday Nov 27th 1863
Arose this morning much fatigued from the weeks exposure. Wrote the official report of the regiment in the engagement. Wrote letters to the Gazette and Patriot.

Saturday Nov 28th 1863
Under orders to march. Raining and wet. Wrote a letter to the Attica Ledger. At 3 o'clock we took up our line of march. It is rumored we go to Knoxville. Marched about three miles and camped.

Chapter Eleven
On to Knoxville

Sunday Nov 29th 1863
The Sabbath again dawns. Very cool. March slowly along the fore part of the day but move up briskly during the afternoon. March till about nine o'clock when we go into camp near Harrison a river village twelve miles from Chattanooga. The country is rough and broken and the roads bad.

Monday Nov 30th 1863
Move out at five o'clock. Very cold. Pass Georgetown and go into camp after marching about 20 miles. The country is much better. Looks as though we were getting into the verge of civilization.

Tuesday Dec 1st 1863
The first day of stern winter dawns clear and bright though very cool. Would that I could enjoy this day at home. O would that peace would again spread its chastening influence, yes
    Let sunshine pierce the gloomy air
  Let verdured wreaths our ____ deck
    Let monster War no longer stare
  With bloody eyes upon our wreck.
Would it not then be a happy time? Ploughshares would then take the place of the sword and industry's hum be heard instead of cannon's roar. Perusing old letters from dear friends at home. Necessity compels that I consign them to the flames but before I do I must transfer some precious words - precious because they come from the hearts of those I most love. "Lide" writing says she would like to sit "and hear you tell of the dangers you have passed through. The victories you have won - when the joy of success shall gladden our hearts and the bright light of heaven shine down calm and steady on the nation's long darkness. When the master of Tyranny shall be banished from the presence of man and the heroes of Rebellion be remembered only for their crimes - their transient names be eclipsed by the glowing images of those whose names will forever live in the memories of a grateful nation. Thoughts of the absent soldier call forth bright dreams of a fairy land a little way off in the future to be explored when our gallant band of brave youths shall have accomplished their mission and secured for us a permanent peace. A solemn awe pervades my heart when I think of the many scenes which would this moment meet the eye could we but glance in upon the evening hour of many a dear one for away. I see away off in that land of the sun a

young man seated in the evening shadows and as one by one the heavenly train comes forth his mild blue eye kindles his bosom heaves and a tear steals down his sun-browned cheek. I turn away to weep for I know that the dream was as blissful reality. The glad day will come when it will be realized. From the same letter I would like to extract more but here at my feet one from "Mate". She writes of the reunion of the old students and says "the Academy halls were well filled and every countenance there beamed with delight and the hours passed swiftly by. But amid the scenes of mirth and gayety the absent were not forgotten. Their names were often pronounced by many lips and the wish that they were with us was often expressed. Especially are our soldier friends remembered on such occasions as this. We contrast their present life of danger and hardship with the past when they mingled with us and shared our happiness and a shade of sadness comes over the heart because the necessity for their absence still exists." "Mary" writing after the battle of Chickamauga says "I think however the fight will be resumed at a day not far distant. Then the brave noble hearted Federal Soldiers will have won the bright laurels and go forth covered with victory". Prophetic were the words spoken by Mary. And now comes "Mollie" "Tis true as you say this whole game of war is absurd and when we think of the many, many brave noble hearts that have been stilled, and the "household gods" that lie shivered on every hearth stone - and "Rachels that will not be comforted" the heart cries out in 'tis enough. But on the other hand we see our nations honor trampled on - our "banner of stars" trailed in the dust and our drooping eagle, we lay aside all selfishness and stand up for God and our country". Noble sentiments of Mollie.

Now comes the last letter from "Annie". She says "I remember other beautiful starry evenings like this when the heart beat high with hope and "eye looked love to eye" and all went merry as a marriage bell. Oh! happy days! Oh! blissful moments. Will you never more return? Has it all been a feverish fitful dream? Was it all ideal and nothing real? Must the faithful trusting heart at last be broken? Shall the bright buds of hope be forever crushed? I sometimes wish I was a child again.

"Oh the merry hours of childhood
And bright hopes of youthful glee
Oh the well remembered wildwood
When we wandered wild and free
Youthful hopes have long been broken Hushed the friends of early love
But kind memory bears a token
That we'll meet them all above."

I know it is wrong to be looking on the dark side of the picture but we all have our sad moments as well as our joyous ones and at such times the heart longs for a sympathizing friend. I have some times thought that these outbreakings of the heart's bitterness and sorrow were a kind of safety valve to our souls for we always feel better after we have raised the flood gates and permitted the bitter waters to flow out."

Tis true, as Annie says, that we all have our sad moments as well as our joyous ones. I love to be melancholy there seems something so holy so calm so pure about it.

Remained in camp nearly all day. At 8 o'clock the bugle sounded and revealed the fact that we must move. Came to the Hiwassee river and crossed on a ferry boat after which we marched about a mile and went in to camp.

Wednesday Dec 2nd 1863

Again on the move at sunrise though the buildings are somewhat old fashioned the spirit of progress seems not to have taken hold of this portion of the country, though like all the southern states they are several years behind the times. Passed through Decatur a pleasant country village the county seat of Meigs county. At sunset we went into camp after having marched 20 miles. I am writing by the blazing campfire which glimmers and flickers from the fast decaying rails. On every side the campfires thickly dot mother earth. To the east the western slope of a gentle hill is thickly bestudded with what might likened to earthly stars - each ray sending forth an influence like unto the mission for which he whom it comforts has gone forth to perform.

Thursday Dec 3rd 1863

Started this morning about 8 o'clock. Passed through a beautiful country on the Loudon road. We are met everywhere with various manifestations of joy. The glorious emblem of their country's honor the flag of the free heart's only home proudly danced in the breezes and winds of heaven as the Federal Soldiers trod - yes wearily trod with blistered feet the red soil of east Tennessee proclaiming that their deliverers had come. That the traitors who had so long prowled through the country would now be driven therefrom. After marching perhaps eighteen miles, taking dinner at Pond Spring we went into camp near Sweet Water a pleasant railroad village in the midst of a most beautiful country. Rock and hill and brook and vale each seems to have a pleasing smile.

86th Regiment, Indiana Volunteer Infantry, abridged

Pop, Pop, Szip, Szip

*I*mmediately after the successful assault on Missionary Ridge, the Fourth corps, commanded by General Gordon Granger, was ordered by General Grant to march at once to the relief of General A. E. Burnside and the Army of the Ohio, besieged at Knoxville by Lt. Gen James B. Longstreet.

Forced marching, meager rations and little rest were again the soldier's lot, but they were aware of the object of the march and the little murmuring indulged was not proportionate to the hardships endured.

On December 2 they came to a nice little town called Sweetwater, situated in Sweetwater valley. Wood's Division passed by the town one mile and bivouacked on a slight elevation of ground in an open field with a higher wooded hill three hundred yards to the southeast. The men quickly had a snug pile of rails and were busily engaged in making themselves comfortable for the night as a limited "commissary department" would permit.

It was at this camp that a thrilling incident occurred which all who were on the march will remember. The principal actors were W. W. Barnes and John D. Packer of Company H, 86th Indiana Volunteer Infantry.

Packer was an original character, the like of which is seldom seen engaged in the exercise of all of his fully developed powers in the respectable walks of civil life. Tall and well proportioned, he was young, active and apparently tireless, generally good humored but sometimes irritable, venting his ill-humor on his comrades.

A natural straggler and forager when on the march, he refused to be confined to the ranks, always looking for and scenting plunder. He would pillage on the left flank in the morning and bestow his plunder upon his comrades at the noon halt with unrivaled prodigality.

He would renew his ravages in the afternoon on the right flank despoiling larders, sacking smokehouses devastating barnyards and poultry roosts, bribing messmates to carry the spoils to camp by the prospect of a feast, but guarding and hoarding the loot when it once reached the bivouac with a miser's care, for he had a soldier's stomach and heart. He had fairly earned his titles of "pot-hound," "jay-hawker," "poacher," and "bummer."

A lark in the morning, a hawk at noon, and an owl at night, he could double discount skunk, weasel, and fox combined in catching chickens. He would filch from the rich or poor with equal indifference. In the very wantonness of this "pirooting" spirit, he would take the choicest goods from the table of the most beautiful and refined lady, who, out of the goodness of her heart and in the most gracious manner, had bestowed upon him enough of excellent food to satisfy for days. All of this he would receive with the greatest humility. His manner of buffoonery of action both astonished the beholder and forced him to laugh. Such was his indifference that it was often a question whether it arose from a heart devoid of sympathy or from a lack of intelligence.

A few minutes after reaching the bivouac, Barnes was ready with nothing but a large butcher knife, and Packer his gun and a few cartridges in his pocket. Not thinking of the hard march just finished, but anticipating the nice piece of fresh Tennessee pork they would bring back to camp, they sallied forth in high hopes.

They had passed out into a lane that ran alongside the right of the bivouac, and were rapidly nearing the woods on the hillside, when a shot was heard, and someone remarked, "Why the boys soon found a hog." Barnes too, at this time remarked to Packer, "We'll have to hurry up, John, someone is ahead of us," and they pressed forward with still greater alacrity. Somebody was ahead of them, sure enough, but they were not hunting hogs. The boys were now drawing quite near the woods and were somewhat startled to hear the challenge thundered close to them in rather more than ordinary military sternness.

"Halt, you blank Yankee blank of blank," and two mounted rebel cavalry men rode down the hill, out of the woods, almost upon the boys, and opened a brisk fire upon them from their revolvers and carbines. It looked like certain death for both of the blue-coats right in the face of the whole division.

Pop, pop went the revolvers, szip, szip came the balls. Barnes had no gun and at that distance had no means of either attack or defense, and of course limbered to the rear at once in a more rapid pace than he had gone forward. Pop, pop, went the carbines. He came down the lane as he had gone out in the advance of the column of two.

Pop, pop went the carbines, szip, szip came the balls. The boys came flying down the lane. Pop, pop, szip, szip came the balls in close proximity to their ears, and tired legs could not carry them half fast enough. The balls hissed spitefully and unpleasantly near the boys as they came running. Packer kept Barnes close company for perhaps half the distance to the bivouac, then taking shelter in a fence corner returned the bushwhackers' fire. Not knowing but that these fellows were the skirmishers or scouts of a strong cavalry force near at hand, Colonel Dick ordered the regiment to stand to arms, and at the same time ordered a company to be thrown forward and deployed as skirmishers.

The company at once opened fire on the valorous enemy to develop his strength, but it proved to be just two adventurous spirits who saw their chance to have a crack at a "Yank." The skirmishers rapidly pressing forward succeeded in killing one of the horses, and as a trophy brought in the saddle; but the men made good their escape by doubling on the remaining horse.

The menu was exceedingly scant that night. There was no savory smell of fresh pork, only a very small supply of hard tack, parched corn and coffee.

Friday Dec 4th 1863
Again on the march by sunrise. The country grows more beautiful as we advance. Foot sore way worn and weary I trudge along scarcely to keep with the regiment. A detail was made this morning from the regiment to forage the country for subsistence as orders have been received that rations will not be issued until we reach Knoxville. Went into camp about half past three o'clock though our regiment went on picket. Marched about thirteen miles.

Saturday Dec 5th 1863
Cloudy. Indicates rain. Orders came to march before we had time to get breakfast but orders for the soldiers are imperative and must be obeyed. Accordingly we started hungry but halted when we arrived at the river which was about eleven miles. I feel much depressed this morning both physically and mentally. I am now experiencing one of the sad pictures. The cause I cannot tell. O would that I had a comforting friend to whom I could tell all. Crossed the little Tennessee at which place is a deserted village, Morgantown. The country begins to grow more rough and broken. Traveling on the Maryville road. Went into camp about nine o'clock after having marched perhaps eighteen miles. Hungry, faint, foot sore, way worn & lay down to rest.

Sunday Dec 6th 1863
Started again before daylight. Cloudy and foggy. The atmosphere fully represents my heart. A cloud and fog seems to obscure all my happiness. Would that I could spend the day in some lone sequestered spot uninterrupted by the weary tread of the soldier's march, but I cannot therefore I must trudge along. Passed through the pleasant town of Maryville

in Blount county. Took the Knoxville road and came to Little river after marching perhaps ten miles and within eleven miles of Knoxville. The country is good generally speaking though in some places it is rather inferior in quality of soil.

Monday Dec 7th 1863

At an early hour this morning the bugle sounded to "fall in" but we did not get started till about ten o'clock when we crossed Little River and proceeded on our way toward Knoxville. Passed Rockford a little village ten miles from Knoxville. The road is rough and much cut up by army wagons. Go into camp when within two miles of Knoxville on a rebel farm. Met with many union men who met us with a glad welcome. They told us that Longstreet had been badly repulsed in a charge he had made on Burnsides works and that he had fallen back to Strawberry Plains eighteen miles from K. and that Wilcox had him nearly surrounded.

86th Indiana Regiment, Volunteer Infantry, abridged

A Laughable Incident

A laughable accident occurred at Little River. The command crossed just above a mill-dam on two hewed logs, the ends of which were chained together in the middle of the stream, while the other ends were safely anchored to the banks. Of course the force of the current carried the ends of the logs in the stream down with it so there was an angle formed in the middle of the stream where the water was quite deep, the logs lying almost at right angles with one another, Consequently the distance to be traveled in crossing was increased and the progress delayed. Besides the logs lay in the water and every step taken gave them more or less motion and rendered then not a perfectly sure and stable footing to one inclined to be timid.

The majority of the Eighty-sixth were becoming impatient at the long delay and hurried across as rapidly as possible when their turns came - most of them at a brisk trot.

When Company H's turn came all were in a hurry but one man, Leander W. Friend, known the regiment over as "China," on account of his being so fat and "chuffy." As a natural consequence of his superabundance of adipose tissue he was a clumsy as a bear. When his turn came, and he was among the first, he passed along very slowly and deliberately, notwithstanding the

---

calls of comrades to hurry. His best pace was decidedly slow and he was afraid of tumbling into the water and being drowned. Just behind him was a comrade of the exact opposite physical make. John Worden was one of the quickest, most active, nervous men in all the regiment. Whatever he did, he did with all his might and with lightning like rapidity.

"China" waddled along like a fat pig, Worden dancing along behind him on nettles, as it were, at his delay, until they reached the angle made by the logs in the middle of the stream. Here Worden's impatience would brook no further delay without an extra effort on his part, so he made a spring to get ahead of "China" as he turned from one log to the other. But the second log being somewhat broader than the first one gave "China" more confidence and he quickened his pace and reached the point of Worden's landing a second too soon for the latter who only succeeded in striking his more bulky and weighty comrade and bounding back into the water.

He went down like a shot up to his neck. With knapsack, haversack, gun and cartridge box he was pretty heavily handicapped for a struggle in the water, but caught hold of the log quick as a flash and thus saved himself until the clumsy "China" very deliberately stooped over and pulled his agile comrade out of his ludicrous predicament amid the shouts of laughter of all those who saw it.

Tuesday Dec 8th 1863
Cloudy morning. Very sick in the forenoon. In the afternoon in company with Ben Carpenter I took a stroll from camp in the direction of the city. Went on the hills overlooking the town. The scenery is indeed grand beyond description. The River Holston beautifully winds its course through crags and rocky dells until it is lost to sight by towering heights of those monuments of Eternity. The wild pastures of the "Switzerland of America" is beautifully dotted with hill and vale and as far as the eye can reach their atmospheric heights magically adorn the ethereal canvas and last but not least is the romantic and well renowned city of Knoxville whose inhabitants all concur to excite our admiration for their firm devotion to the union.

Wednesday Dec 9th 1863
"Beautiful and clear". In company with W.P. Hickson I took a jaunt to the city of Knoxville. Rambled the city over but found nothing but soldiers. The town has been a lovely place but from the fact of its having been devastated by two armies it is rather shabby looking. Called in the old printing office of

Barry & Co.. Passed the Whig office but as Brownlow was not "at home" I did not call. Returned to camp well satisfied with the jaunt.

Tuesday Dec 10th 1863
Remained in camp all day. Wrote a letter to Lide in answer to one I received from her on Mission Ridge. Feel lonely. Would that I could find a confiding friend. In the evening went to a house near camp to get some milk but failed.

Friday Dec 11th 1863
Still cloudy. Took a stroll from camp in company with Jim Darrow. Felt relieved to get away from the noise and the bustle of the camp. Reading the Bible. Wrote the "Dog Tent Visitor" a manuscript paper to while away a weary moment. No news from Longstreet yet. Relieved the 59th on picket at 43 (?)

Saturday Dec 12th 1863
The noise and bustle of the camp is heard in the distance. Here all is quiet and calm. My heart still longs for a congenial friend. Dreamed last night of seeing mother. Would that the dream could be real. Relieved by the 18th Ohio. Rainy.

86th Indiana Regiment, Volunteer Infantry, abridged

Sick Flour

*A*t this camp opposite Knoxville, the Eighty-sixth made its first batch of flapjacks out of that abominable stuff known in East Tennessee as "sick flour." It would be futile to attempt to describe the sensations one experiences from eating it. Ipecacuanha, or lobelia, is not more sickening. The suffering one endures from it is of the depressing and nauseating character with various extras thrown in.

The regiment had a good supply of rails [for firewood] and only lacked in rations to be reasonably comfortable when the first supply of this flour was procured. The men were delighted and expected to live well so long as the flour lasted. All were soon busily engaged baking flapjacks, and there was not a great deal of ceremony wasted until they were disposed of, for the time being at least, but it did not prove to be the final disposition.

Soon the fun began, if fun it may be called. First the saliva began to flow, then the stomach began to have its misgivings, then rebellion and tumult became evident and the poor weakened stomach insisted on throwing off the vile mixture.

It was soon very evident that these stomachs did not propose to be imposed upon in any such a manner. Their function was to digest food, but this was no food, but a poison. In fact, many of the boys imagined that some rebel fiend had actually attempted to poison them by poisoning the flour, and concluded that in his efforts to poison a whole army he had mixed the poison with so much flour that it was so divided up until each one only got enough to sicken and disquiet him instead of enough to kill as was intended. But it certainly would have been laughable to a person not interested to have watched one who had eaten heartily of these flapjacks.

First, he would be a little uneasy and restless. If sitting by the fire he would change his position frequently, probably get up and stand by the fire, turning a few times this way or that as if he were undecided as to the position he wished to assume for comfort.

But the decision was soon made. He would battle against fate and strive at first to control the internal commotion and put the rebellion down. But the sufferer would soon turn deathly pale, take a few steps away from the campfire - a sudden upheaval from the stomach, a volcanic eruption, minus the fire, and the climax was reached. To the hungry soldier it was a calamity. There were his flapjacks on the ground, and nothing else to eat except this same sick flour.

Again, at a later time, the men were again out of rations and drew for breadstuff on the 26th a miserable lot of flour. It was alive with worms, and it is quite safe to say that the picking of worms out of the flour was the business of at least one man in each mess of the entire regiment until all were tired. The flour proved to be not only wormy but "sick" and was a abomination to any half civilized stomach. The filthy pools of stagnant green-scummed and rank water of Kentucky, in which decaying mules festered and rotted in the sunshine, were not more trying to the stomach than this despicable, maggoty, "sick flour." loaded with other nauseating and poisonous qualities, which every soldier well knew were quite sufficient to make him a fit subject for the hospital.

More Culinary Delights

Gradually rations grew more scarce and the men had in a great measure to depend upon themselves. Many of the regiment, almost every mess, went to the Holston River, obtained boats, crossed the stream with ice running dangerously thick, and went miles beyond, procured corn and carried it on their backs, re-crossed, and returned to camp that they and their comrades should not suffer the pangs of starvation. Sometimes a little meat could be foraged, but it was rare. The beef issued was of the poorest conceivable quality. General Jacob D. Cox in his history of the Atlanta Campaign, speaking of the destitution of the army in East Tennessee, during the winter of 1863-64, says: "The country was stripped bare, and during the month of January the cattle that were turned over to the troops for beef were so poor they could hardly stand up. It is literally true that it was the custom of the commissaries to drive the cattle over a little ditch in the field where they were corralled, and those only were killed which could not get over, their weakness proving that it would not do to keep them longer, whilst the others might last for future use.

Of the beef cattle of the division many which were killed were so poor that they had to be lifted up to be knocked down. But mark now the destitution of the men. Often would soldiers gladly pay one dollar a piece for the head of such a beef. Sometimes they would get the head and the melt for one dollar, but usually only the head. The head would be cleaned, the eyes taken out and then the whole head boiled in a camp-kettle, and the bones picked clean of every fibre of meat. Thus did the Eighty-sixth subsist, suffer and endure, almost without a murmur, during this dreadful winter.

Sunday Dec 13th 1863
Cloudy and rainy. Spent the day in reading the Bible. Profitable employment of time.

Monday Dec 14th 1863
From the busy hum which pervades camp this morning one is reminded of a new and flourishing colony. Industry's hum is sounding throughout camp. Quarters are being fixed for the better accommodation of our stay. I was

engaged in putting up a chimney to a log shanty.

Tuesday Dec 15th 1863
Calm and beautiful this morning. The click of the ax and the scrape of the trowel again enlivens the air with - marching orders. Get ready and "fall in". Wait patiently an hour or so when the order is countermanded though to march at six in the morning. Lay down in my shanty of logs and slept sweetly.

Wednesday Dec 16th 1863
At the appointed hour we were on the move. Crossed the river and passed through the city of Knoxville where we took the Strawberry Plains road. The country is rough and broken. Passed near Andly and House mountain. Went into camp after a twenty miles march. Very tired.

Thursday Dec 17th 1863
Rained last night. Remained in camp till 3 o'clock when we relieved the 59th on picket at the base of House mountain. Read 29 chapters in Exodus.

Friday Dec 18th 1863
Cold and windy with flying clouds. Relieved from picket by the 19th O. Came to camp.

Saturday Dec 19th 1863
Remained in camp. The cold chilly blasts howl around reminding one that stern winter has come. Passed the time in reading the Bible.

Sunday Dec 20th 1863
Still in camp near House mountain. The Sabbath dawns clear and cold. What the movements of the army will be next I am unable to say. Reading.

Monday Dec 21st 1863
After foregoing the pleasure of a mail for nearly a month we received one today and many a heart was made glad by the perusal of a missive from the dear ones at home. When it was announced that the mail had arrived it was a scene for a poet. The soldiers eye lit with a sudden flame as though new life the dead had received, and the more so while perusing the words penned by a father, mother, sister brother or maybe sweetheart. But then how sad was the countenance of those while waiting in eager expectation to hear "none for you". If friends at home could but have seen their countenances they would take more pains to write more frequently. Received missives from J.H. Smith, J.M. Cast, "Mollie" and sister Melvina. They all were welcomely

received. Also received the "Gazette" with a letter from Chattanooga together with many others. Read the Pors Message.

Tuesday Dec 22nd 1863
Wrote home. Perusing the papers I received yesterday.   Gen. Manson has been relieved of the command of the 23rd.

Wednesday Dec 23rd 1863
Wrote John M. Cast. Reading the accounts of the Chattanooga battles. Clear, cool.

Thursday Dec 24th 1863
Clear, pleasant. Wrote letters to the Cin. Commercial. Relieved the 59th on picket.

Friday Dec 25th 1863
"Merry Christmas" Not merry either because I am a soldier boy. If I could enjoy Christmas in civilized life perhaps then it would be merry. Feel lonely, a silent melancholy pervades only interrupted by the whoop of the soldier n the distant camp or rustle of the fallen leaf, or the murmuring of the gentle streamlet which courses its way through the rocky hills and dells of the House mountains. Went into a new camp.

86th Indiana Regiment, Volunteer Infantry, abridged

Christmas - 1863

"As Christ died to make men holy, Let us die to make men free."

*T*his may not have been the sentiment of every private soldier and officer of the Eighty-sixth, but it was what they were virtually offering to do by serving in the army at that time. Many claimed that they only fought to maintain the country's unity and constitution as it was, but President Lincoln has said, with that prescience for which he was so remarkable: "This country cannot endure part slave and part free." It was for the freedom of the slaves they fought, thus making possible the unity of the country - all free. It is doubtful if such thoughts entered the minds of many of the rank and file of the Eighty-sixth on Christmas morning. 1863, when first aroused from their slumbers. The conditions and circumstances of their environment claimed most of their thoughts rather than the general purposes and causes of the war.

That environment was not a joyous one. No glad shouting of merry children, no cheerful greetings and the wishing for each other "A Merry Christmas." The spiritual barometer was too low for this.

But the stern command of officers broke the slumbers, for they had slept soundly even if it was Christmas morning. Their commands were: "Prepare to go on outpost," and, "Prepare to go on the line immediately." This was the Christmas greeting. And in the gray of the cold, bleak morning the Eighty-sixth went on the line and gazed upon the rugged heights of House Mountain as the darkness disappeared. The Christmas dinner of 1863, for the most part in the Eighty-sixth, consisted of a small piece of corn bread made of unsifted meal, mixed with water and a very little salt, and baked or fried in the irrepressive army frying-pan, and a small bit of third or fourth grade army bacon. It is hardly necessary to say that is was not a banquet or a feast. Turkey, cranberry sauce, or scalloped oysters could not be had.

Saturday Dec 26th 1863
In camp fixing up our tents. Rainy and wet. Saw some of the 116th boys. Wrote a letter to Will Martin. Feel lonely. Wish I had a confiding friend.

Sunday Dec 27th 1863
Again the day of rest - the day sweetest of all the seven dawns. Welcome Sabbath. But on the tented field I am sorry to say no Sabbath is known. Would that it were not so. Spent the day in reading the scriptures. Rainy.

Monday Dec 28th 1863
Stormy day. The fierce winds howl and whistle around which renders it very disagreeable.

Tuesday Dec 29 1863
Passed the day in chopping wood and reading the Bible. The soldiers heart was made glad this afternoon by the arrival of the mail. Received mail from Annie C. and Josey Foxworthy. Glad to hear from them. Wrote Mollie T.

86th Indiana Regiment, Volunteer Infantry, abridged

Happiness

*H*ow welcome was a letter from home to the soldier, and how sad he felt when those at home neglected to write. The differences on the countenances of those who received and those who did not were particularly noted on the arrival of this mail, so long had it been since one had been received. The features of the one lit up with pleasure, as he perused the epistle in his hand - doubtless the letter of some dear wife or mother,, or may be sweetheart - and as he read it, a smile of joy illumined his weather-beaten face. This was happiness.

It was an oasis on the desert of his rough life of danger and suffering. With the other the opposite effect was observed; as soon as the word "none" had passed the lip of the regimental postmaster the look of anxiety faded away, and an appearance of extreme sorrow could be seen plainly stamped on his features, while a feeling of envy at his more fortunate comrades was plainly apparent. This was unhappiness.

The song of hope that had illumined his heart when he inquired if there was any letter for him had died away, and a feeling of loneliness and regret of the neglect of those at home took possession of him. Happy were they who had homes and loved ones to hear from!

Next to the scarcity of rations the hardship incident to being poorly clad during the extreme cold weather were most severely felt. It was often so cold that then attempting to write letters or make entries in diaries the ink would freeze on the pens. It would often be necessary to heat the pen and write as rapidly as possible until it cooled off. Another plan was to sit near the campfire which was a veritable log heap, and roast oneself while writing, placing the ink bottle in the hot ashes.

Wednesday Dec 30th 1863
Clear and pleasant after the storm and week through which we have passed. Read "the news". Wrote to Wm. L. Bowman. Relieved the 13th Ohio on picket.

Thursday Dec 31st 1863
Cloudy and wet. The scenery from the picket station is beautiful. In the

distance can be seen House mountain rearing its majestic height toward the throne of the Great Eternal while still nearer the wandering streamlet glides murmuringly around its base. The curling smoke from the rude cabin, and the meadow, the orchard of the still nearer farm house each dressed with its winter's robe excites our admiration. And nearer still stands the lone sentinel like a statue at his post. Such is the picture of our picket station. The old year is wasting away. The death knell will soon be heard, and the funeral dirge be sung.

Chapter Twelve
East Tennessee

1864

Friday Jan 1st 1864
Happy New Year? The new year was ushered in this morning with rather a cool air. The wintery winds of E. Tennessee howled and whistled around the rude shelter of the Union Soldiers. Each one was busily engaged during the day in preparing wood to protect him from the chilly blasts which blew so fiercely from the bleak neighboring mountain tops. Instead of being "Happy New Year" unhappy New Year would be more expressive and more truthful. My New Year's dinner consisted of a Johnny cake, fried beef and coffee. Supper a half pie and apples.

Saturday Jan 2nd 1864
"Cold as Greenland", expresses it this morning. The day was passed in endeavoring to keep myself comfortable.

Sunday Jan 3rd 1864
Old Winter's forces are evacuating their stronghold at least his front does not appear as formidable as yesterday. Perhaps he is falling back till reinforcements shall arrive. Mail arrived again today. Many a heart was made glad by a missive from home. Received letters from home. Mate, Anna K., Mary, & Ollie and several Gazettes.

Monday Jan 4th 1864
Cloudy indicating rain. Passed the day attending to various duties both domestic and official. Finished reading the book of Deuteronomy.

Tuesday Jan 5th 1864
Orders came yesterday evening to be ready at a moments warning to move on the enemy and drive him from of Tennessee. Preparations are being made this morning. 100 rounds to a man are drawn which means a battle. The 13th Ohio has reenlisted as veterans and start north this morning.

Wednesday Jan 6th 1864
The first snow of the season visited our camp. Rather an unwelcome visitor, but it became necessary through compulsion that it be entertained. Wrote John M. Cast. "On picket again". Saw the "Knoxville Whig and Rebel Ventilator" It hauls the rebellion over the coals.

Thursday Jan 7th 1864
Cloudy and cold while mother Earth is robed in white.

Friday Jan 8th 1864
Did nothing worthy of note. Too many such days to be noted in making up the great diary of life.

Saturday Jan 9th 1864
Remains cold. Wrote letters to Mate and W.A. Haworth. Cold writing too.

Sunday Jan 10th 1864
The Holy Sabbath dawns clear and cold. The forenoon was spent in trying to keep warm. Went through a thorough ablution of the outer man. Had a rabbit for dinner, quite a luxury. In the afternoon reading the Book of Joshua.

Monday Jan 11th 1864
The morn is beautiful. Reading the "Wabash Magazine", a monthly published by an association of students at Wabash College. It contained an address to the Alumni by Prof. Campbell - subject - Major Gen O.M. Mitchell. Also a poem by D.G. Roderick, The Death Message
  Fell many a youth whose hopes were high,
   In the blood stained fields chose rather to die,
   Than live mid the ruins of Liberty's —

Tuesday Jan 12th 1864
The regiment, or rather half of it march on picket. Wrote Mary Cool.

Wednesday Jan 13th 1864
Had orders to march tomorrow morning at 7 o'clock, accordingly preparations were immediately made, drawing rations, etc.

Thursday Jan 14th 1864
At 7 this morning we were on the move. Crossed the Holston river at Strawberry Plains. Passed through a rough and broken country and after marching about sixteen miles encamped.

Friday Jan 15th 1864
Again on the move early. Marched about eight miles when we came to Dandridge the county seat of Jefferson County and encamped.

Saturday Jan 16th 1864
The day is beautiful. In company with C. Waddell I took a stroll through the town of Dandridge. This is a beautiful mountain town 32 miles west of Knoxville and contained at the breaking out of the rebellion about 1800 inhabitants, but now like most southern towns it bears the impress of war's desolation. I accidentally met a young lady who was quite intelligent and from I learned that the rebel force under Longstreet was about 25000 strong at Morristown 16 miles north. She also told me that the town was about equally divided in regard to the great questions of the union. After an agreeable and pleasant half hour I left her impressed with the conviction that she was in favor of the union to a man. Returned to camp and partook of frugal soldiers supper.

Sunday Jan 17th 1864
The Sabbath again dawns bright and beautiful. The day was spent in camp near Dandridge. My spirits are not as light and gay as they usually are. Feel lonely. Heavy skirmishing in front. Indications are that the enemy is in force and will make a stubborn resistance. At dusk we are ordered to fall in and be ready for any emergency. Marched to the edge of town where we remained perhaps an hour and returned to camp. Soon after had marching orders. News has been received that the enemy is too strong and a retreat is on foot. The consequence is no sleeping is done and the night is spent awaiting the word to march. At 3 o'clock we commence to beat our retreat toward Strawberry Plains.

Monday Jan 18th 1864
At 3 o'clock the army commenced a retreat in the direction of Strawberry Plains. The day was wet and rainy. After a hard march of 30 miles we reached the Plains at dark and encamp in an open field where there were no rails. The night was cold consequently it was passed unpleasantly.

Tuesday Jan 19th 1864
Morning dawned and revealed the fact that an additional cover had been spread over us during the night in the shape of a white covering.

86th Indiana Regiment Volunteer Infantry, adapted

Bivouac In the Snow

The morning of the 19th dawned, but it was a rude awakening for the soldier, tired in every limb and muscle, stiff in every joint and lank as a fox-hound after a long chase. The men had slept soundly, and not a gun or bugle note disturbed their repose. It was a January morning long to be remembered by the Eighty-sixth. There lay the command on open ground and covered with snow five or six inches deep! The words of Margaret J. Preston came vividly to mind:

"Halt - the march is over,
 Day is almost gone;
Loose the cumbrous knapsack,
 Drop the heavy gun.

Chilled and wet and weary,
 Wander to and fro,
Seeking wood to kindle
 Fires amidst the snow.

"Round the bright blaze gather,
 Heed not sleet or cold;
Ye are Spartan soldiers,
 Stout and brave and bold."

The various bunks lay around over the ground like so many logs rolled together and buried in the snow. No sign of life revealed itself for some time. First one, and then another, would gently lift the blanket covering his head and stretch his neck out like a turtle from under his shell, take a brief observation of the appearance of things, utter some exclamation of surprise, and quickly withdraw his astonished countenance from sight. Carefully tucking the blanket around his head, to keep the snow from tumbling about his ears, he meditates.

But there was work to be done. More rails had to be procured for fuel, and it was a particularly unpleasant task for weary soldiers to turn out into the snow and trudge a half mile or more. But difficulties never vanish by trying to evade them. They must be met and overcome.

Finally all were up and at work. Here, too, was an occasion where work was a benefit to the laborer in and of itself. Not that he particularly needed the exercise for the sake of exercise, but the work was highly beneficial both for the physical well-being of the soldier and for the morale of the command.

At the first look to the half-rested, half-starved, poorly clad, sore-legged soldier it was a gloomy morning indeed - a disheartening prospect that well-nigh overmastered him. Under such depressing conditions and circumstances the renewal of work is the great panacea - the one great safeguard, the surest cure, and so it proved with the Eighty-sixth. When the effort was made to meet the difficulties, great as they appeared to be at first, it was soon seen that they were not insurmountable, and as the blood began to flow more freely from exertions put forth, the spiritual barometer began to indicate fair weather, figuratively speaking, and the gloom began to disappear.

Wednesday Jan 20th 1864
After lying in camp nearly all day again started and marched about four miles in the direction of Knoxville and went into camp.

Thursday Jan 21st 1864
The day is beautiful reminding one of a spring day "at home". On march at seven. Came to K--. Bought a shirt and suspenders. Marched two miles east of the city and encamped.

Friday Jan 22nd 1864
Clear. What a lovely day. Such days as this make one feel happy. Mailed a letter to Mary. Wrote cousin "Bette"

Saturday Jan 23rd 1864
Received orders to move at 8 o'clock. At the appointed hour we were on our way. Traveling in the direction of Maryville. Encamped on Little River.

Sunday Jan 24th 1864
Twenty five years ago today I was born. I am indeed placed under different circumstances to what I was on my birthday one year ago. Then I was a prisoner in the hands of the enemy. Now I am trudging along with wearied limbs in pursuit of that same enemy. I trust that my twenty fifth year may be spent in endeavoring to become a better man. Went into camp near Maryville. At night in company with John Michaels I attended the village church. Upon entering the threshold of the sanctuary my thoughts

inadvertently reverted back to the old church at home. I thought of the friends who at this hour were wending their way to the house of God. Pleasing thoughts were these but my reverie was disturbed when the man of God arose and announced that the old familiar hymn would be sung commencing

"When I can read my title clear
    To mansions in the skies"

Singing concluded and the congregation knelt in prayer. The preacher then announced the text "What is man that thou art mindful of him". While those words were being expounded I thought truly that God had indeed been merciful to me. He had preserved my life for twenty-four years and had permitted the dawning of the twenty-fifth birthday. I truly should be thankful. Services concluded and the doxology sung. I wended my way to camp feeling that I was much profited by the evening's exercise.

Monday Jan 25th 1864
Weather continues mild and pleasant. Camp resounds with industry's hum. Like a young and flourishing colony shanties are being erected for the accommodations of the soldier. Looks very much as though winter quarters are being put up.

Tuesday Jan 26th 1864
The work goes bravely on . Our shanties are nearly all completed. Wrote home.

Wednesday Jan 27th 1864
In company with Ben Carpenter I took a stroll through the town of Maryville. Visited the town school kept by a male of the backwoods style. His machine ran on the old pod auger system. Visited the library and obtained "Ossian's Poems" - "Walts on the mind" - and "Life" a poem in three books. Also Walker's dictionary.

Thursday Jan 28th 1864
The weather continues mild and pleasant. The right wing of the reg't went on picket. Wrote a letter to J.H. Smith enclosing two dollars for paper and envelopes. Mail arrived bringing a letter from home and one from M.H. Belknap.

Friday Jan 29th 1864
Reading the Chicago Tribune. Wrote to M.H. Belknap.

Saturday Jan 30th 1864
Reading "Walts on the Mind" and copying an article from the Louisville Journal in regard to the 86th at Mission Ridge. Also read a poem dedicated to the 86th by J.W.C.

Sunday Jan 31st 1864
Sabbath morning again. Visited the village church and heard an excellent sermon by the pastor from the LXXX Psalm. In the afternoon wrote a letter for Wm. Wiley. Went to the Presbyterian church at night.

Monday Feb 1st 1864
Remained in camp but nothing occurred worthy of note.

Tuesday Feb 2nd 1864
Wrote to friend Ollie. Passed the day in reading "Ossian".

Wednesday Feb 3rd 1864
Running round through camp doing everything and nothing either.

Thursday Feb 4th 1864
Writing in the office. Making out a Register of Commissioned officers belonging to the regiment on the first of January 1864 together with a list of casualties that have occurred since the organization of the regiment.

Friday Feb 5th 1864
Still writing on the register. In the afternoon baking.

Saturday Feb 6th 1864
Finished the register. Reading in "Ossian" Rainy day.

Sunday Feb 7th 1864
Wrote letters to Anna K. Flora W., sister Melvina and home. Attended church in the village. The text was "Remember now thy Creator in the days of thy youth."

Monday Feb 8th 1864
Wrote letter to "Lide". Reading in the Northwestern. It contains a piece of poetry "The Old Year of the Nation" For Freedom on the title page wrote
   "Glory" And on the last with firmer pen "Amen"
Attended church at night in town.

Tuesday Feb 9th 1864
Wrote a letter for Sam Hoxlin. Again visited the village church. The series of meetings are well attended and good seems to be accomplished.

Wednesday Feb 10th 1864
Weather continues beautiful. Word received that the pickets are driven in.

Thursday Feb 11th 1864
Wrote a letter to the Indianapolis "Gazette". Clear and beautiful.

Friday Feb 12th 1864
Did nothing worthy of note. Camp equipage came up from Chattanooga.

Saturday Feb 13th 1864
Making out the ordnance reports for Lt. Gorham, also Capt. Ream.

Sunday Feb 14th 1864
The Sabbath dawns cloudy. Making out muster rolls.

Monday Feb 15th 1864
Finished the muster and payrolls. The paymaster is here and will give the troops stationed here two months pay. Finished up the ordnance returns. Rain came in torrents all day. At night I lay down in my comfortable quarters and was preparing to take a dose of "kind nature's sweet restorer" when a sudden attack of marching orders seized me from which I suffered much mental pain. The contagion spread from soldier to soldier until it spread throughout camp. After suffering sometime we were relieved by the command to "fall in." A thousand conjectures are on the lips of the boys as to where we go and what we go for. Trudge, trudge through the mud about knee deep until the dawn of the morning in the direction of Knoxville.

Tuesday Feb 16th 1864
The day has been cold and raw, but still we go heedless of cold and mud. About nine o'clock we came to within a mile of Knoxville and camped in a hollow. Slept on the hillside but it was too steep to rest comfortably. The night is cold.

Wednesday Feb 17th 1864
The morning dawns clear and cold. Windy too which renders it very unpleasant. The boys in the regiment suffer much from cold. Received letters from home and Frank.

Thursday Feb 18th 1864
Still continues cold. Standing around in the weather until two o'clock when the regiment was ordered across the river. Crossed on the pontoon, marched through the city and encamped about half a mile west. Slept out doors without tents.

Friday Feb 19th 1864
Clear and cold. In company with George Chizum I took a stroll through the city of Knoxville. Called at the office of the Brownlow Whig. Subscribed for the paper to send home. Learned that the parson was quite ill. Came to camp and assisted in building a chimney to a dog house.

Saturday Feb 20th 1864
Started to the city early this morning for the purpose of making out muster and pay rolls for Capt. Gregory. Writing in the U.S. Sanitary Building. Took supper at a fifth rate boarding house for which paid the real little sum of seventy five cents. The regiment was inspected today by Maj. Comstock, A.I.G. of Gen. Grant's staff.

Sunday Feb 21st 1864
The Sabbath dawns cloudy indicating snow. About 8 o'clock it commenced snowing which continued coming in great white flakes until about 12 o'clock. Attended the Methodist church in Knoxville. A chaplain of the army officiated. Returned to camp and wrote a letter home.

Monday Feb 22nd 1864
Washington's Birthday! The regiment had made arrangements to celebrate the day but conflicting circumstances prevented. Paid off by Maj. Price. Received two month's wages.

Tuesday Feb 23rd 1864
Making out monthly returns. A detail was made of 240 men for fatigue but about 11 o'clock we received marching orders to be ready to start at daylight.

Wednesday Feb 24th 1864
At 8 o'clock the general call was sounded and we soon were on our way. Moved through K - on the Strawberry Plains road which lays up the valley of the river Holston. The country is beautifully diversified with hill and dale. The soil fertile and the farms well improved though it bears the impress of war's desolating footsteps. The fences are burnt and the many fine mansions

which once were the homes of affluence and wealth are now vacant. In the distance the lofty monuments of nature, the ridges which divide Tennessee and N. Carolina attract the mental vision. These ____ possess awful magnificence while they rise in all their oriental dignity and beauty to heights inaccessible, the skyward peaks of which none will dare approach. Near the Plains went in camp.

Thursday Feb 25th 1864
Remained in camp all day. Read a dime novel. Novel reading as a general thing is not profitable, though just out of every thing else this was a last resort. Mail arrived bringing a letter from my friend Ollie.

Friday Feb 26th 1864
The day is lovely. Writing letters to my friends Frank and Ollie. Rations were issued for four days. The 23rd and 9th Corps. have marching orders with 15 days rations.

Saturday Feb 27th 1864
So much like spring. About 10 o'clock orders came to move. In a moment we were ready and on the move. Crossed the Holston river in a pontoon boat. Went into camp near the river's bank. Mail arrived but I was among the unfortunate and received nothing. In the evening had orders to leave knapsacks and all extra load and prepare for a light march. It is supposed we are going on a reconnaissance. Citizens say that Longstreet is 75 miles and still on the retreat.

Sunday Feb 28th 1864
    Hail, Sabbath morn sweet day of rest
     Whose rising sun has charms divine
    To cheer the weary soldier's heaving breast
     Through danger's toil and battle's time
Yes, tis the lovely Sabbath morning and a solemn awe pervades each soldier's heart as silently he prepares for the weary march. No Sabbath bell calls his willing feet to the house of God. No loving smiles from friends at home greet the eye. Nothing but groups of soldier boys sitting around the camp fires. Some talking of the latest fight. And others of the sights they saw. About noon we were on our way to New Market, a distance of 10 miles. The day was fine and roads good and we made the trip quickly. Went into camp near New Market. Our road still continues up the valley of the river Holston. The country is beautiful.

Monday Feb 29th 1864
Awoke this morning and found it raining. Hurriedly breakfasted and started for Morristown, a distance of 12 miles before daylight. The country still is good though the roads are very muddy. Rainy day but after a weary and toilsome march we reach Morrestown and are quartered in rebel barracks. I lay down very tired. Indeed I thought the bed very sweet. I thought of these lines.

"When the hurried showers gather
  Oe'r all the starry spheres
And a melancholy darkness
  Gently creeps in rainy tears,
'Tis a joy to press the pillow
  Of an Humble Soldier's bed
And listen to the patter
  Of the soft rain overhead."

Tuesday March 1st 1864
Still in our rebel quarters where we remained all day. The rain came unceasingly all day. Nothing definite can be obtained from the enemy. He is said to have halted at Bull's Gap 18 miles distant.

Wednesday March 2nd 1864
At four o'clock the camp was all astir preparatory to leaving. The soldiers had partaken of their frugal morning meal and were busily employing their prophetical powers as to which direction we would move. Soon how ever their curiosity was satisfied when our faces were turned backward. The morning was beautiful and but for the wind we would have had pleasant marching. Halted at Mossy Creek and took dinner. At three o'clock went into camp near New Market having marched eighteen miles today.

Thursday March 3rd 1864
At an early hour this morning we were expecting to move at day light. Remained in camp. Feel lonely. Wish I could hear from some loved friend at home.

March 4th 1864
Eighteen months ago today the 86th was mustered into the United States service at Indianapolis. The boys pass away the time in reading novels though many of them are at their low and degrading game of Chuck a Luck not only squandering their money but their morals and their virtue. I spent the day reading "Ella Adams" a tale of the Charleston Conflagration. At night

the mail arrived bearing precious missives from loved ones at home. Received letters from the chaplain and Frank Cones.

Saturday March 5th 1864
Rained last night. Co "I" "F" "A" & "H" were on picket. Cool morning this. A genuine March day. Reading the Indianapolis Journal. Gov Morton was renominated for the gubernatorial chair. His nomination is hailed with delight among the soldiers. His election is regarded certain. Still near New Market, bivouacked awaiting something nobody know what. While seated by a small campfire picking gray backs which had dared to intrude themselves upon me who should make his appearance but Geo Storms recruiting officer of Co I just fresh from Indiana. As a matter of course it did the boys good to see a person from just from their native state.

Sunday March 6th 1864
This Sabbath dawns fresh and beautiful. How sad it seems to see the soldiers spending the holy day at the card table instead of improving it as should be, reveling and gambling reigns supreme. They seem perfectly infatuated even forgetting that this is God's holy day. Passing through the regiment I saw the "Religious Telescope" spread upon the ground while surrounding it was a group shuffling the spotted cards, - for what? For money? Yes, for money. This crime is growing to an alarming extent. Many young men who left their homes with the tearful injunctions from fond parents not to be led astray by the many vices incident to camp life now travels in the path to ruin. It is a fearful fact to record, yet such it is.

Monday March 7th 1864
Mailed a letter to the Indianapolis Gazette. Co "E" was placed on provost duty in New Market. Received the Gazette with a letter from Camp Beatty.

Tuesday March 8th 1864
The daily routine of camp duties continues. Expecting orders to march every moment. The weather is pleasant. Scarce of reading matter.

Wednesday March 9th 1864
Companies "B" "C" "I" & "K" on outpost duty. Nothing occurred to change the monotony of the camp.

Thursday March 10th 1864
Today an extensive raffle takes place in the northern states. 500,000 men to

be raffled for. The soldiers hail this day with delight. Wrote letters.

Friday March 11, 1864
Private Dixon Company C applied for furlough. Capt. Gregory sent in resignation. Sent regimental history to Washington City. John M. Cast came up yesterday evening. Received letter from home. Sorry to learn of the illness of my mother. The day has been windy. Rec'd orders to march at six in the morning.

Saturday March 12, 1864
At an early hour the camp was all astir making preparations for the days march. The adjutant being absent on business I rode his horse. At six o'clock we start in the direction of Morristown. Go 12 miles and encamp at "Panther Springs" the day is indeed beautiful.

Sunday March 13, 1864
Early this morning the reveille sounded and the camp was soon all astir making arrangements to march. XXXXXXX A letter from Abbie. Marched as far as Morristown and encamped. Took possession of the shanties the rebs had put up. Regiment ordered on picket. About sunset half of the regiment returned to camp.

Monday March 14, 1864
Cool morning writing in the office. Lieut. Yount resigned.

Monday 14, 1864
Cold day. In rebel barracks near Morristown Yount started home.

Tuesday March 15, 1864
Still continues cold. Received a letter from Mollie S. What the next move will be no one can conjecture.

Wednesday March 16, 1864
Capt. Geanner went to Knoxville. Wrote a letter to Mollie. Reading "Marion's Brigade" a tale of the Revolution.

Thursday March 17th 1864
Changed camp this morning. Our encampment how is about a half a mile east of Morristown. About 11 o'clock P.M. orders were received to be ready to move at 5 1/2 on the morrow.

Friday March 18th 1864
At the appointed hour we left Morristown and marched toward New Market and arrived at the latter place at 2 o'clock and encamped on the old camping ground. The day was very windy and disagreeable Mail came but nothing for me.

Saturday March 19, 1864
On the move early this morning. Came to Strawberry Plains and encamped. Here met Nate Hammel just from home.

Sunday March 20th 1864
The morning is indeed beautiful. The sun sheds brilliant luster o'er hill and dale. A holy stillness pervades camp. About eleven o'clock the assembly sounds. Start for Rutledge distant about 12 miles northwest. After traveling about 9 miles encamped.

Monday March 21st 1864
At 6 o'clock we started. About 12 o'clock reached Rutledge, the county seat of Grainger County. The village is a dilapidated mountain town of about 200 inhabitants. The country through which we passed is rough and hilly. Our regiment was detailed for picket duty. Near the picket station a farmer had asked for a guard. Three men from Co H were detailed. I visited the home and was kindly entertained by Angie L. Godwin, a bitter little rebel. She was a good singer and performed on the piano well. (She wrote her name in this diary page 156) Received a letter from W.L. Brown.

Tuesday March 22nd 1864
It commenced snowing this morning and continued all day. When it ceased the ground was covered to the depth of about 4 inches. Relieved from picket about 11 o'clock by the 17th Ky.

Wednesday March 23rd 1864
Real wintery morning. Did nothing in the forenoon. In the afternoon called to see Miss Angie who favored me with some good music among which was Lalla Roohk, "Forget me" "Thou hast learned to love another Lassie" together with some southern songs. Also called to see Miss Smith by the way a union lady who entertained me with good music. Evening closed.

Thursday March 24th 1864
Clear. Took a stroll away from camp among the rocks and crags bordering

the knobs. Visited a cavern from which issued a stream of water which was curiosity. Returned to camp and read "Tales of Waterloo". At noon had orders to march. Moved down Richland Valley 10 miles toward Knoxville and encamped.

Friday March 25th 1864
Arose this morning from my humble couch and found the ground all covered with snow. Dismal morning. Remained in Camp. Received a letter from Ollie and the Indianapolis Gazette containing a letter from New Market.

Saturday March 26th 1864
Cloudy and dull morning. Attending to official duties. Had orders to move at one o'clock. The brigade is ordered on a scouting expedition over in Clinch Valley. Crossed Pool Knobs down the Valley and over Clinch Mountain. Our road lay up Clinch Valley until we came to within about 13 miles of Clinch River where we came to halt and went in camp.

Sunday March 27th 1864
Again on the move toward Tazewell. This morning our cavalry encountered about 50 guerrillas. Killed one and captured another. Marched about 12 miles up the valley when we retraced our steps. Toward night three rebel scouts were captured on the side of the mountain.

Monday March 28th 1864
Co "E" was detailed to scout Clinch mountain. Returned to camp in Richland valley about 12 o'clock. The weather indicates rain.

Tuesday March 29th 1864
Rained last night. Dog tents leaked. Water ran under our beds. Wet, wet, wet all over. Felt like a drowned rat. This is indeed one of the beauties of soldiering.

Wednesday March 30th 1864
Wrote home. Writing in the office. Weather changeable. Still encamped at Powder Springs Gap.

Thursday March 31st 1864
The day is pleasant. Writing for Capt. Carnahan! Sent up recommendations for promotion. Wrote Wm L. Bowman.

Friday April 1st 1864
All fools' day. What the origin of this is I know not. The weather continues cool and unpleasant. Took a stroll away from camp. Plucked the first flowers of spring. Wrote to my friend Ollie. Laid off camp with more regularity . Rainy afternoon.

Saturday April 2nd 1864
Cold and damp morning. Reading in the "Waverly".

Sunday April 3rd 1864
Bright and beautiful is the Sabbath. From Company B.C.D. and I were detailed for picket. Reading Harper's Monthly. Wrote a letter to the Gazette and Prof. Smith.

Monday April 4th 1864
Rainy day. Benj. F. Lytle started home on furlough. An order has just been issued permitting five per cent of enlisted men to go home on furlough. This is welcome news to the soldier. Suffering with the tooth-ache. Jacob D. Bazzle who was wounded at Mission Ridge and a good soldier of Co. I. came up today.

Tuesday April 5th 1864
Reading the Wabash Magazine. Furlough came for Wm Sems Co. K. and John S Bennet. Fife major received orders to march at 6 o'clock tomorrow morning. The day has been drizzly. Mail came in but brought nothing for me.

Wednesday April 6th 1864
At the appointed time the two brigades which had lain for a week or so at Powder Springs Gap were on the move toward Strawberry Plains. For a while the wind rendered it unpleasant marching but it soon cleared off and the road dried up beautifully. Reached the Plains at one o'clock and went into camp. The country is rough and broken. The rumor is that we return to Chattanooga. At least we have orders to move tomorrow morning at 5 1/2 o'clock.

Thursday April 7th 1864
At 5 1/2 we started though rather tedious in moving out on account of the wagon trains which have been considerably increased by the addition of four or five trains to each regiment. The peach trees are in full bloom everywhere

which indicates the approach of merry spring time. The birds are caroling their sweetest songs and all nature smiles. Marched through the city of Knoxville and encamped about three miles west of town. Mail came in bringing me missives from home, Frank, Mother and Prof. Smith.

Friday April 8th 1864
Slept sweetly last night. Awoke this morning and found it raining. Arose and partook of my frugal breakfast. Read the poem of Fanny Lamborn, "After the Battle". Tom Dicker Co. I. came to the regiment today. He was wounded at Mission Ridge and consequently received a furlough home. He brought many presents from home. It is really amusing to see the gratefulness manifested on the part of the recipients. Even though small they were gratefully received. At 1 o'clock the Division moved out after marching 5 miles encamped.

Saturday April 9th 1864
Rained again last night and still continues to pour in torrents. At an early hour moved out. Still going in the direction of Loudon. The road was muddy which rendered it wearysome marching. At 2 o'clock we encamped at Lenoir Station.

Chapter Thirteen
Sherman's Campaign in Georgia

Sunday April 10th 1864
At 6 o'clock we moved out. Still continues to rain. Reached Loudon 6 miles distant at 10 o'clock and went into camp near the Tennessee River. Feel considerably depressed this morning. The cause I know not. Received a letter from Lide last night. Belknap came to the regiment today. He was wounded at Mission Ridge.

Monday April 11th 1864
Clear and beautiful after so many rainy days. Hope spring days have come at last. I am tired of the dreary and gloomy days through which we have just passed.

Tuesday April 12th 1864
Crossed the river yesterday and lay in camp all day today near Loudon. Received a letter from Annie K. together with a programme of the exhibition of the Union Literary society. Wrote a letter to James H. Smith.

Wednesday April 13th 1864
Very sick last night but the division moved in the direction of Sweet Water. I marched 6 miles when I had to take the ambulance. Day beautiful.

Thursday April 14th 1864
Cloudy again this morning. At an early hour on the move toward Athens 13 miles distant where it is said we will encamp. The country hitherto passed through is one of the finest have seen in Tennessee. Today however it was not so good as we traveled most of the day on a ridge. Encamped near Athens.

Friday April 15th 1864
Started early this morning. Cloudy in the morning but cleared up during the day. Passed through Riceville & Calhoun. Crossed the Hiwassee and encamped near Charlestown having marched 18 miles. The country is rough and broken.

Saturday April 16th 1864
Moved out early. Reached Cleveland 10 miles about 10 o'clock. Cleveland is a beautiful town of about 1,000 inhabitants. Passed through and

encamped about 6 miles on the Chattanooga road.

Sunday April 17th 1864
Again it is Sabbath morning. The day is a beautiful one. Thoughts of home enter my mind and I cannot help but wish that I was there. Wrote sister Lizzie a letter.

Monday April 18th 1864
Writing for Capt. Ream. Still in camp. Will change camp tomorrow as a detail was made to clear off a camp about a mile distant. Received the Indianapolis Gazette.

Tuesday April 19th 1864
Changed camps. The regiment is busily engaged in fixing up quarters. Writing letters to Lide, Prof. Smith and W.A. Haworth.

Wednesday April 20th 1864
Attending to official duties. The men are busily engaged putting up quarters.

Thursday April 21st 1864
The same duties have to be performed.

Friday April 22nd 1864
Making out the quarterly returns of ordnance and ordnance stores for the quarter ending March 31st 1864.

Saturday April 23rd 1864
Received a letter from Wm L. Bowman. Still on the ordnance returns. Spent the evening reading Polloks "The Course of Time".

Sunday April 24th 1864
Cloudy morning. A good index of my mind. A moral cloud obscures all the sunshine of happiness. Wrote letters to Mollie T., Annie C., Mary H., Annie K. and Wm. L. Bowman. On dress parade. Received letters from Flora and Frank.

Monday April 25th 1864
Making out the monthly returns of clothing.

Tuesday April 26th 1864
Received a letter from Frank Cones.

Wednesday April 27th 1864
Did nothing worthy of note. On battalion drill.

Thursday April 28th 1864
The inspector of the 3rd Division inspected and condemned ordnance in the regiment.

Friday April 29th 1864
Gen. Howard reviewed the 3rd Division today.

Saturday April 30th 1864
Was mustered today for pay. Writing on the monthly returns.

Sunday May 1st 1864
Happy May Day. Not happy to me however. Assisting Capt. Ream.

Monday May 2nd 1864
Was sent to Chattanooga to turn over ordnance stores, but the stores did not arrive until dark. Put up at the Central House.

Tuesday May 3rd 1864
Arose this morning and made my toilet and after breakfasting finished my business. The remainder of the time I have for looking round. Took a stroll to our old encampment among the tombs. How changed the spot, yet for all that it roused old memories. There was the grave yard with its grass grown mounds, its simple stones and its towering monuments and last but not least its long lines of rebel graves. Then too were the stumps where the trees once stood which adorned the city of the dead. But now no tree, no stump, no clambering vine nursed by a sister's hand invites the unobtrusive visitor. There too, are the rifle pits dug by union soldiers but all, all are now marked by desolation. It made me feel lonely when I visited the spot. I cast my eye to Mission Ridge which now stands dressed in lovely green. Its cloud crested summit too reminded me of days vanished.
"'Twas here they fought
    And Martial peals
Peace thundered o'er the ground
    And gash and wound and plunging steel
Bedewed the battle mound."
Oh! That these gloomy hours were past. Oh! That the time would come when the clashing of arms will be heard no more, when the cannon's mouth shall be hushed, when peace on pure and gentle pinions shall be wafted from

shore to shore, and when we shall learn to war no more.

Wednesday May 4th 1864
At 7:30 took the train for McDonald's Station. Arrived there and found the Division had moved out. Started after it. Took dinner by the way at a frame house. Came up to Division supply train.

Thursday May 5th 1864
Started early to overtake the regiment. Passed the Catoosa Springs a fashionable watering place. It is said that these springs afford 60 different kinds of water. I procured the names of 18 or 20 different kinds commencing with Alkali, Epsom Coffee, Bedford, Healing, White Sulphur, Blue Sulphur, Red Sulphur, Black Sulphur, Red Sweet, Emetic, Chanitine bonaga, Chalybeate, Maguizia, Congress, Freestone Buffalo. Tasted of each but could see no difference except in the sulphur. Found the rgt up.

Friday May 6th 1864
The regiment lay still. Visited the 40th Indiana that had just returned from Indiana on 30 days furlough. Had orders to march tomorrow morning at 5.

Saturday May 7th 1864
Moved out slowly in the direction of Tunnel Hill. A large force is marching upon Dalton consisting of the 4th, 14th, 15th, 16th, 17th, and 20th Army Corps. Also the 23rd. Occupied Tunnel Hill without much resistance. The railroad passes through a tunnel here 1457 feet long.

Sunday May 8, 1864
The morning is lovely. Would that I could enjoy the day among friends at home. About 8 o'clock the regiment was formed and marched out in the valley below about a mile where we lay all day awaiting something I know not what. Perhaps the purpose is to draw the enemy's attention from the flanks. Occasional shots are exchanged by the pickets. Rebs can be seen plainly on the summit of Rocky Face mountain. News from the Potomac is that Grant has severely whipped Lee. It inspires fresh confidence in the soldier's heart. The utmost confidence is reposed in our western army sure that victory will crown our efforts. Bivouacked in the valley.

Monday May 9th 1864
Early in the morning the Brigade was ordered forward. It advanced to the base of the mountain where we halted. Brisk skirmishing was kept up during

our stay and several were wounded from the rebel sharpshooters on the mountain. Later in the day it was ordered to the right. The Division seems to be moving about to puzzle the enemy in regard to our movements. After remaining in line about an hour we again moved to the left where the regiment was ordered on picket. Hastily partook of some coffee and hard tack. The result of the day's fight is that thus far no new position has been gained. Some of the regiments lost heavily. Three were wounded in the 86th among whom was Silas N. Skaggs Co. G.

Tuesday May 10th 1864
Did not rest well last night. Arose from my stony couch and hastily ate my frugal meal which consisted chiefly of coffee and hard tack. The rebel sharpshooters on the mountain soon opened fire and constant shots were exchanged all day. The day has been cloudy. It also rained about an hour. It makes one feel rather uncomfortable to be placed under a continued fire not knowing at what moment a leaden missive will bear to him the tidings that his part of the scene in life's great drama is finished and that he must make his exit. A dispatch from Gen. Halleck to Gen. Sherman announced that a complete victory has crowned the army of the Potomac. Gen. Grant has driven Gen. Lee ten miles leaving his dead and wounded on the field.

Wednesday May 11th 1864
A heavy rain fell last night. Slept on the hillside. The result was I was completely drenched. Had orders to move to the rear about half a mile. Remained till after dark when the division moved back to the top of Tunnel Hill. Very cool.

Thursday May 12th 1864
Cleared off today. As yet I have not heard of the result of the movements of Sherman's grand army in front of Dalton with the exception that everything thus far has proved a success. Orders came very suddenly to move to the left to the support of Sherman's cavalry which it is said is very hard pressed by the enemy. Perhaps ere this battle closes many eyes will moisten and many hearts grow sad as the news hastens on its sorrowful mission that a friend, a brother has fallen a sacrifice on the alter of our Union.

Friday May 13th 1864
Clear morning. Orders came about 8 o'clock to move. The enemy evacuated Dalton last night. Marched about ten miles in a circuitous route and entered the forsaken town about 11 o'clock. But few citizens are left in

the place they having skedaddled with the army. In their retreat much was left such as baggage, etc. Our army is in full pursuit. It is said the enemy will make a stand at Resaca 15 miles distant at the crossing of the Coosa river. At any rate it is considered as a signal victory for our arms. Our Division marched perhaps 8 miles south of Dalton halting at sunset to refresh ourselves with hard tack and raw meat.

86th Indiana Regiment, Volunteer Infantry, adapted

"The Greatest Bunishment"

The Fourth corps was after Johnston early on the morning of the 13th of May, the cavalry pressing on at full speed, followed by the infantry. The corps rounded the north end of Rocky Face Ridge and passed near the mountain down Crow Valley and crossed the enemy's line of intrenchments, which were very strong, and soon came to a general camp. Near this camp were seen eighteen or twenty posts and as many graves. They were said to have been used to which deserters were tied to be shot. Twenty men were said to have been executed here at one time by the order of General Braxton Bragg during the winter or spring.

In the camp itself were many "stocks" used for punishing more trifling offenses. These were the first of the instruments of punishment the Eighty-sixth had ever seen, and many had no idea for what purposes they were intended to be used. General Willich said to a crowd that was examining the "stocks." "Phoys, you don't know what ees the greatest bunishment to these poor devils. Dey can't scratch when de lice bites 'em." This was received with a shout of laughter and the General rode on.

Saturday May 14th 1864

Drew rations and again started about 9 o'clock. Had not gone far until we learned that our advance was engaging the enemy a couple miles ahead. Had skirmishing along the lines. It is supposed that the enemy are crossing the Coosa river and it is merely a feint to get away. Formed in close column by Divisions and moved out in an open field where we awaited further orders. The front lines are heavily engaging the enemy. Among the killed and wounded are Col. Stiles and Gen. Manson. Night closed the contest to be renewed perhaps by the dawn of tomorrow's sun. It is said our corps is to support Hooker who has orders to take and occupy Resaca at all hazards. Into the hands of Him who ruleth all things for the best I commit myself trusting in His protecting Power to shield me from all danger and preserve me both soul and body.

Sunday May 15th 1864
Another Sabbath dawns but it dawns on two contending armies facing each other perhaps soon to be engaged in deadly conflict. Many perhaps who witnessed the rising of this morning's sun have seen it for the last time. Hooker has moved to the left to the support of the 23rd corps. The battle raged furiously the most of the day. All went well. The enemy made several charges but were repulsed every time with heavy loss. At length he is driven about two miles. Gen. Willich is severely wounded. Others fell - yes as a sacrifice upon the union's altar.

Monday 16th 1864
News just reached camp that the enemy retired last night, crossed the Coosa river and is in full retreat southward. We soon were in hot pursuit. Came to Resaca a village of perhaps a dozen houses where we halted a couple of hours after which we crossed the river. The position chosen by the enemy here was a strong one by nature and every spot had been improved by the pick and spade so that it was rendered almost impregnable. Thanks to Gen. Sherman and our large army for the splendid maneuvering by which the enemy was compelled to retreat or else be surrounded. Soon after our entrance into Resaca we were followed by a train of cars from Chattanooga bearing the construction Corps with the material to put up the yet smoking bridge. The air was made to ring with the voices of a hundred thousand Yankees when the whistle announced the arrival of the train. The report is that Hardee is killed. A scalp was found by a 13th Ohio boy taken from a Federal soldier by a barbarous rebel. Verily they must be fiends in human form. The news also comes that Lee is at Lynchburg with Grant after him.

Tuesday May 17th 1864
Encamped last night near Calhoun, the county seat of Gordon Co. It bore the resemblance of being once a lovely village. But few citizens remain to tell its more prosperous days. Near the courthouse was a monument erected to the memory of Gen. Nelson a soldier of the Mexican war. But few slaves are to be seen along our march. Came across one or two today. One old slave I was particularly amused at. He was standing by the roadside shouting at the top of his voice, thanking God that the Yankees had at last come and that he now was a free man. The scene was indeed affecting as the tears trickled down his cheeks while he implored the blessing of God upon the Yankees.

Came but four or five miles when a little excitement was caused by our flankers suffering our train on another road to be rebel fired. The guards returned fire. Fortunately no harm was done before the proper discovery was made. Scarcely was this excitement over until skirmishing commenced in front with the enemy's rear guard. They have proved to be rather stubborn. Immediately were deployed in line of battle on the front lines. Brisk skirmishing was kept up till dark. He threw several shells but our batteries soon silenced them.

Wednesday May 18th 1864
A heavy fog obscured the atmosphere this morning. Start again this morning. Enter the village of Adairsville and remain two or three hours. While there the 15th corps came in from our right. About one o'clock we again start and march in line of battle until we encamp which is about six miles from Adairsville. On our way many prisoners are taken who have given themselves up.

Thursday May 19th 1864
At an early hour we are again on the move and march very briskly until we reach Kingston the junction of the Rome railroad. The country begins to become more broken and underbrush very thick when about two miles below Kingston we came across Johnny Reb who seems to move before us rather stubbornly. Batteries are immediately opened upon them and they slowly fell back. We form in line of battle and march out to meet the enemy - first going to the right - but afterwards more to the left. It is now near sundown. The last rays of the setting sun linger on the long lines of men stretched across the open valley as if loathe to leave them. Some beheld those rays for the last time. At a signal given our skirmishers advanced followed by these dark blue lines. The firing was heavy. One captain was killed in the 17th Kentucky and two privates. After advancing about 3/4 of a mile the lines halted and immediately commenced throwing up breastworks to protect them from balls from the enemy. The firing ceased about 10 o'clock. Lay down to rest feeling thankful to God that my life thus far has been preserved. I commit myself into His hands.

Friday May 20th 1864
Remained in the same position all day. What the next movement will be I am unable even to conjecture.

Saturday May 21st 1864
Orders have been received to the effect that we will remain until the 23rd when we again start with 20 days rations. Wrote home. Saw John Perrin of the 10th.

Sunday May 22nd 1864
This Sabbath day was mostly spent in writing letters to Annie, Mate, Ollie and the "Mail". The day has been warm.

Monday May 23rd 1864
Early this morning Hooker's corps commenced moving to the right. We had orders to move at noon. At the appointed time we started following the Corps. Passed through a country mostly broken by rocky barriers. Came to the Ettowah river and crossed and after marching till nine o'clock went into camp.

Story from the 84th Regiment
Indiana's Roll of Honor, Volume II, abridged

One Rail Fence

The 84th Regiment crossed the Etowah river at sunset on the 23rd of May, 1864. On the 24th they crossed Pumpkin Vine Creek. On the 29th they were in the front line and built works. On the first of June 120 men worked all night on the breastworks. Working and fighting, halting and marching, the soldiers of the 84th kept mind and body busy and reached Ackworth, GA on the sixth of June.

When the base of Kenesaw mountain was reached, the rebels were found in heavy force upon its towering summit, in an impregnable position from the front. The 84th built a line of works across a corn field in the afternoon. At dark they relieved the 21st Kentucky on the skirmish line; advanced after dark, approaching so close to the enemy's lines that the rebels quarreled with our men about the rails we were making breastworks with. In fact, the darkness of the night prevented the color of the uniform being detected, and the belligerents became mixed together, each party industriously building temporary defenses from the material furnished by the same rail fence.

Chapter Fourteen
New Hope Church,
Pickett's Mills, Kenesaw Mountain

Tuesday May 24 1864
At 8 o'clock we moved out. Halted about a hour waiting for Hooker to pass
after which we again started. Our road lay today through a mountain forest
thickly bestudded with stately pines. Upon these grounds the red man years
ago hunted the deer and buffalo unmolested, but the white man intruded
and drove him from his camp fires, his hut and his game and he sought a
home further west. It had been much better had the Indian still inhabited
these forests. Encamped in the hills.

Wednesday May 25th 1864
A refreshing rain made glad these hills last night. Had orders to march at 10
o'clock. Went perhaps a half a mile and lay till about 3 o'clock when we
again started. Our road still lays through a mountain forest - consisting of
gullies, gorges, ravines, hills, mountains, chasms and swales, and looks as
though the foot of man had never before trod. Night came on but our march
did not cease. Move a few steps and halt. Heavy firing in front. Hooker has
run upon some Johnny Rebs. Dark comes and rain comes in torrents. Pass a
wagon train and cross a river said to be the "Punkin Vine". On we trudge.
Pass a hospital where the wounded are being cared for, and another still we
pass. Finally we have orders to bivouac till 3 in the morning.

Thursday May 26th 1864
Ate a hurried breakfast after which we moved to the front line on the left of
the road. Formed in close column by division. Remained in this position till
noon when our brigade moved forward perhaps half a mile and halted till
night when we bivouacked. Brisk skirmishing has commenced all along the
lines today. Among the notable personages I saw today was Gen. Sherman
who commands the Grand Division of the Mississippi. Whether of not the
enemy will make a stand here remains to be seen. It may be that he will. If
so I look for the ball to be opened tomorrow morning.

Friday May 27th 1864
The sun arose clean and bright as if smiling at the absurdity and wickedness
of man. Lay till about 10 o'clock when evolutions commenced, a series of
which no man can tell. At 4 o'clock the skirmishers commenced firing heavily
indicating an attack. Marched out in line of battle about half a mile when

the regiment was ordered to halt. During this time the regiment was exposed to a heavy fire from a rebel battery wounding about 20. Among the wounded is Col. Dick severely in thigh by a shell. A heavy stroke on the regiment and one which is almost irreparable. The division has been heavily engaged losing many killed and wounded. The enemy was too strong and it was compelled to retire under cover of night. Moved back on a hill when the regiment was placed on picket. This reverse it is to be hoped is only momentary. Late at night I took a stroll through the grounds where the wounded had been collected. It enshrouds the heart in gloom to look upon the mangled wounded as they lay suffering in all the agony that humanity could endure. See here a man with one leg torn off by a shell; another with arm torn off; another shot in the head; and here a youth who two hours ago with bright dreams of home gave his life as a sacrifice for liberty and right, is now weltering in his life blood.

86th Regiment, Indiana Volunteer Infantry, **abridged**

The Battle of Pickett's Mills

The 86th was placed upon the extreme right of the division, and was not in the assaulting column proper, but was advanced close up to the enemy's intrenchments - a narrow open field intervening between its position and the enemy's works - in the edge of a woods in plain view of the batteries of the enemy. The 86th was thus exposed to a most terrific fire of artillery during the whole battle. As the 86th threatened the enemy's line and his batteries, by its proximity, it drew his fire which should otherwise been turned against the storming column. The 86th lay under a sharp musketry fire and the most terrific cannonading the regiment had ever experienced.

In the midst of a particularly fierce blast of the enemy's batteries the word ran along the line of the regiment that Colonel Dick had been killed. Fortunately this proved to be a mistake, but he was very badly wounded and had to be carried from the field, severely and dangerously wounded by an exploding shell. His life was probably saved by his saber, which broke the force of the stroke of the flying fragment. His steel scabbard was shattered by the terrible blow.

Saturday May 28th 1864
At a late hour partook of a frugal breakfast. Lay down and took a nap feel much fatigued from constant exposure. The loss of the regiment yesterday

was 15. At 2 o'clock the skirmishers charged front and advanced. The day is lonely indeed.

> "Sad memory brings the light
> Of other days around me".

The soft winds gently sighing through the trees breathes a melancholy air, the echo of which finds a place in my heart. Accidentally came across a stray volume of The Sacred Mountains by J.T. Headly which interested me the remainder of the afternoon. Relieved from picket by the 19th Ohio.

Sunday May 29th 1864
Had a night's good rest. This Sabbath morn dawns clear and bright reminding one of the Sabbaths of the past. Spent most of the day in perusing the sacred volume. All quiet along the lines.

Monday May 30th 1864
Still the fight goes on. Heavy skirmishing in our immediate front. Expecting orders at any moment to move but did not receive them until dark when they came but were countermanded till morning. This truly might be called a second Wilderness.

Tuesday May 31st 1864
At sunrise our lines were advanced. After this and before they had time to from the toils of the day. In the afternoon wrote home. Operations will soon be resumed, at no distant hour.

Tuesday June 7th 1864
Morning clear and beautiful. Mail came in with letters from M.H. Belknap and W.L. Bowman. Glad to hear from them. The regiment is resting today as is also the army.

Wednesday June 8th 1864
Still resting and replenishing preparatory to another advance. Wrote F.M. Cones. Spent the day in reading papers from home.

Thursday June 9th 1864
Wrote a letter this morning to Prof. Smith. Feel somewhat lonely. Still recuperating. Expect to start tomorrow morning. In the afternoon visited the 40th Ind. where I met many old friends. Saw a map of the country of our operations, gotten up by the U.S. Top. Eng. The only difficult obstacle now to Atlanta is the Chattahoochee river whose banks are bluffy and cliffy.

Friday June 10th 1864
Received orders to march at 8 o'clock. At the appointed hour the assembly was sounded by "Dock" and all fell in. Patiently we waited till noon but still we did not start. The dinner call was sounded when we partook of coffee and sow belly after which we moved slowly out but soon came to a halt awaiting the advance of troops in front. It commenced raining and for sometime it came in torrents thoroughly drenching the soldiers who patiently endured it protected by a rubber blanket. There was not a murmur. After going about a mile and a half went into camp to rest during the shades of the night.

Saturday June 11th 1864
The morning is cloudy. Read a poem entitled "Our Heros" from which I extract
    "Yet loved ones have fallen
      And still, where they sleep
    A sorrowing nation
      Shall silently weep
    And spring's fairest flowers
      In gratitude strew
    O'er those who have cherished
      The Red White and Blue"
How true, but there is in waiting for those who fall with faces toward heaven unfading chaplets of immortal glory.
    Lay in bivouac till noon when orders came to advance a mile which orders were complied with through rain and wind rendering it unpleasant.

Sunday June 12th 1864
This day was spent in bivouac near Acworth. An unceasing rain fell all day. Spent the time in reading the Bible. It would indeed be pleasant to spend a Sabbath at home. Skirmishing on the front line.

Monday June 13th 1864
Rained all day. Reading and meditating the scriptures. Still bivouacked near Acworth. Cool. The evening has the appearance of clearing.

Tuesday June 14th 1864
Clear morning. Spent the forenoon in writing letters to the Indianapolis Journal. W.A. Haworth and sister Mellie. Had just partaken of a frugal dinner when the "General" was sounded and soon our brigade was moving to the

left. Moved perhaps a mile when we halted. Heavy skirmishing in our front. Night came on and we lay down to rest. Firing was heard all night but when the morning of

Wednesday June 15th 1864
dawned, it found the enemy had evacuated his works. Took a stroll from camp and accidentally came upon two freshly made graves. A rude board was placed at their heads by sympathizing and bereaved comrades bearing their names and regiment. Two lone graves. What thoughts are awakened by these lonely mounds where two heroes lie who have laid their lives as a sacrifice on the altar of our union. Doubtless they fondly dreamed of home and loved associations, but alas they fell too soon to realize their fondest hopes. Anxious parents and loving brothers and sisters will await their coming, but they will wait in vain. At noon drew rations and have orders to move at 2 o'clock. Advanced southward perhaps a mile when the Divisions of Newton and Stanley commenced heavy skirmishing with the enemy. Bivouacked on a knoll from which can be seen Lost Mountain and surrounding country. The enemy is said to be strongly fortified in his present position. Clear moon-light and skirmishing continued all night.

Thursday June 16th 1864
Morning clear. Came across my old friend J.R. Dean and had a long and pleasant conversation. Old times were talked over - old friends were spoken of and old memories and old associations found a place in the pleasant hour's talk. Our forces took possession of Mossy Peak upon whose summit Gen. Polk was killed. From here creation is spread before the eye like a map. The scene is one of grandeur and magnificence and awakens thoughts mingled with awe and admiration. At noon the mail came in bringing me a missive from my friend Ollie Higgins. Night came and the moon's pale beams seemed to weep at man's ambition. Truly "how like a mountain devil in the heart rules this unresigned ambition.

Friday June 17th 1864
The skirmishing has ceased on our immediate front, though on the left shots are exchanged as though the enemy was still present. Moved out passing the enemy's works which he had evacuated. They were formidable and could resist any attack that could have been made against them. Indications are that the enemy are not far off. Our regiment is thrown out as skirmishers. Advance, driving them about half a mile when he resists stubbornly. Relieved at dusk. Received a letter from sister Mellie. The casualties in the regiment

today are three wounded.

Saturday June 18th 1864
When I awoke from my bivouac sleep the rain was coming down in torrents and the regiment in line ready to advance. Took possession of the works about two hundred yards in front. Remained there till about 10 o'clock. During the time our left (Newton's Division) advanced driving the enemy "skyhooting" and took possession of their first line of works. The rain continued to come in torrents. At ten orders were received to advance when we moved about half a mile and hastily threw up breastworks. The battle rages all day. The history of the war will not furnish a parallel to the picture that this day presents. The mind of man is not capable of even conceiving the reality. My pencil cannot portray therefore I will desist. The enemy artillery opened a raking fire on our works wounding three among whom was Capt. Ream. In the evening moved to the left a short distance when we bivouacked. Slept with Capt. Sims.

86th Regiment, Indiana Volunteer Infantry, abridged

Mud Creek Coffee

On the 18th of June, in a conflict later designated The Battle of Kenesaw Mountain by the rebels, the 86th had taken an exposed position on a probably unimportant tributary of Mud creek, now running full and strong. It was an uncomfortable position. The waters of the little stream came up almost to the works on the right flank of the regiment. A short distance to the rear of the line of works the ground was low and water plentiful. The men were water and mud bound, yet this was no protection. Shells were dropping here and there, all around in a murderous manner.

A comrade was hungry and the more he thought about the matter the sharper grew his appetite. His longings for hard tack and old government Java overcame his caution and made him brave, and during a moment when fire had slackened, he prepared his coffee, made a fire in the rear of the works, and placed the coffee on to boil.

Unfortunate move, luckless moment, he had scarcely succeeded in getting his pot adjusted on the rails when a shot came screaming, tipped the rails and upset the pot in the fire and frightened the hungry soldier back to the works where he remained while his coffee roasted and the spout was melted off his coffee pot. Never did a soldier lose his appetite more suddenly.

Another comrade proceeded to prepare his coffee. He was watching, ready to remove it as soon as it was sufficiently boiled. The aroma of the coffee was beginning to be distilled when there came a mighty shriek, and there was a scattering of rails, coals and ashes.

The soldier! Where was he? Two feet deep in water in the stream at the rear of the regiment!

He was demoralized and was only just pulling himself together when another terrific scream and the plunging of a shell into the water immediately to his front, fairly immersed him with a mighty upheaval of the water. He had snatched his coffeepot from the fire before the shell had struck, and it was his boast as long as he lived that he saved his coffee and drank it.

Sunday June 19th 1864
The Sabbath dawned not under as favorable auspices as I have seen it in other days, yet, still I am rejoiced to know that the enemy has again modestly retired leaving us in possession of their works. Advanced but a short distance till we again encountered the enemy. Heavy skirmishing continued all day. Rain came in torrents. Bivouacked in a wood about a mile in advance of where we were last night.

Monday June 20th 1864
At one o'clock the brigade moved to the left about a mile relieving a brigade of Hooker's corps. The rain still comes in torrents. When will it cease.

Tuesday June 21st 1864
Still rainy and wet. Fighting seems to be heavy on our left. At about one o'clock an advance is made driving the enemy. This places us in possession of the enemy's picket line in our immediate front. An advance is ordered. Co's "F" "C" and "R" are placed on the skirmish line. Advance perhaps three hundred yards when breast works are hurriedly thrown up to protect us from the enemy's fire. About one hundred yards in front of our former line and the same distance to the rear of our present stands a farm house. The inmates have all fled. No not all. An old man perhaps 80 years of age is left. I approached and kindly propounded some questions which he willingly answered. He said his family had fled before the rebel enemy and he had remained to take care of his few earthly possessions. Everything was turned topsy turvy and if any valuable had been there they had been carried off. There he sat crouched in a large stone chimney which served as a fort against

the bullets of rebels which continually poured into the house from rebel pickets. He said the majority of the poor people of the south were union people but were afraid to say their mind was their own. Thus carried away in the vortex of secession. Thousands today in rebel ranks are those who because poor were forced into their army. Distance from this point to Marrietta three and one half miles.

Wednesday June 22nd 1864
The day has been beautiful. No rain. The works have been much strengthened and are now well prepared to give the enemy a warm reception, should he come. Spent the day in perusing the pages of Holy Writ. Reading of Job's afflictions, sorrows and troubles. Truly here is a good lesson of patience. Amid all his losses and sufferings Job could still exclaim "The Lord giveth and the Lord taketh away. Blessed be the name of the Lord." Quite a little stir was enacted on the lines by a demonstration made to diverge the enemy from the right where Hooker is said to be engaging him heavily.

Thursday June 23rd 1864
Beautiful and clear morning but while beautiful and clear above the clouds of battle are lowering and at some points the storm is now raging. At about 3 o'clock heavy cannonading commenced around the whole length of the lines.

Friday June 24th 1864
Clear and very warm. Comparatively quiet along the lines though skirmishing is still kept up. Wrote a letter to the Lebanon Patriot.

Saturday June 25th 1864
Spent a portion of the day in writing letters to friends at home. Wrote Mate Belknap. Sent for the "Advocate". Still quiet along the lines. Nothing but an occasional shot between the pickets. Saw the Patriot.

Sunday June 26th 1864
The morning is beautiful. All nature seems to chime with music. The mating songs of the birds are gently wafted on each gentle breeze. Just such a time as this thoughts involuntarily rush into the mind of the days of long ago. Wrote a letter to Ollie. Sent resolutions expressive of civil affairs at home.

Monday June 27th 1864
Orders came for our regiment to support a battery about 400 yards to our right. After going there it became evident that a charge is to be made still farther to the right. The battery opened on the enemy wounding Lt. John Moore Co. E, and Sergt John W. Cosby Co. I. The charge was made on the right but it met with a disastrous result. The 40th Ind. lost heavily. We were relieved and returned to our former position.

86th Regiment, Indiana Volunteer Infantry, abridged

Friendly Fire

On Monday, June 27 the 86th with the rest of Wood's Division received marching orders for battle. The 86th was in the front line of the supporting forces.

Just to the rear of the left of the regiment, in the second line of works, was the 11th Indiana Battery. The regiment had not been long in this position when the battery opened a terrible fire on the enemy's intrenchments. However, the ammunition was defective and the shells exploded almost as soon as they cleared the mouths of the guns, raining a hailstorm of destruction on the 86th.

After one or two rounds had been fired and men wounded, a protest was sent to the battery, which then changed its ammunition, which proved to be no better.

This made the 86th hot, and the men threatened to face about and charge the battery in order to silence it, and thus save themselves. A peremptory cease fire order was sent to the battery after a shell exploding to the rear of Company I knocked over a stack of guns, severely wounding Sergeant Cosby. The order was promptly obeyed.

Tuesday June 28th 1864
Wrote a letter to sister Mattie. Cloudy indicating rain. Nothing more of importance occurred during the day.

Wednesday June 29th 1864
Wrote my friend Jas. H. Smith - sent for the Waverly Magazine. All quiet.

Thursday June 30th 1864
All quiet along the lines this morning though the enemy made a charge on

the right. The men handsomely repulsed. Received a letter from sister Mellie, replied. A refreshing shower made glad the earth.

Friday July 1st 1864
Beautiful morning this. Feel much indisposed having caught a severe cold. The day passed quietly. Our batteries are shelling Kenesaw Mountain constantly. Saw the Atlanta Confederacy. Orders came to move but afterwards countermanded.

Saturday July 2nd 1864
Our pickets received orders this morning to keep up a fire. A feint demonstration was made this morning but it proved of no effect. Through the guard agreement between the pickets they do not fire at each other. The remainder of the day was spent in quietude . A refreshing shower fell. After dark we moved to the left about a half a mile and took a position on a high knoll commanding rebel works. About 12 o'clock when I lay down to rest.

Sunday July 3rd 1864
Tranquil and clear the sun arose announcing that another Sabbath morning had dawned. The time seems a holy time notwithstanding the pride, the pomp and all the circumstance of war which surrounds. The very air seems to breathe a lonely requiem attended with a sigh and each sigh finds an echo in my heart. At such a time as this my thoughts inadvertently wander back to the sunny days of "long ago." Another link to memory's golden chain is added by this the dawning of another Sabbath morn. My reverie is broken when it is announced that the enemy has evacuated his position which he has so strongly held for the last two weeks in our front. Soon after the order comes to move and accordingly all things are placed in readiness and the army is again in motion. March in the direction of Marietta which place being occupied our march is continued in pursuit of the retreating enemy. About three miles from Marietta we go into camp weary and nearly exhausted. The day has been extremely warm. The intensity of the heat caused many to fall by the way.

Chapter 15
Kenesaw to Peach Tree Creek

Monday July 4th 1864
Today is the Nation's Birthday! Eighty eight years ago today the colonies then forming the infant United States declared themselves free and independent. Now we are vindicating that freedom which our fathers handed us to perpetuate. About two o'clock our brigade moved out about a mile and took a position where fortifications were hastily thrown up. Shots are exchanged by skirmishers indicating that the enemy is close. Stray shots wounded several in the brigade.

86th Regiment, Indiana Volunteer Infantry, abridged

Fourth of July Celebration

*A*s the command waited for a forward movement toward Atlanta, they drew a ration of whisky and continued the celebration of the Fourth of July. The spirits enlivened camp somewhat, if tipsy men can ever be said to enliven anything. Songs were sung and a hilarious good time experienced by those who indulged in the flowing bowl.

One commissioned officer of Company H, grew eloquent and courageous, mounted a stump and proceeded to deliver a patriotic and fiery oration, regardless of the enemy's spiteful humor and the sharp fire he maintained.

This gallant and patriotic speech was loudly cheered by the boys , which drew from the enemy a perfect storm of musketry, and so the glorious Fourth of July, 1864, passed for the 86th.

Tuesday July 5th 1864
The enemy is again reported to have again retreated. We are soon again in pursuit. Follow up the railroad about 4 miles to a point on the river where we halt and go into camp. Skirmishing with the enemy ensues. Near the camp stands an eminence from which Georgia is laid before the vision like a map. Toward evening I scaled its precipitous heights and viewed the landscape o'er. The camps trains etc. of our erring Southern brethren were in full view. Atlanta, the city for which we strive is in sight. Just a few steps down the hill a man was found hanging to a tree. He has the appearance of having hung himself as the sapling from which he stepped off is still bending down. His name D.B. Duncan as papers on his body show. The cause of

such a suicide none can tell. I have since been informed that he was hung by the rebels for giving information to the Yankees. Such inhumanity is but the offspring of a barbarous race. A Christian country would not tolerate such. One could scarcely believe that one half of these Christian United States could be so steeped in guilt as to perpetrate such outrages. But so it is.

Wednesday July 6th 1864
Very warm. Remained in camp till noon when I took another stroll to the top of the hill. Wrote a letter to the "Lebanon Patriot".

86th Regiment, Indiana Volunteer Infantry, abridged

Friendly Enemies

In the evening of the sixth a heavy detail, under the command of Capt. James R. Carnahan, was made from the 86th for skirmish duty along the bank of the Chattahoochee river and at Pace's Ferry.

The men had been on the line but a short time when a conversation arose between the lines on the opposite sides of the river. All firing soon stopped in the vicinity of the ferry, as everyone wanted to hear what was said on both sides. The principal speakers were Orderly Sergeant J. M. Cast, Company H, and Captain Walker, Ninth Mississippi, of Pat Cleburne's division, Hardee's corps.

"How far are you going to retreat before you get to the last ditch?"

"We have the pontoons already on which to cross the Gulf."

The political issues of the day in the Northern States were broached. The Captain seemed quite willing to talk, and to the question of his Presidential preferences, for Lincoln or McClellan, he answered that McClellan was a good man, the friend of the South, and would suit the Southern people in general admirably. He intimated that peace would soon be established if McClellan were elected.

Thursday July 7th 1864
Continues warm. Still no tidings reach us from other portions of the army. Took a good wash and felt much better. Writing for the Adjutant. Making out May monthly returns. Brigade moved to the right a short distance and as the regiment is on picket it will not leave until relieved.

Friday July 8th 1864
Early this morning the regiment moved about half a mile to the right. Most of the day was spent by the boys in putting up their dog tents and shading them over with brush. The day was extremely warm. Visited the 10th Indiana where I saw Jim Heickison and Elisha Little. Glad to see them. Returned and went to the branch and took a bath.

Saturday July 9th 1864
Took a nap in the forenoon. Very much lost for want of something to read. Writing in the office on a monthly return. Wrote home.

Sunday July 10th 1864
The enemy has again fallen back. The phrase "fallen back" seems to have grown as familiar as household words. The morning is cloudy indicating rain. About 11 o'clock the "General" was sounded and we soon were wending our way up the river. Marched perhaps seven or eight miles and encamped. A refreshing shower fell during the afternoon.

Monday July 11th 1864
Morning cloudy but as the day grew it cleared off and the sun shone brilliantly. Mail came in but no missive for me. Wrote my little friend Annie Kramer a letter. Can hear no word from other portions of the army. The 23rd corps in on the opposite banks of the river.

Tuesday July 12th 1864
Had the pleasure this morning of perusing the pages of the "W.C. Advocate" It is now edited by the Rev. J.M. Reid. It seemed like meeting an old friend whom I had not seen for many long months. Orders were received to march at 10 o'clock. At the appointed hour the bugle sounded but through some delay in the advance we were ordered to get dinner. Dinner over we started and came to the banks of the rolling and swelling Chattahoochee. It is a wide but shallow stream with a rocky bed. Its waters are of a muddy caste doubtless caused by the red clay through which its tributaries pass. Crossed the river on pontoons and encamped near its banks in the midst of an unbroken wilderness of thick underbrush of oak and pines.

Wednesday July 13th 1864
The lines were changed this morning consequently the regiment moved out some distance, formed in line and immediately set to work constructing breastworks. Mail came in bringing me missives from Frank Cones and Lide

G. They perhaps little dream of the amount of good such letters do in the army. Very glad to hear from them. Weather continues warm and sultry. The day will be gladly hailed when this campaign will close. Had the pleasure of taking by the hand Ed Wetherald, fresh from Indiana. He came looking after the remains of his brother Henry who fell mortally wounded on the 18th of June. Glad to see him.

Thursday July 14th 1864
Orders were received last night to march this morning at five but they were countermanded this morning. A detail was made of 150 men was made for picket to go out at seven o'clock. Spent the forenoon in perusing a couple numbers of the "W.C. Advocate" which chanced to find their way to the regiment. The time was indeed well spent. In the afternoon wrote a letter for A. Hanael.

Friday July 15th 1864
Last night a heavy rain storm visited this portion of the country. This morning the agent of the Christian Commission visited the regiment distributing paper envelopes and religious reading matter. His visit was truly a welcome one and doubtless result in much good. Wrote a letter to Frank Cones. The day passed with no perceivable improvement in mental culture.

Saturday July 16th 1864
Wrote a letter to the Lebanon Patriot. About noon the regiment greeted the return of Col. Dick who has been absent since the 27th of May on account of wounds received in action that day. His return was gladly hailed by everyone. Received a letter from home.

Sunday July 17th 1864
At 5 o'clock this morning the 3rd Division was sent down the river five miles from this place (Powers Ferry) to enable the 14th corps to lay their pontoons and cross at that point. Met with little or no resistance and the object was accomplished without the loss of a man. From the best information I can get our army is across the Chattahoochee and on a secure footing. Returned to camp in the evening bringing with us fifteen or twenty Johnny Rebs who were somewhat surprised at the Yanks coming down the river on this side. They report Johnson's whole force between here and Atlanta. That city is seven miles from Prices Ferry the point at which the 14th corps crossed. Weather warm and sultry. Capts Gorham, Spellman and Odell and Lieuts Kelso and Sylvester, and quartermaster Underwood went through the ordeal by due

process of being mustered into the service of the U.S.

Monday July 18th 1864
Late last night orders were received to be ready to move at 5 this morning. All ready at that time but hour after hour till noon when we slowly moved out going in the direction of Atlanta about five miles through a rough and broken country with but few farms indicating that march of civilization had passed, though we encamped. It was a weary march the weather being so very warm. Various rumors afloat in regard to the advance. None however are reliable.

Tuesday July 19th 1864
Orders were received to move out at five o'clock leaving our tents and blankets in camp. The road we marched out on led in a southern direction. The main road leading to Atlanta. After going perhaps three miles without any opposition our pickets encountered those of the enemy. The enemy was strongly fortified just across a little stream called Peach Creek. Our advance was checked by the stream which is narrow but deep, and the enemy who occupied works on the opposite side. Heavy skirmishing continued till about two o'clock when a portion of our Brigade was sent to the right to cross at a point where would be little or no resistance. It proved a success and the enemy began to retire in considerable disorder, he being now exposed to a flanking fire. Our captures numbered 58 prisoners among whom were a Lieut. Col., Capt., 2nd Lts. The day wore heavily on until we were relieved which was at nightfall. Returned to camp.

Wednesday July 20th 1864
At five this morning the division was again in motion. At Buckhead Cross-Roads we left the Atlanta road in the direction of Decatur a point on the Georgia R.R,. After going perhaps four miles struck another road leading to Atlanta near which we encountered the enemy. Our Division formed on the right of and our brigade facing Stanley. Breastworks were hastily thrown up as is always the case now when we halt in the face of the enemy. Two men from each company were thrown as skirmishers.

Thursday July 21st 1864
The lines of Stanley were advanced early this morning to within a short distance of the enemy. About ten o'clock Wood moved out his invincibles on a line with Stanley. A deserter came in and reported that the Johnnies were making preparations for a charge.

Although not much dependence was placed in a deserter's story our officers thought it prudent to make the necessary arrangements for their reception. The hastily thrown up works were strengthened, ammunition brought forward and the regiments so disposed that they could meet with a warm reception. While the men were carrying up rails, one of our regiment was instantly killed having received a ball in his head while in the discharge of his duty. Thomas McCartney Co. D. now sleeps on the verdured hill crest near Atlanta a sacrifice upon the altar of our beloved union. One by one as the leaves of the forest they fall. With Walter Scott we can only say

"Soldier, rest, thy warfare o'er
Sleep the sleep that knows no waking
Dream of battlefields no more
Days of danger, nights of waking."

Friday July 22nd 1864
Early this morning it was discovered by the pickets that the enemy had evacuated his works sometime during the night. Prisoners and deserters say he began falling back about 11 o'clock. Soon an advance was ordered and we were slowly wending our way in pursuit, each step bringing us nearer Atlanta. Had gone perhaps a mile and a half when our skirmishers again encountered the enemy's. Took a position on one of the ten thousand little hills with which this country is blessed or cursed, (don't know which,) and as usual commenced throwing up works for our defence. I just now learned that the enemy made three charges against the Divisions of Butterfield's 20th corps and Newton's 4th corps and were handsomely repulsed with a loss of fourteen hundred killed and four thousand wounded. Our loss was slight as our men were behind works - said to be fifteen hundred killed and wounded. Mail came in this evening bringing me precious missives from sisters Mellie and Mattie, Ollie and brother Jo Foxworthy. Also from my comrade in arms J.W. Cosby who was wounded on the 27th of June.

Saturday July 23rd 1864
The news was current in camp this morning that Gen. McPherson was killed yesterday while engaging the army yesterday on the left. Sadly is the news received by the soldiers as he was regarded as among the best of our generals now in command. His loss will be deeply felt by the nation but more deeply by those who were under his immediate command - the army of the Tennessee. The enemy continues to throw shells along our line which occasionally come too close to be healthy. It makes the boys lie close to the works. Gen. Wood complimented the Division very highly today in an order

for the brilliant exploit in crossing Peach Creek in face of an intrenched enemy, and especially the 3rd Brigade as they led the exploit. It is reported that the rebel Gen. Hardee is wounded and in our hands. It is also said the enemy's loss yesterday will not fall short of ten thousand. Gen. Sherman accompanied by his staff rode along the line today. Hood is Johnston's successor in command of the rebel army. It has been clearly demonstrated during this campaign that either party to assault a well defended works is exceedingly dangerous and generally results in a repulse. The call by the President for 500,000 more men is hailed with rejoicing by every soldier. It indicates that the government is waking up to the true state of affairs.

Sunday July 24th 1864
Bright and beautiful this Sabbath dawns though instead of the chiming of church bells calling the good to the house of God the boom of the Cannon and the sharp crack of the musket is heard. The echo reverberates from hilltop to hilltop, saying in unmistakable language to our erring Southern brethren that, as you've sown so shall you reap. Rec'd a letter from Mate. Pickets keep up a constant racket reminding each other that they are still there.

Monday July 25th 1864
Spent the day in perusing the late papers with an occasional game of checkers. Artillery keeps up a constant duel.

Tuesday July 26th 1864
Received a letter from M.H. Belknap. The enemy keeps up a constant skirmish fire which receives a hearty reply from ours. Wrote a letter home. Weather pleasant and agreeable.

Wednesday July 27th 1864
Situation unchanged in our front though the army of the Tennessee now commanded by Major General Howard is moving to the right. The struggle is now in progress for the possession of Atlanta. Already much blood has been shed, yet it is to be hoped it has not been shed in vain.

Thursday July 28th 1864
Heavy fighting has occurred today on the right. News has reached us that the rebs charged our works seven times and were repulsed each time with heavy loss.

Friday July 29th 1864
This morning Stoneman's cavalry started on a raid. It is said they intend to strike at Macon and Andersonville for the purpose of releasing prisoners. Opposite our lines the enemy has several large guns which occasionally throw over a whole blacksmith's shop scattering the tools in every direction.

Saturday July 30th 1864
Stray shots from rebel pickets occasionally find their way over. A soldier in Co. B was struck by one today which was severe though not serious. Was E.F.L. Rec'd a letter from W.A. Haworth.

Sunday July 31st 1864
Clear and pleasant morning. Wrote my friends Lide and Mate. Reading in the Psalms. Pickets still keep up a constant banging. The enemy occasionally throws over a 60 pounder though as yet causing little damage.
Rainy afternoon.

Monday Aug. 1st 1864
Orders were received early this morning for the regiment to report to Gen. Wood's headquarters for fatigue duty. After reporting I learned that two regiments in each brigade in addition to the pioneers were detailed to throw up new works about 400 yards to the rear of our present line with the left refused. Wood's division will be the extreme left of the Army. The 23rd corps and our 1st Division move to the right. Something may be expected soon from there. Captains Sims, Rodman and Moore joined the regiment today after an absence of three week's sickness. They look well.

Tuesday Aug. 2nd 1864
Every now and then a man is wounded on the skirmish line. Three were wounded in the 59th Ohio today. We were agreeably surprised today when Prof. J.M. Coyner of Lebanon Ind. made himself present in our midst. He is acting agent for the Christian Commission and intends remaining some three weeks yet before returning home. This is the second time our regiment has been graced with the presence of an agent of this great work of love. Hope he has been the means of doing such good during vacation days. Recommendation sent for C.L.C.J

Wednesday Aug. 3rd 1864
Nothing unusual occurred till three o'clock when a demonstration was made along the lines to ascertain whether the enemy was still there or not. The

enemy's pickets were driven in except those who were captured and the enemy found to be in force when our skirmishers fell back.

Thursday Aug. 4th 1864
Making out a quarterly return of ordnance. Wrote to W. A. Haworth and T. A. Goodwin. Visited by several boys of the 72nd. Mr. Delemater, was among the visitors.

Friday Aug 5th 1864
In the morning wrote a letter to the Rev. Jo. Foxworthy and sent for the "Advocate". At about three o'clock an order came that the 23rd Corps was heavily engaged on the right and a demonstration must be made to create a diversion of the enemy's forces. The 86th was sent on the skirmish line to reinforce those already out. I presume it had the desired effect as at dusk we were relieved and returned to camp. Found a letter from home which was gladly received.

Saturday Aug. 6th 1864
A detail of seventy men went on picket this morning. Rainy afternoon making it a disagreeable night for picketing.

Sunday Aug. 7th 1864
Another Sabbath morning dawn and finds us still unchanged in our situation. Spent a portion of the day in reading in Psalms. The regiment was relieved from picket by the 19th O.V.I. During the 24 hours they were out the 70 shot away 9 boxes, each box containing 1,000 rounds, on an average of 128 rounds to a man. In the afternoon a soldier from the 124th Ohio held religious services in the regiment - the first sermon I have heard for six months. Quite refreshing to have preaching again. Would that it were so that religious services could be held regularly.

Monday Aug. 8th 1864
The same detail for picket as yesterday. Writing for Lt. Codrey on Quartermaster Stores. Mail came in but brought me nothing.

Tuesday Aug. 9th 1864
Rainy morning. Writing for Lt. Codrey. Heavy cannonading along the lines. Nothing of more than usual occurred. Had the pleasure of taking by the hand Webster Johnson of the 72nd.

Wednesday Aug. 10th 1864
The adjutant went to Bridgeport yesterday to be gone ten days. I am acting in his absence. Seventy nine men and six noncommissioned officers were detailed for picket this morning. Writing on invoices and receipts for ordnance. Joseph Lukens, Co. I transferred to engineer corps.

Thursday Aug. 11th 1864
Attending to official duties. Wrote a letter to mother. Sent a photograph of Col. Dick. The news reached here that Fort Gaines and Mobile have fallen. The situation here is assuming the shape of a siege.

Friday Aug. 12th 1864
Reading a novel in the morning. Lieut. Cravens from the 72nd visited the regiment. Glad to see him. Another demonstration was made in our front today. The regiment marched out with flying colors to make the Johnnies think that the Yankees were coming. Returned to camp up a hollow.

Saturday Aug. 13th 1864
Seventy nine men and six noncommissioned officers were again detailed to go on picket this morning. Many little troubles are attendant upon those who try to do their duty though perplexing at the time, yet if conscious that we are right all will be well. Writing on invoices and receipts for ordnance.

Sunday Aug. 14th 1864
Another Sabbath dawns. Thus adding another link to the golden chain of eternity. Wrote a letter to Frank Cones. In the afternoon hear a couple of soldiers preach in the regiment. It was indeed interesting to listen to the glad tidings of salvation.

Monday Aug. 15th 1864
Nothing occurred today to change the monotony of the camp. A sprinkle of rain fell in the afternoon which made glad the earth. The military situation is unchanged. The army generally is in good health and spirits and ready for the move "forward", though the word is significant and the meaning terrible yet when it becomes the imperative duty of the soldier to comply with its requirements each man is ready and willing to perform his part. Was visited by Wm. Carnett from the 40th. He looks well. His time expires in two months and a half. Received a letter from my friend Ollie Higgins.

Tuesday Aug. 16th 1864
A detail of 22 men and 2 noncommissioned officers were ordered on picket from our regiment. Writing on Lt. Gass Quarterly Returns of ordnance. News came this morning that Wheeler's rebel cavalry were in our rear and have cut off northern communications. The future will determine the truthfulness of the story. It is also reported that Fitzpatric is having his own way on the Macon road thus sundering reb communications. The enemy is said to be massing his forces in front of Geary's division of the 20th Corps.

Wednesday Aug. 17th 1864
Morning pleasant. Same pickets detailed as yesterday. Chess seems to be growing popular. It is a pleasant amusement and tends much to relieve the dull monotony of the camp. In the afternoon made out the quarterly returns of ordnance pertaining to Co. C. Another demonstration was made by the 17th Ky., 13th Ohio and our regiment. Marched out in front of the works with colors flying and made the Johnnies believe we would be on them in a short time. Doubtless they were scared (?). The grape vine news in camp is that the army with the exception of the 4th Corps will be issued 20 day's rations and start in the direction of Macon 107 miles south of Atlanta. The 4th corps will fall back to the Chattahoochee river.

Thursday Aug. 18th 1864
Mail communication has been cut off. Same picket detail. Made out an inspection report for the month of Aug. Commenced writing a letter home but business called me and I had to defer. Orders came after night that our regiment and the 19th Ohio would move a couple of miles to the left to make another demonstration.

Friday Aug. 19th 1864
At 3 o'clock we marched out. Reaching the camp of the 99th Ohio in the 1st division and occupied their works while they moved still further to the left. From this point it is just 1800 yards to the city which is in plain view. A battery is established here which pays its respects to the city every five minutes. Remained here about an hour when we moved back about a mile and remained till 3 o'clock when we returned to camp. Of the result of the demonstration I am not able to say. Perhaps good has been accomplished.

Saturday Aug. 20th 1864
Again this morning at 3 o'clock we made the same demonstration as yesterday. The regiment received a barrel of dried fruit and a couple of

barrels of pickled onions from the sanitary department. These are the first stores ever received from that source. About 10 o'clock we returned to camp. A drizzling rain fell during the day.

Sunday Aug. 21st 1864
This lovely Sabbath morning thoughts of home inadvertently enter my mind. Perhaps the more so this morning on account of Captain Sims resignation who will start for Indiana this morning. When any person is starting home at that time I think more about starting myself. Capt. Sims has been a faithful and efficient officer yet through ill health he has been compelled to quit the service. Wm Wiley is quite sick this morning with diarrhea. Perhaps will be sent back. Capt. Sims on taking leave of his company made a short but appropriate address. Both speaker and auditors were much affected and the separation moved hearts unused to weeping. After the Captain was through with his address a series of resolutions was written giving expression to the high esteem in which he was held by the men under his command. At two o'clock a meeting of the officers of the regiment was also held to pay a tribute to Capt. Sims who has left for his northern home. High encomiums were pronounced upon him as a gentleman, an officer and a soldier together with regrets for the separation of a fellow officer. He returns to his happy peaceful home with the kind and good wishes of both officers and men.

Monday Aug. 22nd 1864
Morning dawns pleasantly. The picket detail was 40 men and four noncommissioned officers. Sent an letter to the Patriot also finished writing home. Mail came in bringing me missives from home. Annie, Lide, and Mate. Glad to hear from each. Answered Annie's. Weather pleasant.

Tuesday Aug. 23rd 1864
The teams were ordered on a forage expedition this morning for the purpose of getting roasting ears. It came in this evening well loaded. Received the Cincinnati Gazette from home and W.C. Advocate from the office. Busily engaged in making out the Ordnance returns for the 2nd quarter. The adjutant returned last night.

Wednesday Aug. 24th 1864
Engaged today in making out the Quarterly Returns of Ordnance for Lieut. Haugh C. R. Wrote a letter for "Jim". Also made out a list of deserters.

Thursday Aug. 25th 1864
The 6th Ohio Battery which has been near us for some time moved out this morning. Wrote a letter to Ollie. About 4 o'clock we received order that the corps would commence moving to the right at dark. At 10 o'clock our regiment started. Moved out slowly marching till 3 o'clock when we bivouacked for the remainder of the night.

Friday Aug. 26th 1864
Breakfasted, after which we were ordered to throw up temporary works to protect our rear. About 10 o'clock the march was resumed. The day was intensely hot almost unendurable. Many had to fall by the way. Passed the 15th, 16th, & 17th Corps. Halted half an hour for dinner but it was so hot and I very tired I satisfied my hunger with a cracker and a cup of water. A shower fell but the atmosphere remained hot. Passed the 14th Corps and reaching the left of the 28th corps, marching today perhaps 10 miles we went in camp.

Saturday Aug. 27th 1864
After a pleasant night's rest I awoke with indications of rain. Hurriedly breakfasted when orders came to move at 8 o'clock. Indications of rain vanished resulting in only a demonstration of the elements. In our march this morning I, for the first time in the state saw a pretty girl. She was indeed pretty and reminded me of the fair sex away up north. After going two miles and a half from our last night's encampment we again pitched our tents within borders of a rich country a point just eleven miles southeast of Atlanta and 6 from East Point. Hastily threw up works as the enemy seems to be prowling in our front though of what-force is not known. Received a couple of letters from Dock Adair who is in Gen. Field Hospital in Chattanooga. I have just learned that he has been transferred to Nashville.

Sunday Aug. 28th 1864
Once more I am blessed with the privilege of beholding the arising of another Sabbath's sun. With what effulgent beauty and resplendent glory its rays gladden each soldier's heart. This morning recalls other Sabbath mornings at home, Sabbath mornings when were all happy and free enjoying the privileges which this day then guaranteed us. But oh bitter thought to contrast the present with the past. Which ever way we turn commotion succeeds commotion all looking toward war. The golden chain of peace which over bound us as a nation together as in a bond of fraternal love seems to be now severed link by link. The sad tidings daily reach us of discordant

elements working together for the destruction of our union and the complete overthrow of peace in every section. These discordant elements are blending and the news may at any time reach us that, too, the North is submerged in the sea of blood. Would it were not so. O God, put to naught the designs of wicked men. Hasten the time of a pure and lasting peace - a peace that men and angels and God will smile upon. Orders were received to march. Wearily the hours passed on. Noon came at last and dinner call was sounded. The wagon train of the army commenced coming and parking in the fields in front of us which is considerable of a valley. They roll in as a wave until the valley becomes submerged as it were in a sea of wagons. No pencil picture could portray the scene. The imagination of man could not conceive what an immense wagon train it takes to supply the army with food, baggage etc. Even with this each regiment is limited to but one wagon. The afternoon passes away and we are not off yet. The frugal meal, supper, is eaten and the bugle sounded the assembly. It is now sunset. Fall in and go perhaps half a mile when we halted and to await the supply to pass. Thus we went till 12 o'clock when we bivouacked for the night.

Monday Aug. 29th 1864
Arose this morning and after breakfasting we moved half a mile and drew rations. After which orders were received for the Division to go to the railroad three miles distant and destroy the track. Upon reaching the R.R. which was the road leading to West Point the work of destruction commenced. The ties were built up and the railing thrown across and burned which render both unfit for use. Eight miles were thus torn up. Returned to near where we encamped last night. The weather is indeed sultry. Furnished a detail of 45.

Tuesday Aug. 30th 1864
Early this morning orders came to march. At six o'clock we slowly moved east, crossed our work of destruction and bore toward the Macon R.R. Our march was slow though wearisome as we halted so many times in the hot sun which did not rest us. During the evening we went into camp three times before we finally settled down. Each time commenced to throw up temporary works. Came to within three miles of the R.R. and camped.

Wednesday Aug. 31st 1864
Cloudy morning. Again on the move toward the Macon R.R. Halted after going 3/4 of a mile and threw up works. Started again and reached the works the Johnnies had evacuated. About 4 o'clock reached the R.R. without

serious resistance. The work of construction again commenced. Works were thrown up and all things betokened active work. The country through which we have passed is somewhat broken though in some places level. The soil is sandy and sterile. Corn is the principal production though many fields are idle. The inhabitants are generally of the poor class - none of them wealthy. Of the males there are none of them at home they being mostly in the army. Females were much frightened having been told that the Yankees were a semi-barbarous tribe that would commit all kinds of depredations on their persons and property.

Thursday Sept. 1st 1864
About 8 o'clock we again moved out going south about 3 miles we again struck the railroad when the work of destruction was resumed. The enemy is retreating south. Heavy cannonading is heard in that direction. It is said that the enemy supposing when we evacuated the works before Atlanta that the Yankees had retreated across the Chattahooche river. Upon this supposition the elite of Atlanta who had fled returned and had a general rejoicing. Scarcely had their lamps ceased to burn ere the Yankees in countless hosts were in the rear of Atlanta thus effectively cutting off their retreat. Verily their rejoicings will be turned to mourning.

Friday Sept. 2nd 1864
Last night a great noise was heard like unto a noise of a great battle. It appeared to be in the direction of Atlanta and the general supposition was that the city had been evacuated and the magazine had been set on fire. Also came upon the enemy last night. Their works were charged and taken. Drew rations this morning and started in pursuit of the fleeing enemy who evacuated last night. Passed through Jonesboro and the county seat of Clayton County and 20 miles south of Atlanta. Five miles south of Jonesboro we again encountered the enemy. Our lines were formed and the advance made. Drove him to his works when we were ordered to charge but it proved a failure. Though if our support on the left had come up they could have been taken. The loss was considerable especially among officers. General Wood was severely wounded in ankle. Col. Manderson 19th Ohio & Lt. Col. Bailey were severely wounded. Capt. Miller AAG on Gen Beatty's staff was killed also. Adjutant Dunn of the 79th, Lt. Colclazier A.D.C. 3rd Brigade were severely wounded. In my own regiment were Eli Duchman Co. F, supposed mortally, and seven others.

Saturday Sept. 3rd 1864
Rainy morning. Saw the Atlanta Macon Intelligencer of the 30th ult. Great rejoicing over the fact of the Yankees evacuating in front of Atlanta. Orders were received that the mail would go out at sunset. Wrote a hasty letter home. Official news was received from Gen Sherman that Atlanta is ours without a doubt. That eighty car loads of ammunition and the magazines of the fort were blown up before abandoning the city. The siege guns and a vast amount of other property which could not be gotten away was also destroyed.

Sunday Sept. 4th 1864
Remember the Sabbath day often enters my mind yet to one situated as the soldier is it is impossible as it should be. Spent a portion of the day in perusing the Psalms. How heart-cheering and soul reviving to read and meditate upon the words uttered by that good man David. Bullets come too close to be healthy. A member of Co. K. was wounded. Washed my shirt, socks and suspenders. Had grapes for dinner. Saw Tom Halloway of the 100th. Fortified my dog tent. Wrote to Ike Adair.

Monday Sept 5th 1864
Received Commission as 1st Lieutenant Co. I. Capt. Carnahan being sick I assumed command of the company. Marching orders were received to get back to Atlanta. Detailed to go on picket. At eleven o'clock we started rearward. Such a night has not been experienced. Broken shins, legs, bones, noses, bruised hands and mud from head to foot of every one. Reached Jonesboro at daylight.

86th Indiana Regiment, Volunteer Infantry, abridged

T. H. B. McCain Commissioned

Sergeant Major T. H. B. McCain, who had been a member of Company I, and Hugh Reilly, of Company K, on September 5, 1864 received their commissions as First Lieutenant of their respective companies. The documents had scarcely reached their hands until they were detailed as officers in charge of the skirmish or picket line. On them devolved the duty of withdrawing the outposts, which was done about 11 p.m. after the command had started toward Atlanta. The night march of the 5th was one of the hardest and most difficult short marches the Eighty-sixth ever made. It had rained very hard and

---

the ground was wet and very slippery. Strict silence was enjoined on getting ready to leave camp. The regiment and column wound their way over steep slippery hills and hollows to the rear painfully slow. "Curses, not loud but deep," could occasionally be heard as some soldier took an extra vicious tumble, rolling down an embankment into a pool of water or fell into a washout gully. These headlong tumbles were innumerable and beyond description. The might was extremely dark and the route wholly strange, therefore the men were at the mercy of every obstacle. If a man took only a half dozen tumbles he did not think himself particularly unfortunate. The fountains of profanity flowed freely when the men were once out of the hearing distance of the enemy. But owing to the peculiarly trying conditions it is to be hoped that at that hour of the night the recording angel was kindly taking a nap, and that those deviations will not be charged up against the boys at the final muster.

Tuesday Sept 6th 1864
Went into camp where we remained all day. Rainy. Mail came in bringing me a letter from Frank C. Much pleased to hear from him.

Chapter Sixteen
Rest In Camp - After Hood

Wednesday Sept. 7th 1864
On the move towards Atlanta by seven o'clock. Marched about ten miles.

Thursday Sept. 8th 1864
Started early this morning. About noon entered the city of Atlanta the city we set out to take four months ago. Our work is now done and we will take a rest. Went into camp east of the city about two miles.

Friday Sept. 9th 1864
The regiment was busily engaged in clearing off the grounds erecting houses and fixing up generally. Secured the services of the train and brought a load of boards. Wrote a letter to Frank Cones. Wrote home up to this date.

Saturday Sept. 10th 1864
Busily engaged in fitting up my little domicile. Went up to Corps Headquarters.

Sunday Sept. 11th 1864
Though Sunday yet, it was a busy day for me. Making out a muster roll for Capt. Carnahan. Religious services by Rev. Mr. Brown of the 124th Ohio.

Monday Sept. 12th 1864
Wrote the official report of the campaign just closed for Col. Attending to other duties in company.

Tuesday Sept. 13th 1864
Morning beautiful. Received letters from Annie, M.N. Belknap and home. Wrote Mate a letter. Reading in the Advocate. Also read the Chicago Platform.

Wednesday Sept. 14th 1864
Spent the day in writing letters and perusing northern papers. It is humiliating indeed to see that the draft has been postponed. It is nothing short of trifling with the lives of the brave soldiers in the field, who have endured all and periled their lives upon the altar of the Union, yet the much needed assistance is again delayed and the war thus prolonged. Read McClellan's letter of acceptance.

Thursday Sept. 15th 1864
Our regiment was detailed to go with a forage train as convoy. Went out in a south eastern direction about six miles through a country where nobody lives. Found two or three fields from which 60 wagons were filled with corn and fodder. The boys went for every thing they could find in the way of sweet potatoes, fresh meat etc.

Friday Sept. 16th 1864
Wrote a long letter home, also my friend Belknap. A general inspection took place in the afternoon. Drew clothing. Reading the Atlantic Monthly.

Saturday Sept. 17th 1864
Did nothing today worthy of note. Yes, nothing: Why simply because I had nothing to read, nothing to work at. Went to Corps Headquarters to get material but before I returned I was taken with the ague and it was with difficulty that I could get to camp. Very sick all day.

Sunday Sept. 18th 1864
Awoke this morning and found it raining. Feel much better today. Heard a part of a sermon but must say I had to leave in disgust. The man was a butternut.

Monday Sept. 19th 1864
Cloudy morning though it cleared up during the day. Took the company out on drill. Capt. C. is detailed on Court Martial which convenes today. Battalion drill in the afternoon. Rev. Mr. Delamater, Chaplain of the 72nd whom I was glad to meet preached to the regiment at night.

Tuesday Sept 20th 1864
Again the drill occupied my time. Studying Hardee's Tactics. Read a speech of Gov. Wright's. Rainy afternoon.

Wednesday Sept. 21st 1864
Spent the day in bed and the chill and fever. Read a letter from Ollie.

Thursday Sept. 22nd 1864
The night was spent more pleasantly. Suffered much from headache, fever, etc.

Friday Sept. 23rd 1864
Wet and cloudy. Feel much better today. Taking some ague preventatives

which don't well accord with my feelings. In the afternoon a heavy dashing rain fell.

Saturday Sept. 24th 1864
Still improving. Took a bathe and put on clean clothes which is indeed refreshing. Reading the Atlantic Monthly. Cleared off and the winds sigh the melancholy dirge of coming winter.

Sunday Sept. 25th 1864
The morning is clear and cool. Everything denotes the decay and death of vegetable life. A somber loneliness pervades. In the afternoon had the pleasure of hearing a sermon by the Chaplain of the 72nd Rev. Mister Delemater. The words spoken were indeed cheering to the wandering Christian heart.

Monday Sept. 26th 1864
Feel very unwell. Reading in the Atlantic Monthly.

Tuesday Sept. 27th 1864
The Division was reviewed today by Maj. Gen. Stanley commanding Corps.

Wednesday Sept. 28th 1864
Went to Atlanta this morning and returned at noon very tired. Nothing to be seen but soldiers. Got a Continental Monthly.

Thursday Sept. 29th 1864
On drill this morning. Reading the "Continental".

Friday Sept. 30th 1864
The same routine of drill and camp duties. Our mail communication is intercepted somehow and consequently we get no mail nowadays. This is provoking especially when a fellow is very anxious to hear from home.

Saturday Oct. 1st 1864
Visited the city of Atlanta and Division Headquarters. Returned very tired.

Sunday Oct. 2nd 1864
Detailed for picket duty this morning. Relieving the 13th Ohio. I was placed in charge of the first relief. About ten o'clock A.M. orders were received to take off the pickets immediately and be ready to march at daylight.

Monday Oct. 3rd 1864
Daylight dawned and we were on our way toward the Chattahoochee River. Crossing over we continued toward Marietta six or seven miles and encamped for the night. The march has been a hard one.

86th Regiment, Indiana Volunteer Infantry, abridged

Allatoona Signal Dispatches

On the morning of the 3rd of October the bugles of Wood's division awoke the echoes at the early hour of 1 o'clock. The men expected some lively times, some fighting or footracing, and very probably ample portions of both. Everything was made ready for marching in good time. At daylight the regiment broke camp and marched back through Atlanta, thence along the wagon road by the railroad to the Chattahoochee river at Bolton, and crossed the river near the railroad bridge. The march was continued over bad roads until near sundown, when the command bivouacked near Smyrna.

The men had learned that Hood with his army was in the rear and threatening a great deal of trouble. It was vitally important that Hood's forces be kept off the railroad and not be allowed time to destroy too much of it. Jeff Davis and Sherman had boasted to the Southern people that Sherman would be forced to retreat or his army would starve, and this was the move made to accomplish their object.

After a night of rain reveille was sounded at 4 am on the 4th. At noon Wood's division marched out on the road to Marietta which was reached about 3 pm. They then continued over the western base of Kenesaw mountain to Gilgal church, but the command bivouacked before crossing the base of the mountain.

On the 5th reville was sounded about daylight and the command entered upon one of the great days of the Atlanta campaign. It was on this day that the assault was made upon the Federals under General Corse and Colonel Tourtellotte at Alllatoona by the rebel forces under General French. It was a desperate and bloody battle for the numbers engaged and fought with the most resolute courage by the troops on both sides. It was not a single dashing charge, but charge after charge, stubbornly fighting over every foot of ground, driven back and yet returning to the battle as if with renewed hope and courage.

The signal dispatches that passed to and from Kenesaw mountain were as follows:

Sherman asked if Corse had reached there. At 10:35 a.m. the reply came, "We hold out. Corse is here."

At 4 p.m. Allatoona was again called and at 4:15 the reply came, "We still hold out. General Corse is wounded. Where is General Sherman?"

The dispatch went back to Allatoona, "Near you. Tell Allatoona hold on. General Sherman says he is working hard for you."

General Sherman communicated with General Elliott, commanding the cavalry, as follows: "I have heard from Allatoona. All right. Corse is there, but wounded. You need not send all of Garrard's cavalry, but send a squadron. Let them make a circuit and they will find nothing there."

On the next day, October 6, Allatoona was asked: "How is Corse? What news?"

Back came this spirited reply signed by General Corse: "I am short a cheek bone and one ear, but am able to whip all hell yet. My losses are very heavy. A force moving from Stilesboro on Kingston gives me some anxiety. Tell me where Sherman is."

Back went the reply: "Saw your battle. Am here all right. Have sent you assistance. Am sorry you are hurt. General is mindful of you."

Sherman said that he reached the top of Kenesaw mountain about "8 o'clock on the morning of the 5th of October - a beautiful day - and had a superb view of the vast panorama to the north and west," and from that point witnessed "the battle and could hear the faint reverberations of cannon." That the day and the contest at Allatoona was a critical one for Sherman and his army few can doubt.

The 86th had a representative in the Allatoona fight. On the 3rd of May, B. F. Snyder of Company K had been detailed to go to Bridgeport in charge of the baggage belonging to the regiment, to store it, and remain with it until further orders. He remained there until October 1 when he was ordered to the front with the baggage. The train on which he traveled made a perilous trip, but finally arrived at Allatoona. The Confederates ate their breakfast on the railroad south of the pass, and began business at once, capturing a stockade with a company of an Illinois regiment. Sergeant Snyder related the following incident in connection with the capture of the stockade:

One of the men did not want to surrender. Prison had no charms for him, so when the company marched out he dropped flat on his face and

> groaned loudly. One of the Johnnies looked back, saw him and said: "Get up, Yank, get right up, old fellow."
>
> Mr. Yank made no reply, but kept to work groaning. Going up to him, the rebel said, "What's the matter?" "Small pox," was the reply. "Oh Lordy," said the rebel, "I don't want nothing to do with you," and he ran out of the stockade as fast as he could, leaving the cute Yankee to walk over to our lines after the enemy had passed on.

Tuesday Oct. 4th 1864
About two o'clock the march was resumed. Passed through Marietta. Many rumors are afloat in regard to the enemy though none reliable. Went into camp near Kenesaw Mountain which place in memorable as around it were fought some of the most sanguinary battles of the war.

Wednesday Oct. 5th 1864
At nine o'clock we again slowly moved out passing over the battlefield where we fought last June. Every tree, bush and shrub bears the impress of a hotly contested field. After marching perhaps five miles encamped near Pine Mountain memorable as the spot where the rebel Gen. Bishop Polk was killed on the 14th of June.

Thursday Oct. 6th 1864
Rain came in torrents. The enemy is said to have a strong force in front of us.

Friday Oct. 7th 1864
Beautiful and clear morning. Took a stroll on Pine Mountain. From here could be seen the broad expansive forests of Georgia with peaks on the monuments of Eternity lifting their heads in stately magnificence and lofty grandeur.

Saturday Oct. 8th 1864
Wind blew fiercely all day. Winter is approaching. At one o'clock we moved toward Acworth and encamped after marching perhaps six miles.

Sunday Oct. 9th 1864
The night was very cold and consequently was passed very unpleasantly. Expecting orders to move but they came not and we lay all day in the smoke. Tis the Sabbath. No chiming bell calling the worshipers to the sanctuary - the place - "Where friend holds fellowship with friend."

Monday Oct. 10th 1864
Changed camp late yesterday evening. Waiting for orders to march. At two o'clock they were received and we struck out in the direction of the Etowah river northward. Marched till nine o'clock at night passing on our way Acworth, Alatoona Pass and Ettawah. The march was a weary one and I lay down on my humble couch very tired.

Tuesday Oct. 11th 1864
Today is election day in the three great states of Indiana, Ohio and Pennsylvania. At daylight we started. Passed Cartersville and some good country in the Ettowah valley, but generally speaking the country is poor and sterile. Passed the Cassville battlefield where we fought on the 19th of May. Reached Kingston thirteen miles from last night's camp at twelve o'clock where we took dinner. Encamped two miles west of Kingston. At night after three long weeks of interruption the mail came in. Received letters from Mattie, Frank and home, besides several northern papers.
Good news in regard to the enforcement of the draft. Among the papers was the much loved Advocate. It was read and reread with much interest. Like an old friend it is ever welcome.
This day closes another volume of my daily journals. Would that the record of each day could say something more done, something more accomplished. But "irrevocable" is written on the pages of the Past.
May each day be a lesson for improvement in coming days. Learn wisdom from the past and improve it is a timely injunction.

[Signed] T.H.B. McCain

Wednesday Oct. 12th 1864
Earth, air, and sky breathe such a loveliness this morning. Thoughts inadvertently wandered back to by gone days - days when a mellow autumn shed a halo of luster and undimmed happiness o'er the paths my youthful feet there trod. I thought of my humble home. I thought of the clambering rose bush that shaded the great front window, of the orchard ladened with mellow fruit, of the barn and the neighing of old "Lize" and Tom - and the lowing of old Cherry, and the crowing of the chickens and the gobbling of the geese, and the meadow where the bleat of the woolly tribe made music, and the pasture where the forest leaves, brown yellow and red are falling to the lap of earth. I too thought of happy smiling faces within that home. My thoughts were interrupted by the sound of the bugle sounding the march. In a moment all were ready and we slowly moved out in the direction of Rome

where it is said the enemy is supposed to be in force.

The country we passed through is rough being principally composed of mountainous wastes and sterile swampy valleys. It was indeed like traveling though the bogs and fears and shades of death. Marched till the wee small hours of the morning when we bivouacked. Lay down supperless and very tired Knew nothing until the dawn of

Thursday Oct. 13th 1864

Arose, breakfasted, and made preparations for the march. No orders however. The immediate country is rich and well cultivated being in the valley of the Castonata and Etowale. The boys go in on the forage - procuring sweet potatoes fresh meat-etc in abundance.

William Michaels and Lane Slaw found secreted in a hollow lyn tree 16 bottles of Quinine and four of morphine besides a good squirrel rifle. At three o'clock marching orders were received. Rumor has it that the enemy with a large force is between here and Resaca playing squash with the railroad.   Immediately we started and marched till nine o'clock in the direction of Calhoun where we encamped.

Friday Oct. 14th 1864

Started before day and continued steadily on till reaching Resaca when we took dinner. Here I learned that the Johnnies were here yesterday but were now rushing toward Dalton.

Near where we took dinner are 49 Federal graves of those who were killed in a charge made on the 14th of May most of whom belonged to the 70th Indiana on the battlefield.

Saturday Oct 15th 1864

Again on the move at an early hour. Marched westward about two miles when we halted and threw up a barricade as it was said that Cleburne's Division was making efforts to get into our rear.   Took dinner here when we again started towards the mountains leaving our train in the rear.   Reaching the base of Taylor's Ridge we commenced scaling the precipitous and rugged ascent. Up and up we went. Some falling by the way. Some falling in the way.

Panting and blowing the top was reached when we descended into a valley through which we passed.   Coming to another ridge the same work must be performed. It was dark when the summit was reached which was much higher than the one we had just come over.   Yet though darkness enshrouded the beautiful domain of scenery I felt as though I was standing where the monuments of Eternity were in towering grandeur above the violence of a wicked and perverse people. Descended into Snake Creek Gap where we bivouacked. The enemy had passed through just before us and had felled the timber in the road which impeded our progress but our pioneers soon cleared the way. Felt quite unwell and lay down without supper.

Sunday Oct 16th 1864
Another Sabbath dawns yet how unlike a Sabbath morn it seems. The moving of a great army, the bustle and excitement which it creates is calculated to make one forgetful of the sacredness of this day. Marched perhaps four miles out into a fertile valley - name unknown, where we encamped for the night. Lieut Cowdrey being sick I was placed in command of Co. "C".

Monday Oct 17th 1864
Remained in camp today. Near where we encamped lived a family who are now tasting the bitter dregs of war. Every thing about house garden and field has been appropriated by the Yankee to his use. Not a mouthful is left for the family. It was indeed touching to see the tears trickle down his cheeks as he saw the last thing taken from his house. Said he "I have lived 35 years and never knew before what it was to want for something for my children. Not a mouthful in the house and God knows I know not where to get any thing and continued he "I fear I am not as humble as a man can be in this world. I don't know". A couple of young ladies passed the yard arm in arm crying and the wife and children too mingled their tears with the young ladies. Night came again and I took a good rest.

Tuesday Oct. 18th 1864
On the march by daylight. Crossed a mountain Ridge into a rich valley down which we marched all day. Forage is plenty and the boys live well. Sweet potatoes and fresh pork in abundance. Encamped after marching about 18 miles.

Wednesday Oct. 19th 1864
About noon after waiting patiently all morning we started going in the direction of Summerville the capital of Chattanooga county Ga. near which place we encamped having marched six miles. Chattanooga valley is guarded by the Pigeon mountains on the one side and the magnificent heights of Taylor Ridge on the other. Its fertile soil betokened that the

productions made glad the husbandmen whose happy lot it was to say he was the owner there of.

Thursday Oct. 20th 1864
Started early. Continued on southwestern course. Country beautiful. Crossed the state line into Alabama and encamped near Galesville Ala. The road was very dusty which rendered marching disagreeable.

Friday Oct. 21st 1864
Mustered this morning to date from Sept. 5th 1864. Remained in camp. Details from the regiment were sent out after forage as notice has been given that we will live chiefly upon the country. The detail brought in fresh meat and sweet potatoes in abundance which verifies the words of Sherman that this army is better off than in camp. Mail came in bringing me a letter from sister Annie. Also one from Mrs. C.A.P. Smith Delphi Ind. informing that she had in her possession a Bible found on the battlefield Chaplain Hills Ky by her brother George E. Armor. The treasure was lost by me on our march through Ky and found by Mr. Armor and sent to his sister at Delphi.
As a matter of course I never expected to see it again but through a curious chain of circumstances I have been able to trace it up. Mrs. Smith learning my address through Prof. Jackson of Stockwell immediately wrote. Though surprised yet I was truly glad to hear from her in regard to the Bible.

Saturday Oct. 22nd 1864
Still in camp. Nothing definite can be heard in regard to the movement of the army. Foragers are again sent out today and we truly live upon the fat of the land. Wrote a letter home. Cool day. Very much like an October morning up north.

Sunday Oct. 23rd 1864
The holy Sabbath again dawns bright and beautiful. Still deprived of privileges that this day once afforded me, and still enjoyed by the good people of the unharmed North. Would that a return of those days would hasten on. Sometimes I think I can hardly wait, but then when I remember that patience and cheerfulness are the surest means of happiness I resign myself and conclude that it is only ten months more. "Only ten months more." Who can tell what may happen in those "ten months more." How many hearts that now bear high with hope that "only ten months more." and they will embrace loving ones at home. But how many of those hearts will cease to throb and they find soldier's graves in the soil of the traitorous South.

Heard a sermon by the Rev, Mr. Brown of the 124th Ohio from the words Awake thou that sleepest and Christ will give thee light.

Monday Oct. 24th 1864
Making out a quarterly Ordnance Return for Col. Dick. Laid out camp in regular order. Straightening up and policing was the order of the afternoon. Weather cool but pleasant. This is indeed a delightful climate and were it not for the institution of slavery would be a pleasant place to live.

Tuesday Oct. 25th 1864
Pleasant morning. Finished the Ordnance Returns. Wrote a letter to Frank Cones. Feel quite lost for want of reading matter. Been some days since we received mail. Orders were received today that only the regular details would be permitted to forage, that the promiscuous foraging that had been going on for the past few days would at once cease.

Wednesday Oct. 26th 1864
Wrote a letter to Mrs. Smith of Delphi who wrote me a few days ago in regard to a Bible I lost in Kentucky. It gave me great pleasure to answer her letter. In company with Capt. Spellman and Lieut. McInerney I took a jaunt to the village of Gaylesville which I found to be a small dilapidated place. Like all southern towns it bears the impress of war's imprints. The inhabitants are gone and the once smiling village is a deserted waste. Chanced to pass near Sherman's headquarters. There set Wood, Jeff. C. Davis, Stanley and last but not least in the center of the group was Wm. T. Sherman. This conference indicated a move of some kind so the great chief seemed to be divulging some of his peculiar notions to the listening trio. Returned to camp and wrote a letter to Mate.

86th Regiment, Indiana Volunteer Infantry, abridged

General Sherman's Farewell

General Sherman was riding round viewing the camps and troops in a quiet, unostentatious way. It was his "good-bye" to the Fourth corps, although the men did not know it. It was the last time many of the men ever saw the Grand Old Soldier. He then had everything in readiness to leave and march back to Atlanta, and with a little more hasty preparation, start on his matchless March to the Sea that was to startle the world. The divisions of the Fourth corps were once more united at Gaylesville, but were now about to separate from its companion corps, the Fourteenth and Twentieth, which were to accompany General Sherman on his march.

Many of the Fourth corps regretted that the corps was not permitted to accompany Sherman, and on January 6, 1886, J. A. Barnes wrote the General in which he expressed this regret. In reply, General Sherman said:

"Of course I hated to send the Fourth corps back from Kingston, but the general plan contemplated Gen. Thomas at Nashville and me marching to Savannah, Columbia, Raleigh and Richmond, with Hood at liberty to attack either. I therefore had to provide Thomas with enough men to fight Hood. All he asked for in addition to the troops he had was the Fourth corps. After sending that corps to make assurance doubly sure, I also sent the Twenty-third corps - Schofield - and you know the result. The battle of Franklin and Nashville were as important to the general cause as the march to the sea. So you may faithfully assume that you performed a full share in the final campaign that ended the war."

Chapter Seventeen
Franklin

86th Regiment, Indiana Volunteer Infantry, abridged

Shhh!

On October 26, amid occasional skirmishing, the Army of the Cumberland's First, Second and Third Division were marching toward Franklin looking for a place to cross the Duck River, whose bridges had all been destroyed. On the 27th they passed through the town of Columbia and crossed Duck River to the north side on pontoons, about two miles below the town.

On the 28th, The 86th was detailed for picket, the sentinels being stationed on the bank of the river and relieved at noon on the 29th. The enemy was seen by Post's Second brigade crossing at a place called Davis' ford, and as soon as the 86th was relieved it was ordered to march in the direction of Post's brigade as support. There was a good deal of skirmishing and cannonading in the direction of the pontoon bridge, where the enemy was attempting to cross. General Cox with his division of the Twenty-third corps held his position and repelled every attempt to cross the stream, which would have allowed the enemy to entrap the three divisions of the Fourth corps and the two divisions of the Twenty-third corps as if in a vise. Cox withdrew his division after nightfall and retired to Spring Hill.

The 86th rejoined the brigade soon after nightfall . There was no moon and the darkness was almost impenetrable. Wood's division filed in after Cox and began its retreat about 10 p.m. on the 29th. Wood was followed by Kimball's First division, which had started northward in the morning but had halted on the hills south of Rutherford creek, four miles north of Columbia. The progress was extremely slow.

There had been a report freely circulated and confirmed that a large body of Confederate infantry had crossed Duck river five miles above Columbia. Wood's division marched on undisturbed until weariness became fatigue, and fatigue exhaustion, when the light of large camp fires broke upon the vision of the men some distance in front, or in the direction they were marching. This was thought to be the camps of the Union forces, and the troops, cheered by the prospect of rest and sleep, stepped briskly forward.

But lo! what a change came over the spirit of their dreams! The column was quietly halted, and Captain M. P. Bestow, of General Wood's staff, rode down the ranks and announced softly, "Boys, this is a rebel camp lying near the road and we must march by it was quietly as possible. Arrange everything so there will be no noise!"

Companies B and H of the 86th were in the advance of the brigade to try the alertness of the enemy.

> *"And the air was so calm, and the forest so dumb,*
> *That we heard our heartbeats like taps of a drum -*
> *"Column! Forward!"*

Steadily, quietly, the regiment proceeded steadily, followed by the brigade. All passed by without notice by the rebels with the exception of one regiment. Temporarily connected with the Third brigade - on this retreat only - was the Fortieth Missouri, a new regiment that had been pushed immediately to the front, and which the boys had named the "Fortieth Misery," on account of their extreme nervousness.

One or two of the rebel pickets on the side of the rebel camp fired into the "Fortieth Misery" as it passed, and such a tumbling of raw recruits, and such a clatter of frying pans and cooking utensils, is seldom heard in an army. Those green levies were piled about five deep in the center of the pike, and tried to pile higher still. There was groaning and lamentations. They had lain down to escape the enemy's fire, having been out long enough to learn that much.

But this halted the column in the immediate rear, which was Major Snyder, with the veteran 13th Ohio. The Major was a man of quick, decisive action who did not care to be delayed long here, so he came forward and saw that the delay was far more dangerous than the fire, and advised the Colonel to march his men on as quickly and quietly as possible so as to clear the road. The Colonel of the 40th hesitated, so the Major rode back to the head of his regiment and gave the order, "Forward March!", and it literally walked over the Fortieth Misery and proceeded on its way. When the Missourians saw, or heard, or felt, the Ohio troops passing on undisturbed, they, too, picked up courage, gathered themselves up from that pile of cooking utensils and canteens and resumed the march, - very cautiously.

Thursday Oct. 27th 1864
Rained last night. Before day arrived came the Col. announcing that we

would march at 8 o'clock for Alpine 15 miles north in the direction of Chattanooga. Truly the indications of yesterday were fulfilled. Though it was a sloppy and disagreeable march yet we reached Alpine in due time. Country is rough and broken though the valleys are rich and well adapted to raising the necessaries of life. Some of the most beautiful natural scenery that my eye ever beheld I witnessed today on our march. The rich valley guarded on either side by the grand old mountains. The reflection of the sun on the mountain side and a beautiful rainbow spanning the valley as if a promise that the flood of hardships was over.

Friday Oct. 28th 1864
Encamped one mile south of Alpine at night. Started early and traveled toward a beautiful country in the Chattanooga valley. The country is well supplied with forage. After marching about 25 miles encamped at LaFayette Georgia.

Saturday Oct. 29th 1864
Started this morning at 6 o'clock. Passed through a good country until we came to Chicamauga creek. Crossed this stream at Lee and Gordon's Mills and came to Chicamauga battlefield. It was a melancholy October day. The soft winds gently sighed through the branches of the oak and the pine that clustered o'er the battlefield. The leaves, brown, yellow and red were falling to the lap of mother earth, carpeting the desolated ground, yes desolation marks that ever - memorable field. Weeds and briars have grown up and the scattered graves of union soldiers only adds to the loneliness. The trees are scarred with musketry and cut down by the cannon as like the sweeping hurricane. Truly sad thoughts were awakened by the memory of the bloody hours of Chicamauga. Encamped at Rossville.

Sunday Oct. 30th 1864
At six we moved out. Came to Chattanooga. The query on the lips of every body is Where are we going? No one can tell. Finally we get on the cars bound somewhere west. We are off at lightening speed, pass Lookout which towers Heavenward as a sentinel for sister mountains of approaching danger. Next after winding round mountains and hills and passing over streams and gullies and precipices and the blue and placid Tennessee we reach Bridgeport. In a short time more Stevenson is in view.

Anxious are we to know whether we take the road to Nashville or the road to Decatur. Soon it is known when the engine is switched off on the Decatur road. Flying down through a livid uncultivated county till dark when we came to a sudden halt occasioned by guerrillas tearing up the road about 300 yards. In about three hours it is repaired by the construction corps and we are again off. It now being night nothing could be seen of the picturesque scenery which is said to adorn north Alabama. Pass Huntsville the home of fair women and brave men and at daylight reach Athens the Capital of Limestone county Ala. on the Nashville and Decatur R.R.

Monday Oct. 31st 1864
At Athens we landed off the train, breakfasted and drew rations and about 3 o'clock started for Pulaski Tenn. a distance of 30 miles. After leaving Athens we struck a wilderness traveling about 12 miles without a sign of human habitation. Encamped in the forest.

Tuesday Nov. 1st 1864
At 4 o'clock we resumed the march. After starting we learned through the telegraph operator that the rebels came into Athens 3 hours after we left and that the federal garrison had boarded the cars and gone back to Huntsville. The wilderness continued until for four or five miles when we struck a more beautiful country. Came to Elk river. The bridge having been burnt some time previous we were ordered to strip for a wade. The scenery was worthy of a place in "Frank Leslie's" or "Harper's". Although it was a cold bath I felt much refreshed after crossing. On the right bank is Elkton, a pleasant little village. From here to Pulaski is a good pike. The country is good and subsistence plenty. I am not one of those who believe that the south can be starved out because in a country where they can plant and the earth bring forth fruit in return without cultivation it is an impossibility. Our hopes are mainly in fighting and whipping them which I am confident can be done if we are but true to ourselves. Arrived at Pulaski the county seat of Giles County Tennessee about five o'clock. The town is a beautiful place and indicates that it has been a place of thrift and business. I think it the most beautiful town I have seen in the south with the exception of Knoxville. One attractive feature was the many smiling faces of good looking females.

Wednesday Nov. 2nd 1864
Rainy, drizzly and wet day. The disagreeable generally plays its part. Remained in bivouac near Pulaski. Charmed to find a stray copy of the "Advocate" which was perused with pleasure. I also read a lecture delivered to the students of H.W.C. University by Professor Henshour. Subject - "We all fall as a leaf" which was indeed interesting.

Thursday Nov. 3rd 1864
Awoke this morning and found it raining. Nature truly has assumed a garb of melancholy. The leaves are fading and falling and Bryant's lines are truly appreciated - commencing
  "The melancholy days are come
    The saddest of the year
  Of wailing winds and naked woods
    And meadows brown and sere."
  Heaped in the hollows of the groves
    The withered leaves lie dead
  They rustle to the eddying gust
    And to the rabbit's tread.
  The robin and the wren have flown
    And from the shrub the jay
  They call from out their wintry home
    Through all the gloomy day".

Friday, Nov. 4th 1864
Cloudy and cold day. Sat down to a small rail fire with a blanket thrown around me. Mail came in bringing me a letter from home.

Saturday Nov 5th 1864
Detailed for picket today to go at nine o'clock. At the appointed time with 75 men I went out- relieving the 13th Ohio. The picket station is on a high ridge overlooking the little village of Pulaski.
The winding stream glides through the valley while its willow grown banks trending far back to the base of huge hills are covered and dotted with the gleaming of white tents presenting to the eye the appearance of a vast city of canvas. Lovely are the hours as they slowly pass on. Night came on cool and chilly. Then I wished for a big straw pile to crawl in. I thought of our old straw pile in the field where oft on such days as this I would seek the sunny side to keep warm.

Sunday Nov. 6th 1864
The morning dawned cloudy and cool. The atmosphere feels very much like snow. Relieved from picket at ten o'clock. Came to camp made my toilet and felt much refreshed. The corps commenced fortifying the town today. The whereabouts of the enemy is unknown. Supposed to be at Florence Alabama a point of the Tennessee River 40 miles S. W.

Monday Nov. 7th 1864
Rainy morning this. Details were sent out to work on the fort. Received orders to make out-orders pay rolls for eight months pay. Received letters from my friends Ollie and Emma. Wrote to sister Mellie. Took a stroll from camp and went up town. Saw Wm. Curnuth of the 40th. One of the peculiar features of plantation appendages is the gin house and cotton press. A cotton press is as unique and peculiar a feature in southern scenery as a thrashing machine in the North. With its sloping roof, long sweeping arms and pagoda caps its heavy beams and great wooden screw, and its adjunct, the gin press, mansard roofed and supported by square pillars, within which you see, or did see, an African urchin driving the mules that turn the machine, it would make a charming sketch for an artist.

Tuesday Nov. 8th 1864
Today the voters of the United States exercise the election franchise in the choice of President and Vice President. Abraham Lincoln and George B. McClellan are the nominees of their respective parties. The one representing the Great Union and the other the so called Democratic. Today will be decided by the people whether the measures for the suppression of the infamous and most most wicked rebellion will be approved or not. A vote was taken in some of the companies of our regiment. Company C gave a majority of four for McClellan. Rainy day.

Wednesday Nov. 9th 1864
Received blank muster and pay rolls. Writing on the rolls of Co. G. as Lieut. Cowdry is absent. Went to the Masonic hall to write.

Thursday Nov. 10th 1864
Continued writing on the rolls. Received my monthly wages for eight months as Sergt. Major which was $188.00. Also having served two years I was entitled to bounty which I received $75.00 making in all $263.00. I will send $50 home, retaining the balance.

Friday Nov. 11th 1864
The regiment was paid today, eight months wages cleared off.

Saturday Nov. 12th 1864
Finished business with the paymaster - such as - making out the allotment rolls, etc. Co. G. sent home $2920.00 dollars.

Sunday Nov. 13th 1864
The day ushers in clear and cool. Finished writing a long letter to sister Mellie. In the evening I received a letter from home and Dr. Bowman.

Monday Nov. 14th 1864
Wrote a letter and receiving pay of men just come up from the rear.

Tuesday Nov. 15th 1864
Rained last night. Very disagreeable day. Commenced to put up a shanty. Ben Lytle, Tife Bailey and John Micherts came up today. Autumn is not so brilliantly tinted and gorgeous in the south as in the north. The frost comes so slowly and so slightly, the verdure lingers so long and fades so gradually and the evergreens are so many that you do not get a scene of foliage all crimson and yellow and brown.   There are shades of these hues but they are softer and more subdued. I love autumn better than any other season - better than spring with its winds and showers - better than summer with its sweat and dust and sultry sky - better than winter with its sloppy thaws and pinching frosts. I feel sorry when the wrinkled fingers of old winter rub out the gorgeous pictures the genius of autumn has been sketching in the valleys, and substitutes his own somber tints of snow and rain, brown and silvern, ashen grey and leaden. In autumn the daydreams of my wanderings have a deeper charm. (Fairy ? swift) tissues of gold add a richer margin to your fancies. The whole being is full of a serene joy, a calm and exalted happiness unalloyed with the base things of life.
   To me nothing is more delicious than these dreamy autumn reveries - these strange undefinable sensations, partaking of the hue of the hazy autumnal horizon, its dim infinities produced by that season, along with the gaudy tints of forest, the rustling of the crispy leaves of yellow and brown, crimson and gold falling through the branches, shooting fitfully hither and thither in the feverish wind - "wind that to and fro drives the thistle in autumn's dusky vale". So calm is the autumn landscape. Old mother earth has drunk a chalice of ruby wine from her vineyards; the tears and cares, the storms and sorrows that marked her queenly countenance have passed away, a voluptuous languor transfuse her limbs; her eyes swim dreamily beneath their heavy lids; she sleeps in the sunshine. Her harvest labors are over.

Wednesday Nov. 16th 1864
Made out a monthly report of clothing for which I am responsible in Co. G. Rainy afternoon. Did nothing more worthy of note. I was glad to hear from Frank Cones.

Thursday Nov. 17th 1864
Made out a return of Ordnance Stores for Capt. Gorham. Still raining.

Friday Nov. 18th 1864
Detailed in charge of a forage party which consisted of 120 men. The train consisted of 64 wagons in charge of J.M. Blythe of the 41st Ohio. Went out the Shelbyville road ten miles and loaded the wagons with corn, oats, fodder and hay. The rain came in torrents all day which made it disagreeable. Returned by way of the Columbia pike and got in camp about ten o'clock.

Saturday Nov. 19th 1864
A continual rain fell all day. Trying to keep dry. Did nothing else.

Sunday Nov. 20th 1864
Although it was the Sabbath yet there are times when it is necessary that work must be performed. Such a time was today. Out doors and a shanty must be fixed to keep me dry. Took command of Co. I. as Capt. Carnahan is detailed as A.C.G. 3rd brigade.

Monday Nov. 21st 1864
Finished my shanty. Rainy and cold. Fixing a chimney. Wrote to Jas. A. Smith.

Tuesday Nov. 22nd 1864
The weather turned very cold last night. Almost like a northern clime. Expecting orders to march. Madam Rumor has it that Hood is marching toward Columbia and that this place will be evacuated.

Wednesday Nov. 23rd 1864
Still continues very cold. Received orders to be ready to march at 12 o'clock N. Accordingly preparations were made and the hours passed slowly by until sunset when we started, though we made but little progress as we were rearguard to the wagon train, which of all bores is almost intolerable. Marched till 3 o'clock in the morning toward Columbia when we had orders to bivouac till 5 in the morning but by the time we had coffee made, orders were received to march. Consequently no sleep to our eyes nor slumber to our eyelids. Arrived at Columbia at 12 o'clock.

Thursday Nov. 24th 1864
Thus we marched getting, during the twenty four hours, a cup of coffee and

a piece of hard tack. Commenced fortifying on our arrival at Columbia. Detailed for picket. Established the lines about sunset. I was in charge of the second relief. What strange emotions are caused by that one duty of the soldier - picketing. Even though danger may be distant yet for all one feels as though - well, well I cannot tell how.

Friday Nov. 25th 1864
Today one year ago will be remembered as the day upon which one of the greatest victories of the war was achieved by federal arms. Mission Ridge was stormed and taken. Relieved from picket by the 19th Ohio. Came to camp. The Johnnies are following close on our heels. Hood's army is supposed to be in pursuit. Night came on and we moved to the left about a quarter, relieving a regiment of the 2nd brigade. Day has been cloudy.

Saturday Nov. 26th 1864
Rained during the night. Suddenly awakened about 4 o'clock by the firing of musketry on the picket lines. The enemy has established his lines and skirmishing has commenced. Rainy day. The spot where Co. "I" lies is in the mud, the field having been recently plowed. During the day we moved back a few rods and took up our abode in the cemetery among the tombs! The cemetery is a beautiful spot - laid off in plots and counterplots, and the sacred ashes that repose beneath know naught of the actions of the living above. Sweetly do they sleep, far from the cares and ills of life. Many beautiful inscriptions upon the stones tell to the living of a happiness beyond the shades of their narrow home. On one was the beautiful promise "And there shall be no night there." What a pleasing thought that when mortal life shall fail if faithful to the teaching of Him who taught "Peace and good will to man" we can have a home where there is no night. Orders were received at dark to be ready to march at daylight tomorrow morning. Lay down under some boards and slept sweetly among the graves. Rained during the night.

Sunday Nov. 27th 1864
With what a glory wakes the Sabbath morn!
What sudden splendors gild the Easter skies!
Now swiftly from the shrouded Valleys borne
The mists dispel and vanish from our eyes!
   On account of the wagon train not getting across the river we did not march this morning. The orders are to go tonight. We go to Nashville. Started about 8 o'clock. Passed through Columbia and crossed Duck river, a narrow deep stream on pontoons. Bivouacked after going two miles down the river.

Skirmishing continued.

Monday Nov. 28th 1864
Moved up the river opposite the town. The regiment was detailed for picket. Picketed on the right bank of the river. The sentinel posts are on the crest of the river's bank and have a full view of the approach of the enemy. Cloudy, indicating rain. Mail came through but brought me nothing. Drew rations, ate supper and lay down and slept, the blue arched canopy as my covering.

Tuesday Nov. 29th 1864
Awoke this morning at 5 o'clock. Expecting to be relieved from picket but no orders were received until about 12 when the word came to us that the enemy were crossing the river about two miles above. Precautionary steps were immediately taken to impede their progress. The first brigade was sent out on a reconnaissance. The regiment moved back into works which had been constructed during the night. The very earth quakes with the roaring of artillery. Orders were received to march in retreat at dark. Slowly we moved out, so slowly indeed that we were till 12 o'clock marching five miles. The cause of our delay being the crossing of Mud Creek. Though after crossing we marched briskly. Where near Spring Hill we were informed that a rebel line of battle was lying to the right of the road about half a mile and that the utmost silence must be preserved in order that we may pass unmolested. The rebel camp fires glowed with light to all around and while passing not a word was spoken, not a clatter -hardly the tramp of the weary soldier could be heard. We passed safely which we considered lucky and a hair's breadth escape. All night the march was continued. No rest until about eleven o'clock the next day.

Wednesday Nov. 30th 1864
Reached Franklin at 12 o'clock. Crossed the river and stopped to rest. The enemy came and met us upon the field and met a bloody fate. Charge upon charge they made but were repulsed each time with a heavy loss. Many fell who were anticipating that ere long they would revisit the houses of their youth and the places most dear to their erring natures. Commenced the evacuation of the town about 12 o'clock however we did not leave till about 3 o'clock. Though we slept not, neither did we eat, and suffered much from cold.

Following the war, Thomas Hart Benton McCain was a member of The Military Order of the Loyal Legion of the United States (MOLLUS) and read this speech before the Indiana Commandery. It was published by the commandery in the year of his death, 1898. Ed.

Franklin's Battlefield To-Day
by Lieutenant Thomas H. B. McCain, Abridged

*I*t is not the province of this paper to enter into a detailed account of the battle of Franklin, fought on the 30th day of November, 1864. Neither the scope of the subject assigned nor the time allotted would permit, however tempting and inviting the field, but I will say that the history of the war records no braver charge than that of Hood's forces in that engagement.

Without cover, that solid phalanx swept over an open plain, through an immense cotton field, in the face of a terrible fire of musketry, grape and canister, not only once, but twice, thrice, and on some portions of the Union lines as many as six and eight times.

Before that withering storm the Confederate hordes fell like grass before a scythe, but the survivors passed on into the ditch, and at the Carter house, over the works, where they were met with clubbed gun and bayonet.

For a moment it seemed that the day was lost, when a superb dash by Opdycke's Brigade drove back over the intrenchments those who remained alive, and the Union line was re-established. The carnage was frightful. Rarely in the war was such deadly work done as during the afternoon of that brief November day.

The line of defense as established by General Schofield was about a mile and a half in length, both flanks resting on the river. This line was chosen for the reason that at the Carter house there is a slight knoll over which runs the Columbia turnpike, and with the crest running east and west.

Between the lines of the two armies a plain extended, broken by slight undulations and little hills, with here and there clumps of bushes. Beyond are the forest and hills where General Hood formed his lines. From the moment of going into position early that morning the Union troops worked energetically in the erection of breastworks of earth and logs, the latter being taken from a cotton-gin and an old log barn.

Franklin, a town with a population of 2,800, is situated on the south side of Harpeth river, a narrow but deep stream with high banks, a bend of which encloses more than half the town, leaving only a part of the south and west sides exposed. Three roads converge form the south, the Lewisburg, the Columbia, and the Carter's Creek turnpikes. One railroad, running north and south, did the business of the town then, and does now. On the north bank of the river was a fort, known as Fort Granger, built two years before the battle, which commanded the town, a stretch of river on the left, and the cut for the railroad. Traces of the fort can still be seen.

The earthworks are yet plainly distinguishable and are likely to remain so for some time, as they are well covered with sod and the ground used only for pasturage. It was here that two spies were hung in 1863 by order of General Rosecrans. They rode up to Colonel Baird's headquarters, then commanding the post, and represented themselves to be Federal officers with instruction from the War Department to make an inspection of the Union forces. They exhibited their authority duly and properly signed.

A loan of $50 and a pass to Nashville were requested and granted. Before reaching the picket lines they were overtaken by Colonel Baird's Adjutant-General with a request that they return to headquarters. The Colonel had entered into telegraphic communication with the Department, and with the assurance that no such officers were known there, he at once placed them under arrest. The evidence against them was so strong that they made a confession, and that night before midnight they were dangling from a wild cherry tree near the fort.

Although thirty-three years have elapsed since the "useless butchery at Franklin," as General Joseph E. Johnston characterized that engagement, there has been but little change in the appearance of the battlefield except that wrought by the ravages of time.

A few saplings have grown to be stately trees, the old cotton-gin has been replaced by a school known as Battleground Academy. The students of the school erected a monument to kindred and friends who fell that day and who sleep in the little battle cemetery a mile and a half to the southeast. Each state also has a separate monument and there stands a monument twenty feet high dedicated to the "Unknown Dead." Many bodies were taken away after the battle, but the number left - 1,485 - are mournful evidences of that evening's awful carnage.

Chapter Eighteen
The Battles of Nashville

Thursday Dec. 1st 1864
Continued the march until noon when we reached Nashville and established our lines making preparations to receive the Johnnies. I visited the city of Nashville. Bought a sword and belt paying therefor the sum of $31.00. Visited the theater where the star actress Miss Alice Kingsbury is edifying the throngs that assemble. Lindorum or the Black Hand of Death was good and Miss Alice, the charming and versatile actress was applauded for the manner in which she acquitted herself.

Friday Dec. 2nd 1864
Changed lines and moved out in line of battle as it was said the enemy was advancing. Again changed lines and threw up entrenchments working till the small hours of the night. Received a letter from my friend Mate.

Saturday Dec. 3rd 1864
Rainy morning. Finished the works and feel well prepared to receive the enemy. Mail arrived bringing me a letter from Dr. Wm L. Bowman. About 3 o'clock the enemy commenced to advance. Every man was to his place behind the works. The different commanding generals were riding to and fro followed by their respective staffs and war bustle, but no excitement. Gen. Wood passing up the lines spoke a cheering word by saying, "Hold fast boys, God and your country today." Night came and no charge was made. He only advanced his lines and fortified.

Sunday Dec. 4th 1864
Detailed for picket. Went out at 9 o'clock. The rebel pickets are not more than 200 yards from our own. The day is pleasant. Citizens from Nashville are pressed to work on the fortifications. Reading the "Advocate"

Monday Dec. 5th 1864
Relieved from picket this morning. Did nothing worthy of note.

Tuesday Dec. 6th 1864
Straightening up camp. Visited by C. Champion. Glad to see him. Received letters from Annie & Ollie.

Wednesday Dec. 7th 1864
Wrote letters to Lide and Frank. Very cold. Trying to keep comfortable.

Thursday Dec. 8th 1864
In company with Capt. Spillman McInerny visited the city of Nashville. Made a purchase of clothing.

Saturday Dec. 10th 1864
Went to the city again this morning. Snowy and cold. Reminds one of winter days at home. What enormous prices are asked by merchants, market men and everybody with anything to sell. Holders seem to be devoid of conscience. Prices too are twice as high since the army fell back here. The poor must indeed suffer for the necessaries of life. What a blessed thing it is to live in the plenteous North. Wish I could live there now.

Friday Dec. 9th 1864
Turned very cold. Rain, sleet and snow fell. Built a chimney to my dog house. Some of the boys are on picket. It is such a nasty ugly day. I feel sorry for them. Folks at home have little idea how disagreeable it is to soldier.

Sunday Dec. 11th 1864
Cold as Greenland. The first thing I did this morning was to get a load of wood to keep from freezing. Remained in my tent all day. Reading the Atlantic Monthly. Drew clothing for the company.

Monday Dec. 12th 1864
Rumor has it the army will shortly move. In the afternoon I went to Nashville. Received a letter from sister Mellie.

Tuesday Dec. 13th 1864
Got my phiz this morning. Preparations are being made for a move. The weather has moderated. Indications point to a battle.

Wednesday Dec. 14th 1864
Thawing out. Wrote letters to Annie, Ollie and home sending photographs.

Thursday Dec. 15th 1864
Had orders early this morning to move. Breakfast over, tents struck and we were ready. Form our lines and move out in front of our works. The attack has been made on the right and the indications are that the work has been glorious. Our lines are ordered to advance when the yell of a charge was

made. Although only a support yet our regiment lost one killed and several wounded. Nobly have they fallen. The enemy's works were charged and taken and he routed and driven from position to position when night fall closed the contest. The day has been a sanguinary though glorious one.

Tonight we rest on our laurels with the probabilities of the morrow being ushered in with a renewal of the contest. Would that the bloody scenes of war would come to an end and a peaceful and glorious finish. Then the nation though mourning for many of the loved and lost could and would shine as a beacon star in the firmament of empires, kingdoms and republics. Free, redeemed from the blackening curse of human bonding. Until then let prayers ascend, let all the people humble themselves in dust and ashes, and wait for the appearance of that happy day.

86th Regiment, Indiana Volunteer Infantry, abridged

The Attack on Hood's Position

General Wood's attack on Overton's Hill had failed. It was too strong a *position and too well fortified to be swept away by a handful of men. But not in the least disheartened, the corps commander, with Gen. Thomas' consent and direction, made preparation for a combined attack.*

The attack upon Hood's position began with General Schofield's command on the Union right, and ran along the blue-coated line like a wave along the shore. Knefler's brigade (79th and 86th Indiana; 13th & 19th Ohio) was still at work on its line of intrenchments when the wave of action reached it. "Forward" was the word that sprang from the lips of Colonel Dick. This was the regiment's only preparation for the assault.

The Third brigade was to attack directly on their front, on Overton's Hill. Now began a charge in some respects almost equal to the wonderful assault on Missionary Ridge.

There was no time to "fall in" and "form a line." All that could be done was to grab one's gun and rush to the front. Not a moment was lost and the men went forward at a full run, no halting, no hesitating, no seeking shelter behind stumps or trees, but right on for the works and the enemy. Cheers far to the right indicated that there too, Union men were pressing the enemy, and that he would have to fight all along the line and could not mass at any particular point.

Over the ground of the previous assault they came, over the bodies of the slain, both white and black, on the regiment went, still at a run for the enemy and his works. The fire of the enemy was not as severe as had been expected, and the men literally ran over the works and many Confederates.

"As ye dance with the damsels to viol and flute,
So we skipped over breastworks and flocked in pursuit."

Capturing the fort, guns and prisoners, and kept right on, scarcely stopping to notice what was captured, but almost treading on the heels of the fleeing fugitives.

Colonel Dick in his report said: "At the point where my regiment gained the enemy's works he had left in good condition four pieces of artillery, over which I placed a guard. Here also the regiment captured fifty-five enlisted men and three commissioned officers."

The prisoners were taken to the rear while the regiment continued in pursuit of the enemy still east of the Franklin pike. Only those who were in first rate racing condition could keep the pace set after the enemy, and many fell behind the regiment. The Eighty-sixth in the very front of the army raced on after the fleet-footed Confederates until dark.

When finally halted, the 86th was within 50 yards of quite a large number of demoralized rebels, who by their officers had been brought to a stand. There were a number of teams and a battery, but all were fearfully shaken up, and it was only by the most strenuous exertions that the officers could hold them there.

The 86th had raced after the enemy with such impetuosity that there were only a handful of the regiment left when the halt was called. By the time the rest of the regiment was present, and could have captured prisoners, the Confederate officers had lost control and the men had scampered away in disorder.

Again the Brigade had earned the right to be termed "rash, inconsiderate, fiery voluntaries," by their assault on Overton's Hill.

Said a captured Brigadier General, "Why, sir, it was the most wonderful thing I ever witnessed. I saw you were coming and held my fire - a full brigade, too - until they were in close range. I could almost see the whites of their eyes, and then poured my volley right into their faces. I supposed, of course, that when the smoke lifted, your line would be broken and your men gone. But it is surprising, sir, it never even staggered them. Why, they did not come forward on a run. But right along, cool as fate, your line swung up the hill, and your men walked right up and over my works and around my brigade, before they knew that they were upon us. It was astonishing, sir,

> such fighting."
>
> Prisoners numbered 2,847 that day; captured were 13 field pieces, 34 guns, many thousands of small arms, and regimental colors of which no count could be taken. All this was accomplished with a loss of 750 men killed and wounded.

Friday Dec. 16th 1864

At early dawn we were again in pursuit of the enemy in line of battle. Had gone perhaps two miles when an occasional shot from our skirmishers indicated that we had not entirely vanquished. Soon on the right where the 23rd corps and A.M. Smith's corps were engaged the contest was growing hot. Heavy skirmishing continued in our front till about 2 o'clock when our corps advanced in mass - the 1st and 2nd divisions in front - they charging the enemy first. Then came the turn for the 3rd when amid smoke and the din of the contest they charged the enemy's works. Through a storm of leaden hail they rushed, halting only to load and return the volley. The fire from the enemy's works became so hot that our line's began to waver and fell back a short distance though not in confusion. Another charge was made on the right and their lines were broken.

The enemy fled like packs of wolves from their den. The 3rd brigade raised the yell and started, captured this line of works and four pieces of artillery. On and on we went but till dark when night came on and we bivouacked, having driven him about five miles. The result of the day has been glorious. In all the two days fifty pieces of cannon has been taken and three thousand prisoners. The enemy has been ingloriously and almost demoralized. But the horrors connected with the battlefield! Who can picture them. The dead and the groans of the wounded and dying is a picture that no pen can describe. Among our losses are many brave who sacrificed their lives upon the altar of our union and their names will be embalmed in the memory of surviving comrades as the noble among the noblest. A grateful nation will hold them in lasting remembrance as deliverers from traitors and tyranny.

86th Indiana Regiment, Volunteer Infantry , abridged

The Heroism of the Colored Soldier

One incident occurred in the Eighty-sixth, but was no part of it, which is worthy of recital because it shows to some extent the depth of the heroism of the colored soldier. It has become a trite saying, "The colored troops fought nobly," more frequently quoted in a spirit of levity than out of admiration for their heroic courage. No one who witnessed the first assault on Overton's Hill will ever question the true courage of the down trodden colored man. When Post's brigade, of Beatty's division, and Thompson's brigade of colored troops, were repulsed, a number of the latter held their ground well up to the enemy's works, not retiring when the columns of assault retired. Here they remained until the onset of Knefler's brigade. They joined the leaders of the storming column and went over the works with the spirit and resolution of veterans. One of these was so elated by the final, but what, no doubt, seemed to him long delayed, success, of the Union troops that he jumped upon a piece of artillery and stroked it with his hand as he might have done with a favorite horse or dog, patting and petting it as though it were a thing of sense and intelligence. Of course he was an ignorant, unlearned colored man, but he knew the victory was gained. At first he and his comrades had been beaten. Many of them lay just over the works - dead. He, however, was unwilling to acknowledge it was a defeat. He waited and watched for assistance to accomplish the work. But these grim monsters - these bulldogs of war roared on, belched forth death and destruction, and it seemed that no body of men could stand before them and live, much less capture the works. But with the spirit of a true hero he persevered in waiting and watching until hope was almost gone. His intrepidity was to have its own proper reward - victory. A handful of men came over their partly constructed works and started for those blazing cannon. He waits. They come abreast of his cover, still on the run. He is unlearned in books and scholastic training, but he is a close observer and has been a student of nature and the human countenance all his life, and now he reads in every line of the rugged faces of these men that they mean to capture these works, that hill, cannon, and all else that do not run away from him. It was enough. He joins the procession, and rushing among the Eighty-sixth he goes over the works with a leap and a shout. The enemy flees. The works are taken. The hill is captured. The guns are silenced. He is satisfied and looks no farther. This to him was the complete victory - the end of the battle, and he was as happy as the laurel crowned hero in the greatest triumph. He himself was a hero as was many of his comrades on that dreadful day on the bloody slope of Overton's Hill. All honor to the colored soldiers although in their magnificently sustained charge they failed, and equal honor is due to the Second brigade.

Saturday Dec. 17th 1864
Again moved in pursuit of the enemy in line of battle. Marching in this manner about two miles when we came to the pike and marched in columns. The day was rainy. The rain having come all day in torrents. At night reached Franklin and encamped. The news from the enemy is that he is still going and no one knows where or when he will stop. Very wet and tired. Though I went to bed and slept sweetly.

Sunday Dec. 18th 1864
Reveille sounded at four o'clock this morning and at six we were in pursuit of the fleeing enemy. For three miles we marched in line of battle, through fields and woods, while rain came in torrents and the mud almost knee deep. Reached Brentwood when the columns struck the pike and learned the Johnnies were still going and beyond Springhill. Encamped four miles from Springhill at nightfall. Detailed for picket duty. Our picket lines extended about 300 yards to the left of our encampment.

HEADQUARTERS 4th ARMY CORPS,
HUNTSVILLE, ALA., Jan. 6th, 1865

TO THE OFFICERS AND SOLDIERS OF THE 4TH ARMY CORPS:

You have received the commendation of his Excellency, the President of the United States, for your glorious deeds in the various conflicts around Nashville on the 15th and 16th ult. You have also received the commendation of the Commanding General of the forces engaged in those conflicts, not only for your splendid achievements on the field of battle, but for your cheerful indurance of privations and hardships, in the most inclement weather, during the long and vigorous pursuit which followed the rout of the enemy in the vicinity of Nashville.

As your actual commander on the field and in the pursuit I desire to add my commendation to the high enconiums you have already received, and to tender you my grateful thanks for your soldierly conduct, both on the field of battle and in the trying pursuit.

Without faltering, at the command of your Officers, you repeatedly assaulted the enemy's strongly entrenched positions and drove him from them in confusion and dismay. When he was utterly routed and no longer durst confront you in battle, you at once commenced the most vigorous pursuit, continued it more than a hundred miles at the most inclement season of the year, over the most miserable roads and across deep and difficult streams, which were passed by your labor alone, and until the enemy was driven in utter disorganization across the Tennessee river.

The substantial fruits of these glorious deeds were twenty-four pieces of Artillery, five caissons, several stands of Colors, many thousand stands of small Arms and two thousand four hundred and eighty-six prisoners. Such noble services entitle you to the lasting gratitude of the Nation. Fortunately this great success was achieved with comparatively slight loss to the Corps. Seven hundred and fifty killed and wounded will cover the entire casualties of the Corps in the two days conflict.

To the friends of the gallant dead and to the wounded - and I am sure you will join me in this tribute of comradeship, I offer my sincere sympathy and condolence.

Th. J. Wood
Brig. Gen'l Vols

Official:
Assistant Adjutant General

Monday Dec. 19th 1864
Before daylight it commenced raining and continued unceasingly all day. Moved out and marched about two miles when we came to a halt. After waiting and standing in the rain for sometime we were ordered to file off in the woods, which we did and encamped. Remained until next morning.

Tuesday Dec. 20th 1864
Cloudy this morning. Remained in camp till noon when the bugle sounded the march. Off we went. Crossed Mudge's creek and encamp near Duck River. Before arriving at camp it commenced raining and continued till long after nightfall. Everything, clothing, blankets and tents are drenched with rain.

Wednesday Dec. 21st 1864
The weather turned cool this morning and the rain ceased. Built up huge fires of rails and wood and dried out clothing and blankets. The boys go for the fresh meat and turnips in the neighborhood. No prospect of moving therefore we prepare for the night by strawing our beds.

Thursday Dec. 22nd 1864
Growing colder. The day is real wintry. Home would be much pleasanter than here. Such a day as this one is often reminded of the cheerful hearthstone with its bright blazing fire lending a ray of comfort to happy smiling faces. Remained in camp till sunset when the bugle sounded the march. Crossed Duck River on pontoons, passed through Columbia and encamped about a mile and a half there-from in an open wood. Slept cold.

Friday Dec 23rd 1864
Clear and cold morning this. Mail left this morning - the first opportunity I have had of writing home since the battle. About noon the bugle sounded the march but afterwards sounded the dinner call. In partaking of my frugal repast today, prepared by "Mat" my intelligent contraband & found several worms in one hard tack. This issue of crackers is worse than usual. Eight men of my company are on picket. The other day one of the boys picked up, or in the army vernacular, "went for" a mule which carries all the blankets of the company. Thus lightening the load of each man materially. The company now numbers 21 for duty. The regiment 190 and the brigade composed of four regiments, viz, the 19th and 13th Ohio and the 79th & 86th Ind. about 600. The brigade is commanded by Col. Fred Kneffler of the 79th Ind. - The Division by Gen. Beatty - the Corps by Gen. Wood.

Saturday Dec. 24th 1864
The bugle sounded the march early but from some cause we did not get off till noon, when we marched about 14 miles and encamped near Lynnville. The cavalry has been skirmishing with the enemy's rear guard as the dead horses lying in the roadside indicate.

Sunday Dec. 25th 1864
Christmas again. The last for me in the army. This is the Sabbath too, but notwithstanding we continue the march. Passed through Pulaski and took the Laurenceburg road, which is about knee deep in mud. In fact the road is almost impassable. The Rebs destroyed wagons, guns and everything pertaining to an army, indicating they were closely pushed.

Monday Dec. 26th 1864
Remained in camp today awaiting rations. At three o'clock they were issued. Rainy.

Tuesday Dec. 27th 1864
At an early hour we started and continued the march till near night, passing through a very poor sterile country and encamped after marching 13 miles. Scarcely a human habitation was seen along the whole route.

Wednesday Dec. 28th 1864
Moved out early and continued the march through the wilderness. The roads are bad and it is with difficulty that the wagon trains are gotten through. Encamped near the deserted village of Lexington Ala.

Thursday Dec. 29th 1864
Received orders that we would not move. Foragers were sent out who brought in everything in the eating line. It is said we are waiting for the train to reach us.

Friday Dec. 30th 1864
Still in camp. Rations reach us about 4 o'clock. The orders are to march at 6 in the morning. It is said we go to Huntsville to winter. At dusk it commenced raining and snowing, and altogether the night was very unpleasant

.
Saturday Dec. 31st 1864
Today is memorable in the history of our regiment as the day upon which

was fought the battle of Stone River in 1862. The ground was covered with snow. Started at the appointed hour and marched in the direction of Athens. At nightfall we encamped having gone about 15 miles.

Sunday Jan. 1st 1865
Many can say "Happy New Year" this morning but the soldier cannot realize the happiness. True he can think of loved ones at home and know that they realize that it is Happy New Year. The army is in bivouac awaiting the building of a bridge across Elk River. The day is a pleasant one. The sun Shines brilliantly which makes it a mild winter day, especially in this southern clime. From here it is said to be 15 miles to Athens. Near night we moved nearer the river and bivouacked on a high hill where wood was plenty though the ground was too sloping on which to make a good bed. Partook of a New Year's supper prepared by a couple of men in my company who invited me to the feast. The supper consisted simply of stewed chicken with dressing, hard tack and stewed peaches. Relished it finely.

Monday Jan 2nd 1865
Orders have been received that the promiscuous foraging for subsistence which has prevailed since the time of our leaving Nashville will at once cease. Details are to be made each morning to be in charge of a commissioned officer to forage in the future. The order is an excellent one and if carried into effect will stop the pilfering and plundering which has been carried on to such an extent that it was a disgrace to the Federal Army.
Straggling soldiers would forage through the country for miles on either side of our route of travel and not only forage but enter dwellings and ransack from garret to cellar in search of money or other valuables. And in some instances the lives of women were threatened in order to make them tell where their money, if they had any, was secreted. The question might be asked who are to blame for this. Superior officers, and they only. Chopped down a big hickory tree and made a comfortable fire by which we could while away the hours. At such a time as this I long for something to read. I look through the regiment but find nothing, nothing. Accidentally I left my Bible in my desk and consequently am without it.

Tuesday Jan. 3rd 1865
Rained last night. After breakfast I came across a novel entitled the Black Mendicant with which I whiled the forenoon away. Just as I had finished it the bugle sounded the march. The day is a gloomy one - fair index of my heart. Would that these gloomy days in the army were over. Then methinks

my melancholy hours would be happiness, no cares of march, of camp or battlefield. No orders military to enforce when most I feel unlike 'twas my mission to command. The duties of a commanding officer are onerous and when so many minds and natures are under him, then he feels as though it required the wisdom of Parnassus, the patience of Job, and the combined qualities of citizen, soldier, teacher and scholar, of statesman and hero to withstand the shortcomings of those he would command.

Wednesday Jan 4th 1865
Having crossed Elk river and marched to Athens yesterday evening we were on the way early toward Huntsville. Passed through a barrenous country and marched 18 miles. Encamped on a little stream six miles from Huntsville.

Thursday Jan. 5th 1865
Started at 8 o'clock. Marched through the city with music and banners flying. Encamped south of the city. It is said we will winter here though it will depend on the movements of the enemy.

Chapter Nineteen
Winter Quarters at Huntsville - Forays Beyond

Friday Jan. 6th 1865
Rainy and unpleasant. Lying in our dog tents. Officials are laying out camp. The orders are to construct winter quarters.

Saturday Jan. 7th 1865
Commenced to form our colony this morning. All are busy.

Sunday Jan. 8th 1865
Operations, notwithstanding, it is the Sabbath. Continue active and the woodman's axe makes music all around. Wrote the official report of the action of the regiment in the battle before Nashville. We captured 55 privates, 3 commanding officers. Also four pieces of artillery. Wrote Lide.

Monday Jan. 9th 1865
Commenced this morning to build a log house for myself. Size 10 X 7. Cut a white oak with the intention of splitting slabs. Afternoon rain came in torrents causing me to cease operations.

Tuesday Jan. 10th 1865
Resumed work this morning. Succeeded in getting enough timber and hauled it in.

Wednesday Jan. 11th 1865
Laid the foundation and notched the slabs down and commenced an old fashioned dirt, mud and stick chimney.

Thursday Jan. 12th 1865
Continued work on my shanty. Finished the chimney. Received a letter from Lide.

Friday Jan. 13th 1865
Daubing my shanty and fixing it. Did some writing in the Adjutants office.

Saturday Jan. 14th 1865
Secured the use of the team and went to the country seven miles from camp and got a load of lumber with which to finish my shanty. Returned to camp

and about sunset we were ordered to march. One regiment from each brigade is detailed for a scouting expedition. It is supposed in pursuit of the rebel Gen. Lyon who is endeavoring to cross the river somewhere above. Marched to the depot and boarded the train. Arriving at Brownsville ten miles from Huntsville we bivouacked.

86th Indiana Regiment, Volunteer Infantry, abridged

Foraging In Bushwhacker Territory

On January 14, 1865, Col. Dick's regiment was ordered on a scout. They marched to Huntsville and boarded a train, which proceeded east as far as Brownsboro and bivouacked at 2 a.m. The scout then resumed in a section of country infested with bushwhackers or guerrillas, those soldiers who strike at the unsuspecting straggler.

In the guise of peaceful citizens, they went about attacking at random whenever defenses were lacking or low. They interfered with the railroad, shooting into cars so that no train dared to travel there without a strong guard. It was supposed that the purpose of this scout was by marching a sufficient force through their neighborhood, threaten their homes if the murderous practices were kept up, or so intimidate them that they would cease or leave this section, going south where they could not interfere with the railroad.

The boys were under no orders against foraging, but were warned to beware of the bushwhackers. The boys who were so disposed were not slow in taking advantage of the rich bounty of meat, molasses, meal and apples in this country which had not recently been overrun by troops. The bivouac near New Market was reached at 3 p.m.

The next day they continued by marching back into town and turning off to the eastward. The pace was sufficiently slow to allow the boys a splendid chance to continue their foraging. It was truly astonishing to see how the men were willing to make pack mules of themselves, always thinking they could carry a little more.

About noon they passed a house where in the yard were a number of beehives. Notwithstanding the goodly number of bees, the honey hungry soldiers rushed in and took their share.

The bivouac was reached about 2 o'clock in the afternoon. The merry foragers brought into camp an ample supply of flour, honey, corn bread, ham, eggs and dried fruit. Everyone in the command had plenty to eat, and a

> *greater variety of edibles than at any other time during their time of service. This bounty was not without danger. After a particularly good haul, one man actually so overfed himself that he never recovered from it, going to the hospital directly upon the return of the regiment to its quarters and dying soon thereafter.*

Sunday Jan. 15th 1865

This morning a detachment of ten men were sent forward to Maysville to obtain some information in regard to the enemy. Upon reaching this place which was but a mile and a half from Brownsville, three citizen teams were pressed for the purpose of transporting the personal baggage of the officers. From Maysville the expedition started northward in the direction of New Market in Jackson Co. Went perhaps three miles when those teams were relieved by the impressment of others. The country we are passing through is good though the citizens generally are enemies to the Union. Reached New Market, a small dilapidated, out of the way village about four o'clock and encamped on the banks of Mountain Fork of Flint River a beautiful mountain stream whose source is a large spring two miles above at the foot of the mountains. This place is famous as the place where Gen. McCook was murdered in the spring of '62. The country is infested by a prowling band of guerrillas who live by robbing and stealing and murdering and committing all kinds of depredations on union citizens.

Monday Jan. 16th 1865

After breakfasting we struck up Mountain Fork valley eastward from New Market and after going two miles struck the road which led to the Baker settlement in Hurricane Creek valley. At Bakers we changed our course southernward toward Golden Hollow named after a man named Golden. This same man was killed last Friday by guerrillas. The citizens are burying him today. Upon reaching Hurricane meeting house a distance of two and a half miles from Golden Hollow we encamped.

Tuesday Jan. 17th 1865

After a pleasant night's rest by a huge fire of green beech we started homeward or rather campward. Reached Brownsboro ten miles distant from last night's encampment and took dinner; after which we crossed Flint river on the R.R. bridge and after marching perhaps four miles encamped on the banks of a beautiful little stream. The weather has been pleasant throughout.

Wednesday Jan. 18th 1865
Moved in the direction of Huntsville. Reached there about 11 o'clock and camp about twelve, very tired. Drew clothing.

Thursday Jan. 19th 1865
Making out the quarterly return of ordnance for the Col. Received a letter from my friend W.A. Haworth.

Friday Jan. 20th 1865
Detailed for camp guard this morning. The duty is very irksome and the hours pass sluggishly by. Received word from John W. Cosby. News from every quarter is cheering.

Saturday Jan. 21st 1865
Relieved from picket or guard this morning. Received letter from sister Annie. Reading in Arthurs Home Magazine. Made muster rolls.

Sunday Jan. 22nd 1865
The Sabbath again dawns but with it comes no change. The dull monotony of camp life continues. Wrote a long letter to sister Mellie.

Monday Jan. 23rd 1865
Made out muster rolls for Dec. 1864. Booking clothing acc't of company. Wrote James Mivangle and home. Sent an account of the battle of Nashville.

Tuesday Jan. 24th 1865
The years how swift they fly. The months how short? A few short fleeting years ago I was young, but now   "I'm growing old. I'm growing old"
Perhaps this is only the reverie of a bachelor, but when I say I am today twenty six, the reverie is disturbed by stubborn facts that assert the right of being the most truthful. The days are now spent mostly in company and battalion drill.

Wednesday Jan. 25th 1865
Cool weather this. The same routine of duty every day. An order was read on dress parade this morning reducing I. ____ to the ranks.

Thursday Jan. 26th 1865
On coming in from Co. drill this morning I was gladly surprised on meeting my old friend James A. Darragh. Wrote a letter to Mrs. C.A.P. Smith.

Friday Jan. 27th 1865
Today was mostly taken up in roll calls and drills. Read a story entitled "The Traitor's Doom", a story of New Orleans. Weather cool, though clear.

Saturday Jan. 28th 1865
Relieved from drill today as this is Saturday. The twilight shades of a Saturday evening reminds me of early childhood.

Sunday Jan. 29th 1865
Reading this morning. Musing upon past joys and past sorrows. "If mother would but come" steals through my thoughts as I sit by my lonely tent fire. Sometimes I can almost see her. Yes
"I look for her when morn is near
   With all the golden light
When birds are singing sweetly clear
   And all is pure and bright.
Yet I hear not her well known step
   Her smile I cannot see
Oh! if my mother would but come
   How happy, yes how happy I should be."
My reverie was disturbed by the order to make out pay rolls at which I put in the remainder of the day.

Monday Jan. 30th 1865
On drill in the forenoon. About noon the order came to be ready to march at 2 o'clock. Bid adieu to winter quarters and marched to Huntsville where we boarded a train for Nashville by the way of Stevenson. It is said we go to Eastport Miss.
   [An error is recorded here. The army started Tuesday Jan. 31st from Huntsville to Nashville.]

Wednesday, Feb. 1st 1865
This morning found us in Stevenson 59 miles from H. and 111 from N. Up we fly over the rough N. and C.R.R. and reach N. about ten P.M.

Thursday Feb. 2nd 1865
As transports are not here will have to await their arrival. Camp on the battlefield two and a half miles from the city.

Friday, Feb. 3rd 1865
Went to Nashville. Heard Macbeth. Wrote a letter home.

Saturday Feb. 4th 1865
Again went to Nashville. Saw the "Rebel Chief" and "Outschdemchent".

Sunday Feb. 5th 1865
Still no transports ready for us. Had inspection this morning.

Monday Feb. 6th 1865
Started early this morning for the cars with the intention of returning to Huntsville. The order for our corps to go to Eastport has been countermanded. The cars are both inside and top and ready to go though we did not get off till two o'clock. Whisky rules the hour. Everybody, be it said to the shame of our soldiery is drunken.
Passed Murfreesboro when night came on. Dawn found us at Stephenson 111 miles from Nashville. Here we are switched off on the Huntsville road at which place we arrived and stopped at old camp about night. Found every thing torn up but went to work and put every thing to rights.

Tuesday Feb. 7th 1865
Tinkering around our shanty. Fixing things to stay awhile. Cold day.

Wednesday Feb 8th 1865
Spent the day reading the "Atlantic Monthly" and "Waverly Magazine".

Thursday Feb. 9th 1865
Attending to official duties etc. but nothing else of interest transpired. Weather clear and cold.

Friday Feb. 10th 1865
Beautiful day. Reminds one of Spring at home. Wrote a letter to sister Mattie.

Saturday Feb 11, 1865
Made out monthly muster rolls for 1862, and other writing.

Sunday Feb. 12th 1865
Sabbath dawns beautiful and clear. Inspection this morning. Wrote letters to Dallas and Thomas Moore. Read the article in the "Atlantic" - "The Chimney Corner".

Monday Feb. 13th 1865
Writing on unfinished business of the company. Weather pleasant.

Friday Feb. 14th 1865
Today is Valentine day but I sent none. Some of the boys are experimenting.
Drilling.

Wednesday Feb. 15th 1865
Still busy on unfinished business. Making out back muster rolls etc., etc.

Thursday Feb. 16th 1865
Pleasant day. It has been a long while since I received any letters. I am
getting very anxious. These days are spent in drilling - a couple of hours each
day.

Friday Feb. 17th 1865
General inspection of army accoutrements, clothing, camp, and quarters
came off today. Capt. R. L. Walker 19th O T. T. I. Inspector. Started on a
scouting expedition with a detachment composed of the 79th, 19th, and
86th Regiments. Went to Whitesburg, five miles, and bivouacked till two
o'clock.

Saturday Feb. 18th 1865
This morning we embarked on the gun boats Sherman and Stone River and
proceeded up the river to Fearn's Ferry, 25 miles from Whitesburg where we
debarked crossed the mountains into a rich valley and came to Warrenton.
The band of which we were in pursuit had here turned south and
consequently the pursuit was discontinued. We then started to Guntersville,
a point on the river above the Ferry two miles. We had gone but a short
distance until we ran into a squad of guerillas upon which we fired, but they
being mounted escaped. Reached Guntersville and re-embarked on the
Sherman and Stone-River and steamed down the river to Whitesburg
reaching there at sundown. Debarked and marched to camp very tired. Am
now suffering with a severe cold. While on the boat I met some relatives,
with whom I passed the time pleasantly, getting both breakfast and supper.

Sunday Feb. 19th 1865
Wrote the official report for the Col. as he commanded the expedition. The
day is warm. Feel quite unwell.

Monday Feb. 20th 1865
Making out monthly returns of clothing camp and garrison equipage for the
month of Dec. 1864. Day pleasant and mild.

Tuesday Feb. 21st 1865
Weather continues pleasant. Wrote sister Lizzie a letter. Drilling. Heard the news of the fall of Charleston Glory. News is good from every point.

Wednesday Feb. 22nd 1865
Today is the anniversary of the birthday of the great and good Washington. It is the day welcomed by all loyal American hearts. Would that the day could be celebrated throughout the length and breadth of the union in peace.

Thursday Feb. 23rd 1865
Raining and stormy. The day was spent in doors. Wrote a letter to Annie. Also the "Patriot".

Friday Feb. 24th 1865
Received a letter from Emily. Glad to hear from her. Wrote a letter to brother Billy. Day rainy and wet and drizzly.

Saturday Feb. 25th 1865
Reading Leslie's Ten cent Monthly. The hours pass slowly by. The mail has been delayed a couple of days on account of bridges washing away.

Sunday Feb. 26th 1865
The morning is pleasant. The day beautiful. I was somewhat surprised this afternoon by the appearance of my old friend Howard Cones. I was indeed glad to see him and learned much from him that I was pleased to hear. It does a soldier good to meet old friends, to hear direct from home etc.

Monday Feb. 27th 1865
Made out muster rolls for February. On drill. The hours pass pleasantly in company with Howard.

Tuesday Feb. 28th 1865
The regular bimonthly muster took place today. Mustered by Captain R. L. Walker 19th Ohio Vols.

Wednesday March 1st 1865
Winter is over and spring comes again. The day is beautiful. Drilling.

Thursday March 2nd 1865
Raining and stormy. Received a letter from home and Frank McCain. Answered Frank's. Did nothing worthy of note. Good bye old journal.

Friday March 3rd 1865
Reading Bayard Taylor's last novel, "John Godfrey's Fortunes". Taylor delineates character well, none better.

Saturday March 4th 1865
Today Abraham Lincoln is re-inaugurated as President of the U. S. Mr. Lincoln enters upon his second term under auspices for a speedy close of the war. Received a letter from Frank Cones. Wrote in answer. Also wrote Emily.
 Now permit me to say, Good-bye old journal, thou recorder of my joys and sorrows.
End of a volume

Sunday March 5th 1865
Bright and beautiful does the morn appear after the storms and clouds of the week just closed. All nature smiles and I can but wish I was away up north enjoying the day with friends and partaking of their privileges. I feel lonely a shade of sadness comes over me when I remember bright Sabbath days at home.

Monday March 6th 1865
The days pass drearily by. This day was spent in reading "Bitter-sweet" a poem by "Timothy Titcomb". The poem is good and throughout the author has endeavored to show that man was redeemed through merit of Christ who was tempted alike as we are - that had he not put on immortality man would have been eternally lost.

Tuesday March 7th 1865
Returned Bitter Sweet and got the life of Julius Caesar by Jacob Abbott. Went to Huntsville. On brigade drill.

Wednesday March 8th 1865
Rainy day this. Remained indoors all day. Received letters from Ollie, Annie Kramer and M. H. Belknap.

Thursday March 9th 1865
Writing letters. By it thoughts of absent friend ushered in on my mind.

Memory flowed with love tide back to the beautiful and happy days of childhood - to my gay companions. But where are they?

"All are scattered now and fled
  Some are married, some are dead".

Friday March 10th 1865
The day is cold. Feels very much like winter. Overcoats are in demand and the soldiers hover near their dog tent fires. However in the afternoon brigade drill comes off and running over the fields soon warms one's blood and outdoors is comfortable.

Saturday March 11th 1865
The adjutant started home this morning on "leave of absence". He is to be gone 20 days. I was detailed to act during his absence. Day pleasant.

Sunday March 12th 1865
The day was extremely pleasant, though the day passed slowly by. For the first time I appeared on dress parade as adjutant. The position is new therefore awkward.

Monday March 13th 1865
Rained today. Busily writing on quarterly returns of deceased soldiers.

Tuesday March 14th 1865
Quite unwell. The sick were sent to hospital preparatory to leaving. Finished the quarterly returns of deceased soldiers.

Wednesday, March 15th 1865
The orders came this morning to be ready to march at an hour's notice. We go to Knoxville by rail. Waited patiently all day but no orders came to march. While waiting I wrote letters to Flora Welch and Mrs. C.A.P. Smith.

Chapter Twenty
East Tennessee
The War Winds Down

Thursday March 16th 1865
Started early this morning and reached Huntsville at seven o'clock. Boarded the train and off we started. Reached Chattanooga at dark. Unpleasant day.

Friday March 17th 1865
Received a letter yesterday from Annie. Slept comfortably last night. Awoke at daylight this morning and found ourselves at Charleston on the Hiawassee. On reaching London one of our trains ran off the track which consequently detained us till nearly night. The beautiful valley of east Tennessee is beginning to assume its former prosperity. Farmers are repairing their farms with the evident intention of raising a crop. Reached Knoxville at dusk where we lay all night.

Saturday March 18th 1865
The morning is indeed beautiful. Remained at Knoxville till about noon when the train left eastward bound for New Market though we did not reach there till after dark. Camped near town.

Sunday March 19th 1865
The morning is lovely. The sun sheds a halo of lustre on all around. Wish I was at home this morning. The village church bell announces the hour of Sabbath school. I make preparations to go. I found the school small yet there was an interest manifested though the country is a desolated waste. How much it reminds one of home - of the village Sabbath school - of the little class. Sweet were the associations connected with my reveries while I sat a looker on. Attended church in the afternoon. Services by the chaplain of the 8th Kansas.

Monday March 20th 1865
Writing. Clear and pleasant day. Maj. General Moore has returned and will take command of his Division. Gen. Beatty will command the brigade.

Tuesday March 21st 1865
Arose this morning and found it raining. Continued all day. Received a letter from cousin Ann. Reading the Pickwick Papers. Here in East Tennessee many

loyal citizens are suffering for want of the proper accessories of life. The violence of war admits no distinction, the lance that is lifted against guilt and power will sometimes fall on innocence and gentleness. But the angels of afflictions spread their toil alike for the virtuous and the wicked, for the mighty and the mean.

Wednesday March 22nd 1865
Reading the Vicar of Wakefield. His an interesting story of domestic life written by Goldsmith.

Thursday March 23rd 1865
Read Rasselas the Abasynian chief by Samuel Johnson. This story has a good moral. Learn to be contented in whatever station in life we may be placed. Rasselas learned this after traveling in the world.. Received a letter from Annie. Answered the same.

Friday March 24th 1865
The weather is somewhat cool. So cool in fact that it was uncomfortable. Reading Pickwick Papers.

Saturday March 25th 1865
In camp near New Market. The weather moderates. No news from the east.

Sunday March 26th 1865
The day is pleasant. The balmy breeze of spring lends a charm to the already lovely morning. Reading in the book of Psalms. On dress parade. Received a letter from Lide.

Monday March 27th 1865
Very busy making out an ordnance return for the Col. for 1861-62.

Tuesday March 28th 1865
Continued on the returns. Made out the returns for March.

Wednesday March 29th 1865
Last night we sent our surplus baggage to Knoxville and started toward Morristown. Reached Panther Springs early in the afternoon and encamped.

Thursday March 30th 1865
Rained last night. Started early. Reached Russelville 12 miles and encamped.

Friday March 31st 1865
Reached Bulls Gap and encamped. Made out the monthly returns.

Saturday April 1st 1865
Finished the returns. Sent returns of deserters. Wrote a letter to Lide.

Sunday April 2nd 1865
Pretty morning. Wrote letters to Ollie and Flora. Took a stroll to the depot.
Saw Howard Cones. The 40th passed by on train.

Monday April 3rd 1865
Dispatches from the President announce the fall of Richmond. All is
excitement in camp.

Tuesday April 4th 1865
This morning at seven o'clock we started to Greenville. Passed through a poor
country. Reached G. about five o'clock. It is a pretty little village the capital
of Greene county and the home of Andy Johnson.

Wednesday April 5th 1865
Remained till noon when we received orders to march to Jonesboro.
Marched ten miles to Rheatown and encamped. The regiment was detailed
for picket. The country grows more broken each mile traveled. In the
distance can be seen the Paint Mountains. Day beautiful.

Thursday April 6th 1865
Started early. Reached Jonesboro about 4 o'clock and encamped near town.
The brigade is stationed at different points around town.

Friday April 7th 1865
Rainy morning. Took a stroll over town. The place denotes that at one time
it was a town of business and thrift. It is the county seat of Washington Co.
30 miles from Bristol and 100 from Knoxville, Bushwhackers infest the
county.

Saturday April 8th 1865
Morning is beautiful. The boys are busy constructing shanties. The
indications are that we will remain here till the railroad is repaired. Mr. Hyatt
is here getting the material from which to write the regimental history for

Indiana's roll of honor.

Sunday April 9th 1865 (Lee surrendered)
Rainy morning. Made my toilet this morning and went to church. Services by Rev. Mr. Smith from 1st Psalms. Did not enjoy it as I should like to have done.

Monday April 10th 1865
Rained all day. James M. Hyatt is taking the notes to write the history of the regiment.

Tuesday April 11th 1865
Still rainy and disagreeable but notwithstanding the rainy weather good news continues to come from the east. Great rejoicing in the prospect of peace.

Wednesday 12th 1865
Reading a little and doing a little of everything.

Thursday April 13th 1865
Cleared off. Commenced boarding at Dr. Rhea's, a very pleasant family near camp. It has been several days since we received mail.

Friday April 14th 1865
Beautiful day. Wrote the biographical sketch of Col. George F. Dick for "Indiana's Roll of Honor". Anxiously awaiting mail. Good news continues to come, The white winged angel is in the air. Soon it will spread its folds from east to west, from north to south. (Lincoln shot-killed)

Editor's Note: The sketch referred to in the journal entry does not appear in either volume of Indiana's Roll of Honor, but is printed in the book, *86th Regiment Indiana Volunteer Infantry.* We hold the opinion that the following is an expanded and updated version of the original sketch.

George Frederick Dick

*T*he man and officer, who, by his military skill, by his firmness and courage made of the Eighty-Sixth an organization of which they who still live, are so justly proud, came to the regiment near the close of the Kentucky campaign in the early winter of 1862-1863. This officer was Lieutenant Colonel George Frederick Dick, destined soon thereafter to be the Colonel.*

He joined the regiment at Rural Hill, Tennessee, on the night of November

17, 1862. This was the officer who was in all of the subsequent history of the regiment, whether in camp or on the field, in the trenches, or in the storming of the enemy's works; who was to be the central figure. He was to be the one to make, by strict discipline and thorough drill, a body of soldiers out of the raw material then organized into what was called a regiment.

Colonel Dick, for such soon became his title, came to the regiment unheralded. He came as an utter stranger to all but a very few, and the regiment as such, had never even heard his name. There had been rumors that a Lieutenant Colonel had been commissioned, but who he was, or when he was to report for duty, was unknown. The few who had known him, prior to the war, had known him only as a quiet citizen, and as a man earnestly devoted to the care of his mercantile pursuits. All soon knew him thoroughly as an officer, and quickly respected and admired him for his genuine soldierly qualities. Never in the habit of talking of himself, nor of exploiting his deeds, Colonel Dick was, and is, known to the members of the Eighty-sixth only in his identification with the history of the regiment subsequent to the time of joining it. After he assumed command of the regiment it was not long until officers and men alike learned that a master hand held the sword.

From the moment he took command on the battle-field of Stone's River there was a change for the better. New life was infused in the regiment, new hopes inspired, and a new ambition took complete hold of all to do and be something; to make a record as soldiers that had not before existed with the great mass of the officers and men. Some of the officers in the regiment soon found that they were not fitted to be soldiers in the highest and best sense of the word, and these retired.

George Frederick Dick was born at Tiffin, Seneca county, Ohio, February 22, 1828, of German parents, but from his childhood on he was intensely American in all his thoughts and actions. The family moved to Cincinnati when he was two, and there he attended public schools. Always an enthusiast in military matters, when in his sixteenth year a juvenile military company, the Cincinnati Cadets, was formed, he was chosen as the Captain. He said, "This little experience proved very useful to me in after years when I assumed the active duties of a soldier, in actual and not mimic warfare."

A recognized leader, he was chosen Captain of a volunteer fire company in Cincinnati when still a young man. He brought this experience with drill and discipline with him to his military career.

He entered business as a tobacconist, and remained so until 1855, when he moved to Attica, Indiana, and went into the same business. He closed up his business affairs at the first call for troops by President Lincoln in April, 1861. He was chosen Captain of one of the first companies organized for three months of service. As rapidly as this first company was organized, the rush to arms had been so great and so rapid that the quota of 75,000 men had been filled, so they had to wait until May 3, 1891 for the second call. They were mustered into the service in July as the Twentieth Indiana Volunteers, for three years service. Captain Dick led Company D, and he was commissioned and mustered as its first Captain July 22, 1861.

The Twentieth Regiment left August 2, 1861, going to Maryland, where it was placed on duty for a short time guarding the Northern Central Railroad, a branch of the Pennsylvania road, which was such an important factor to the Army of the Potomac during the war.

Dick saw action in many of the battles in the eastern section including the engagement between the Merrimac, Cumberland and Columbus; the capture of Norfolk, the battle of Fair Oaks; and the Orchards. The regiment covered the retreat of the Third army corps in the celebrated Seven Days Fight, participating in all the battles of that campaign.

In August, 1862 he was commissioned a Major. In October of 1862 he was commissioned Lieutenant Colonel of the Eighty-sixth Indiana. He found on his arrival a regiment without drill, without discipline, without anything that could be called military. The officers and men were most thoroughly pleased at his coming. Even though he was then only second officer, it was a great relief and assurance to have one man at the head of the regiment, who was an officer, competent to command.

In January of 1863 Dick was commissioned Colonel of the regiment. Before moving from Murfreesboro, July 5, 1863, Colonel Dick had been assigned to the command of the Second brigade, Third Division, Twenty-first army corps, and retained command thereof until after the organization of the Army of the Cumberland while at Chattanooga, after the battle of Chickamauga.

Colonels Dick and Knefler (79th Indiana) were commended after the battle of Missionary Ridge November 25, 1863 by Brigadier General Samuel Beatty. He said in his report: "In recounting the operations of my command in the advancing of the lines of the 23rd, and the charging of Missionary Ridge on

the 25th, I have to compliment Colonel Fred Knefler, Colonel George F. Dick
... for the discipline and efficiency of their troops, and for the gallant style with
which each vied with the other in doing their utmost to secure a victory to
our arms. The advance of the Seventy-ninth and Eighty-sixth Indiana was
strongly resisted by the enemy, but led by their gallant Commanders, and
supported by the advance of the Thirteenth and Fifty-ninth Ohio regiments in
splendid style, succeeded in first planting the National flag on the rebel works
at the summit of Missionary Ridge." In the battle of Pickett's Mills, Georgia,
he received a severe flesh wound in the hip and was given a thirty days leave
of absence. Although yet suffering from the wound, he was again at the head
of his regiment at the end of this time.

On March 13, 1865, in recognition of his services, he was brevetted a
Brigadier General by Congress. At the end of the war, he laid aside his sword
and took up the peaceful pursuits of a private citizen. Much to the regret of
his friends and comrades of Indiana, he removed his residence to
Bloomington, Illinois, and was still there at the publication of this sketch, in
1895.

In 1873, he was appointed Postmaster of Bloomington by President Grant
and held the appointment for twelve years. He engaged in business pursuits
after retiring as Postmaster. He was President of the Eighty-sixth Indiana
Regimental Association from its inception.

He was married in 1853 to Anna Mayers of Cincinnati, and they had nine
children, eight of whom died in infancy. Anna died in 1878 and some years
later he married Mrs. Emma Kimball.

In the long list of those faithful soldiers of the Nation in her hour of peril,
none deserve a higher place than George Frederick Dick, Colonel Eighty-sixth
Indiana Regiment.

Saturday April 15th 1865
Rained all forenoon again. Waiting patiently for it to clear off. Spending the
time as best we can though it drags slowly by.

Sunday April 16th 1865
Pretty morning. Went to church. Heard a citizen preach from the words
"Set not your affections upon things upon the earth, but on things above"
Col.3-2. It was a fine sermon. Had dress parade in the afternoon.

Monday April 17th 1865
Nothing going on in camp. Detailed for picket. Received a letter from Mrs. Smith.

Tuesday April 18th 1865
The nation now mourns the death of President Lincoln. He was assasinated the 14th. The command of the rebel Gen. Vaughn has disbanded and is now coming in. They all seem to be very glad. Relieved from picket at 4 o'clock.

86th Indiana Regiment, Volunteer Infantry, abridged

Mr. Lincoln

The lightning-like stroke of assassination stunned the American people as well as the soldier in the field. On Sunday, April 16, the Eighty-sixth was inspected by Captain Walker, the Brigade Inspector for the Third brigade, and everything was dragging along in the usual hum-drum channels of camp life. But in the evening a dispatch came bringing the shocking news that President Lincoln had been assassinated. This fell like a pall. It caused universal sorrow in the army, for no one in all the land came so near the hearts of the soldiers as Mr. Lincoln. They had never seen him, but his kind words had come to them and touched in their hearts a sympathetic cord. His character and greatness has been analyzed as follow by one of America's greatest orators:

"Lincoln was not a type. He stands alone - no ancestors, no fellows, and no successors. He had the advantage of living in a new country, of social equality, of personal freedom, of seeing in the horizon of his future the star of hope. He preserved his individuality and his self-respect. He knew and mingled with men of every kind; and, after all, men are the best books. He became acquainted with the ambitions and hopes of the heart, and the means used to accomplish the ends, the springs of action and the seeds of thought.

"Wealth could not purchase, power could not awe, the divine, this loving man. He knew no fear except the fear of dying wrong. Hating slavery, pitying the master - seeking to conquer not persons, but prejudices - he was the embodiment of the self-denial, the courage, the hope, and the nobility of a nation. He spoke, not to inflame, not to upbraid, but to convince. He raised his hands, not to strike, but in benediction. He longed to pardon.

Lincoln was the grandest figure of the fiercest civil war. He is the gentlest memory of our world." The soldiers of the army of the Union although unable thus to analyze and point out the elements of greatness in the character of their beloved leader felt in their hearts his greatness and his goodness - the influence of his mighty intellect and his great heart, and loved him as man has seldom or never been loved by the rude soldiery and the common people of any country. It was a dark day for the army when it knew Lincoln was no more - foully murdered by the hand of an assassin.

Even the joyful news of the great victories recently won could not dispel the gloom the death of Lincoln caused. Time alone could heal the wound.

Wednesday April 19th 1865
Day delightful. Every thing in nature smiles but my heart is lonely.

Thursday April 20th 1865
About noon we bade adieu to Jonesboro and started toward Greenville. Encamped after going 12 miles.

Friday April 21st 1865
Started early. Reached G. about noon. Passed through and encamped about 4 miles this side. Received letters today from Frank, Mattie, Emily, Belknap and home. I was glad.

Saturday April 22nd 1865
On the march early. Reached Bull's Gap at 11 o'clock. Windy day. In the afternoon visited the 40th Indiana. We are now awaiting transportation to Nashville.

Sunday April 23rd 1865
Unpleasant morning this. The wind renders it disagreeable. Remained in camp till about 9 o'clock when we boarded the train and started toward R.

Monday April 24th 1865
Morning found us at Russelville having run only six miles during the night. The forest trees are beginning to robe themselves in their spring attire. All is beauty and loveliness. We soon are on the way again. Reach Knoxville about noon and remain there till 11 o'clock at night.

Tuesday April 25th 1865
Train in motion when I awoke this morning. Pass through a fine country.

Reach Chattanooga at 4 o'clock. Left there at five. An enormous amount of business is done at Chattanooga by the government.

Wednesday April 26th 1865 (Johnston surrendered)
Still found us on board the cars. Ten miles north of Stevenson we lay by awaiting a train till 8 o'clock in the morning when we started. Traveled all day and reached our camp ground within six miles of Nashville about 12 o'clock.

Thursday April 27th 1865
Went from the railroad to the camp distant about two miles near the M___ pike and near the ground where we encamped two years ago before the Stone river battle.

Friday April 28th 1865
Somewhat rainy and cloudy. Fixing up quarters. Wrote letter to Frank Cones.

Saturday April 29th 1865
Making out muster rolls. Wrote a letter to Annie Kramer and Hattie Posey.

Sunday April 30th 1865
Now that Johnston has surrendered it will not be long until peace will be proclaimed throughout the length and breadth of the land. Every heart beats happily in the prospect of a speedy return to the endeared ones at home. The day is hailed with acclamations of joy. The time is near when Sabbaths will be spent in peace and quiet - when all can worship under their own vine and fig tree. The regular bimonthly muster took place today. Mustered by Capt. Walker.

Monday May 1st 1865
Mayday comes again and still finds us in the field. Received a letter from Ollie.

Tuesday May 2nd 1865
In company with Capt. Spillman I visited Nashville. Saw Laura Keene in the play of The Soldier's Daughter.

Wednesday May 3rd 1865
Preparations are being made for a grand review shortly. I learned today that

Jup Menaugh was in military prison at Nashville.

Thursday May 4th 1865
I again went to Nashville for the purpose of getting J. Menaugh released from custody but could not as the charges against him were serious. Desertion to the enemy. (Taylor surrendered)

Friday May 5th 1865
Received notice that my ordnance return was correct and referred for settlement. The beautiful days of spring pass languidly by.

Saturday May 6th 1865
Wrote letters to my friends Mate, Emily and Ollie. Did nothing else.

Sunday May 7th 1865
Reading the Bible. The brigade went on review. Waiting patiently for something to turn up.

Monday May 8th 1865
Rainy day. Preparing for grand review. The corps will be reviewed by Major Gen. Thomas.

Tuesday May 9th 1865
The morning is bright and beautiful. At 7 o'clock we were on the way to the review ground and arrived there about 9 which was just south of Nashville. Thousands of spectators had assembled to witness the grand pageant of military display. It passed off finely and all were well pleased. Gen. Wood in a general order expressed his thanks to every officer and man of the division for the brilliant display made. The high military bearing and fine appearance of the division were the theme of universal admiration. The reviewing officer, Major Gen. Thomas, expressed his gratification of the command, and of the high state of discipline and efficiency exhibited by it. Such commendation should be cherished by all. The command returned to camp well pleased.

HEAD-QUARTERS DEPARTMENT OF THE CUMBERLAND
Nashville, Tenn., May 10, 1865

General Orders, No. 30.

The General Commanding the Department takes pride in conveying to the 4th Army Corps. the expression of his admiration, excited by their brilliant and martial display at the Review of yesterday.

As the Battalions of your magnificent Corps swept successively before the eye, the coldest heart must have warmed with interest in contemplation of those men, who had passed through the varied and shifting scenes of the great, modern tragedy, who had stemmed with unyielding breasts the rebel tide threatening to engulph the land-marks of Freedom; and who, bearing on their bronzed and furrowed brows the ennobling marks of the years of hardship, suffering and privation, undergone in defence of freedom and the integrity of the Union, could still preserve the light step and wear the cheerful expression of youth.

Though your gay and broidered banners, wrought by dear hands far away, were all shred and war-worn, were they not blazoned on every stripe with words of glory, - Shiloh, Spring Hill, Stone River, Chickamauga, Atlanta, Franklin, Nashville, and many other glorious names, too numerous to be mentioned in an order like this.

By your prowess and fortitude you have ably done your part in restoring the golden boon of peace and order to your once distracted but now grateful country, and your Commander is at length enabled to give you a season of well earned rest.

But, soldiers, while we exult at our victories, let us not be forgetful of those brave, devoted hearts which, pressing in advance, throbbed their last amid the smoke and din of battle; nor withhold our sympathy for the afflicted wife, child, and mother, consigned, far off at home, to lasting, cruel grief.

> By Command of Major General Thomas:
> WILLIAM D. WHIPPLE,
> Assistant Adjutant General

Official:

Wednesday May 10th 1865
Doing and working at the business of the office.   Reading in Tupper's Proverbial Philosophy. (Jeff Davis captured)

Thursday May 11th 1865
Cold and rainy. An overcoat feels comfortable and such are in great demand. Cleared off in the afternoon.

Friday May 12th 1865
Clear though cool.   Filled out blanks for the non-commissioned officers of Co. I. Reading Tupper.

Saturday May 13th 1865
The time drags slowly on.   Waiting. Patiently waiting.

Sunday May 14th 1865
In company with several comrades I went to the hermitage in an ambulance. The place is made sacred by its being the home of Gen. Andrew Jackson. The place is somewhat antiquated and bears the marks of dilapidation. The finger of time leaves its impress on every thing. A carriage drive leads up to the mansion through a thick clump of cedars. We were shown through the hall and parlor by an old negro who belonged to the General and who had been with him since he was ten years old. He said he was with the Gen. while he was president. The furniture of the parlor consisted of the General's easy chairs. Mrs. Rachel Jackson's chair, besides several others modeled after different fashions. A piano too stands covered at one side.   The walls are decorated with several portraits of the Gen., his wife, and also of his adopted children. They are painted in oil by R.E.W. Earl, artist Friend and companion of Andrew Jackson.   Sculpture is not neglected. Busts of Jackson, Cass, Dickenson and others ornament the halls.   There too was the office chair of Washington - the chair he used for thirty years. It was presented to President Jackson by some of Washington's personal friends. The next point of importance is the tomb. Through wandering paths of the garden in the south east corner is where the last of Jackson lies. The monument is plain and the inscription simple. It is native sandstone with the words:
    General Andrew Jackson
      Born March 15th 1767
      Died June 8th 1845

Monday May 15th 1865
Today the regular monthly inspection took place by Capt. Walker.

Tuesday May 16th 1865
A detail of 73 men on camp guard. Through the kindness of a friend I secured a copy of "Tom Moore" which has afforded me infinite delight in the perusal of his Lalla Rookh.

Wednesday May 17th 1865
Rainy day. Went to the Christian Commission and got the May No of the Atlantic.

Thursday May 18th 1865
Reading the Atlantic. Nothing more of interest occurred.

Friday May 19th 1865
At noon in company with Capt. Spilman I went to Nashville and remained over night.

Saturday May 20th 1865
Came out to camp this morning. Found upon my arrival a couple of letters - one from home and the other from Mrs. Smith.

Sunday May 21st 1865
Fixing up camp. Received a letter from Annie. Wrote letters home and to Mrs. Smith.

Monday May 22nd 1865
Changed quarters and fixing around generally. Pretty day.

Tuesday May 23rd 1865
Dull. Nothing worthy of note.

Wednesday May 24th 1865
Reading the Eclectic Magazine.

Thursday May 25th 1865
Went to Nashville and remained over night.

Friday May 26th 1865
Returned to camp. Cloudy and rainy.

Saturday May 27th 1865
Beautiful morning. Had inspection. Wrote a letter to Lide. A delegate of the Christian Church preached to the regiment in the afternoon. Wrote two letters home.

Monday May 29th 1865
Time drags slowly on. Awaiting something to turn up. How lovely

Editor's note: Here the journal ends abruptly as if he were suddenly interrupted.

Mustering Out

*I*n the afternoon of the 6th day of June, 1865, the 86th Regiment, Indiana Volunteer Infantry, was mustered out of the United States Service.

On June 8 at noon the regiment broke camp, marched to Nashville, got on the train at 5 p.m. They reached Louisville on June 9 at 5 a.m. They crossed the Ohio River by ferry boat and landed on Hoosier soil at 11 a.m. They reached Indianapolis about 6 p.m. on the 9th.

The 86th Indiana entered the field with 39 commissioned officers and 917 enlisted men. During the latter part of 1864 it received 41 recruits, making a total of 999. Two commissioned officers were killed and one died from the effects of wounds. Among the enlisted men 238 were killed and died from disease and wounds, 48 men deserted from its ranks, 67 were transferred to the Veteran Reserve Corps, 10 to Engineer Corps, and 5 to the Mississippi Marine Brigade.

There were mustered out with the regiment 302 men, the remainder having been discharged on account of wounds and other disabilities. The recruits were transferred to the 51st Indiana Regiment.

Muster of 86th Ind.

		Officers	Enlisted
Co.- A-	99 men	3	102
Co.- B-	91 men	3	94
Co. -C-	98 men	3	101
Co. -D-	95 men	3	98
Co. -E -	96 men	3	99
Co. -F -	94 men	3	97
Co.-G -	97 men	3	100
Co.-H -	98 men	3	101
Co. -I -	87 men	3	90
Co. -K -	92 men	3	95

947	30	

Regimental Noncoms 5   7

        952 men

          37 officers

Col.

L. Col.

Major   Total

Adj.   regimental

Q. M.   officers - 7

Surgeon

Ass't Surgeon

37 Officers + 952 Enlisted men = 989 Officers & Enlisted men

Also entered in McCain's hand is:

      86th Reg. Muster - P 541 86th Hist.

   39 Com. Officers   917 Enlisted men

          mustered out

         302 men

Editor's Note: These entries were on separate sheets of paper tucked between the last pages. Also tucked in a pouch at the end of one volume were the three general orders which are interspersed with the text of the journal as they occurred.

Lynnville, TN 12-24-64
Lyon, Hylan Gen. CSA 1-14-65
Lytle, Benj. F. 4-4-64; 11-15-64
Macon, GA 7-29-64; 8-16-64;
    8-17-64; 8-30 & 31-64, r.r.
Madison 9-21-62
Manderson, Col 9-2-64,
Manson, Mahlon Gen.
    12-23-63; 5-14-64, wounded
Marble Hill 9-22-62
Marietta, GA 7-3-64; 10-3 & 4-
    64; 6-21-64
Marion's Brigade 3-16-64
Martin, Will 9-4-62
Maryville, TN 12-5-63, road; 12-6-
    63, Blount County; 1-23-64 to 2-
    15-64
Maxwell, Obediah Col. 3-31-63
Maysville, AL 1-15-65
McCain, Frank 3-2-65
McCain, Melvina 12-21-63 & others
McCain, Thomas Hart Benton
    12-31-62, p.o.w. Stones River;
    11-4-63, Sergeant Major;
    9-5-64, 1st Lieutenant,
    assumed command of Co. I;
    9-12-64, wrote official report
    of Atlanta campaign; 10-16-
    64, in command of Co. C.; 3-11-
    65, detailed to act as adjutant;
McCartney, Thomas 7-21-64,
McClellan, George B. 9-14-64;
    11-8-64, candidate for President
McCook, Alexander Gen.
    12-31-62, corps; 6-4-84
McCook, Robert Latimer, Gen.
    1-15-65, murder of '62
McDonald's Station TN 5-4-64
McInerny, Matthew Capt.
    10-26-64; 12-8-64
McMinnville, TN 7-7-63; 9-3-63
McPherson, James Gen.
    7-23-64, killed; 7-23-64 com
    mand of Army of the TN

Meade, George G. Gen. 7-9-63
Meigs County, TN 12-2-63
Menaugh, Jup
    5-3-65, in military prison in
    Nashville; 5-4-65, charged
    with desertion to the enemy
    (Ed. Note: He was mustered
    out 8-24-65.)
Metamora (ship) 1-27-63
Metcalf County, KY 11-1-62
Michaels, John 1-24-64
Michaels, William 10-13-64
Micherts, John 11-15-64
Mikesell, John (roster:Micksele)
    12-24-62
Mill Springs, KY 10-28-62
Miller, Capt. AAG 9-2-64, killed
Miller, John F. 12-16-62, deceased
Miller, Mr. 9-24-62
Mission/Missionary Ridge, GA
    9-22-63; 11-25-63; 12-10-
    63; 4-4-64; 4-8-64; 4-10-64;
    5-3-64
Mitchell, O. M. Maj. Gen. 1-11-64
Mobile, AL 8-11-64, has fallen
Montgomery, AL 1-6-63
Moore, Capt. 8-1-64
Moore, Dallas, Thomas 2-12-65
Moore, John, Lt. 6-27-64
Moore, Maj. Gen. 3-20-65
More's School House 4-9-63
Morgan, Col. 12-12-62
Morgantown, TN 12-5-63
Morrison's School House
    11-27-62; 4-7-63
Morristown, TN
    1-16-64; 2-29-64;
    3-12-64 to 3-18-64
Morton, Oliver P. Gov. (Indiana)
    9-14-62; 3-5-64
Mossy Creek, TN
    3-2-64
Mossy Peak, GA
    6-16-64

Mount Vernon, KY
10-19-62; 10-23-62
Mountain Fork, Flint River
1-15-65
Mudge Creek, TN
11-29-64; 12-20-64
Murdock, James E., Esq. (orator)
10-26-63
Murfreesboro, TN
11-28-62, asylum; 12-26-62,
pike; 12-29-62; 12-31-62,
battle; 5-31-63; 6-24-63;
2-6-64
Nashville, TN
10-21-62; 12-12-62; 5-30-63;
10-3-63, Courier; 8-27-64;
12-1-64; 1-8-65, official
report on battle; 2-3-65;
2-4-65; 2-6-65
Nelson
5-17-64
New Market, TN
2-28-64 to 3-12-64; 3-18-64
New Market, AL 1-15-65
Newport, KY 9-9-62
Newport News, Virginia 1-27-63
Newton Division
6-15-64; 6-18-64; 7-22-64
Noble, Adj. Gen. (Col John
Willock) 3-31-63
North Carolina 2-24-64
North, J. 2-5-63
Northwestern 2-8-64, poetry:
"The Old Year of the Nation"
Odell, Thomas A. Capt. 7-17-64
Ohio River 9-15-62; 9-25-62; 5-
29-63
Ossian's Poems 1-27-64
Our Heroes (poem) 6-11-64
Owensboro, TN 1-13-63
Panther Springs, TN
3-12-64; 3-29-65
Parole Camp 2-9-63 to 3-10-63
Patriot 11-27-63; 8-22-64

Peach Creek, GA 7-19-64
Perrin, John 5-21-64
Perryville, KY 10-9-62; 10-12-62
Pery, P. 3-20-63
Peter's Creek 11-6-62
Petersburg, Virginia 1-27-63
Peterson, Paris H. 11-25-63
phiz (physical) 12-13-64
Picket Agreement 7-2-64
Pigeon Mountains 10-19-64
Pine Mountain, GA 10-5-64,
Pitman,(William) 11-26-62
Pittsburg, Pennsylvania 3-13-63
Polk, Bishop, Gen. CSA
6-16-64; 10-5-64
Pollock's 4-23-64
Pond Spring, TN 12-3-63
Pool Knobs, TN 3-26-64
Poole, Mr. 6-15-63
Pors Message 12-21-63
Port Hudson7-18-63; 8-16-63
Potomac 5-8-64
Potomac, army of 5-10-64
Powder Springs Gap, TN
3-30-64; 4-6-64
Price's Ferry 7-17-64
Price, Maj. 2-22-64
Prisoners 7-17-64; 7-19-64; 7-
21-64
Pryne, Rev. 10-16-63
Pulaski, TN 10-31-64; 11-1-64;
11-2 to 23-64; 12-25-64
Punkin Vine River, GA 5-25-64
Quackenbus 12-6-62
Rash, Andrew 7-16-63
Rash, Mr. 9-13-62
Ream. Littleton V. Capt. 2-13-64
4-18-64; 5-1-64; 6-18-64
Reid, J. M. Rev. 7-12-64
Religious Telescope 3-6-64
Republican (newspaper) 2-7-63
Resaca, GA 5-13 to 16-64; 10-
13-64; 10-14-64, 49 graves
of 70th Indiana soldiers.
Rhea's 4-13-65

Riceville, TN 4-15-64
Richland Valley, TN
　3-24-64; 3-28-64

Richmond 9-5-62; 1-15-63;
　1-16-63; 4-3-65, fall
Ringgold, GA 9-11-63
Rockford, TN 12-7-63
Rose, William B 11-12-62, died
Rosecrans, Gen. 12-26-62; 12-
　30-62; 12-31-62; 6-24-63;
　10-4-63
Rosseau 10-10-62
Rossville, GA 1-11-64
Russelville, TN 3-30-65;4-24-65
Rutledge, TN 3-21-64
Salt River 10-3-62
Saylor, Mert 4-14-63
Sciota River 3-19-63
Scott, Sir Walter (poet) 9-20-63;
　11-13 & 14-63; 7-21-64
Scottsville, KY 11-7-62
Sells, Lt. 7-16-63; 7-17-63
Sems, Wm. 4-5-64
Seqatchie, TN 9-5-63, Valley &
　County
Sheath, Capt. 12-25-62
Shelbyville, TN 6-24-63
Sherman (boat) 2-18-65
Sherman, Wm. T. Gen.11-24-63;
　11-25-63; 5-10-64; 5-12-64;
　5-16-64; 5-26-64, saw him;
　7-23-64, rode along the
　line; 9-3-64; 10-26-64, con
　ference with Wood, Davis &
　Stanley
Shiloh 11-22-62
Silver Springs, TN 11-10-62;
　11-15-62
Simonson, Capt. 9-4-62
Sims, William S. Captain
　6-18-64; 8-21-64, resigned
Skaggs, Silas N. 5-9-64,

Slavery, slaves
　10-6-62; 12-6-62; 12-27-62;
　10-16-63; 5-17-64; 12-23-64
Slaw, Lane 10-13-64
Smith, A. J. Gen. 12-16-64
Smith, C. A. P., Mrs. 10-21-64
Smith, J. H. 1-28-64
Smith, Jas. H. 9-6-62; 3-30-63;
　5-29-63; 10-23-63
Smith, Prof. 11-20-62; 4-5-63
Smith, Rev. Mr. 4-9-65
Smith's Div. 12-11-62
Smyrna Church 12-28-62
Snake Creek Gap, GA 10-15-64
Snepp, Rev. Mr. 8-31-62
Snyder, Bro. 8-24-62
Somerset, KY 10-24-62; 10-25-62
Southard, William M. Captain
　11-25-63,
Spillman, Robert B. Capt.
　7-17-64; 10-26-64; 12-8-64;
　5-2-65; 5-19-65
Spring Hill, TN 11-29-64
Springfield, KY 10-8-62
Stanford, KY 10-14-62
Stanley, David S. Maj. Gen.
　6-15-64; 7-20 & 21-64; 9-
　27-64; 10-26-64
Stark 9-21-62
Stevenson, AL 10-30-64; 2-1-65;
　2-6-65 to 2-17-65
Stevenson, David 10-21-63,
Stiles, Capt. (Col. Israel N.)
　5-14-64, killed or wounded?
Stone River (boat) 2-18-65
Stone River, TN 11-19-62
Stoneman's 7-29-64, cavalry
Stone's River, battle of
　12-30 & 31-62
Storms, George 3-5-64
Strawberry Plains 12-7-63; 1-14-
　64; 1-17 & 18-64; 3-19-64;
　4-6-64

Sweet Water, TN 12-3-63
Tallahatchie River 1-5-63
Taylor, Richard 5-4-65
Taylor, Bayard (novelist) 3-3-65,
Tazewell, TN 3-27-64
Tennessee River 9-7-63
The Traitor's Doom 1-27-65
Thomas, Major. Gen.
    5-9-65; 12-26-62
Thomas, Uriah, Lieut. 10-20-62
Tippecanoe, Camp 8-26-62;
    9-2-62
Titcomb, Timothy (Poet) 3-6-65,
Tullahoma 1-2-63
Tunnel Hill, GA 5-7-64, occupied
Tupper's 5-10-65
U. S. Sanitary Building 2-20-64
U. S. Top. Eng. 6-9-64
Underwood, Robert 7-17-64,
Union Society 4-10-63
Vallandingham (Vallandigham)
    Clement Laird, politician
    11-22-63
Vaughn, John C. Gen. 4-18-65,
Vevay, KY 9-21-62
Vicksburg, Mississippi 7-9-63 Virginia
1-14-63, entered
Voorhees, Dr. 10-9-62
W. C. Advocate 7-12-64
Wabash College 4-5-64;1-11-64
Waddell, C. 1-16-64
Wagner, George D. 11-17-63
Walker, R. L. Capt. 2-17-65
Warner, Mr. 11-27-62
Warren Co. Indiana 6-15-63
Warrenton, AL 2-18-65
Warsaw. KY 9-21-62
Washington City (D.C.) 3-11-64
Watkins, Billy 8-30-62
Watkins, Enoch 11-23-62
Wautauga River 1-12-63
Waverly Magazine 2-8-65
Welch, Flora 10-1-63
Welch, Jesse 9-29-62; 10-1-62;

10-17-62; 10-27-62; 11-26-
62
West Point, GA 1-5-63
Wharton, Mr. 10-9,11,12-62
Wheeler's Cavalry 8-16-64
Whig Office 12-9-63; 2-19-64
Whitesburg, AL 2-17- & 18-65
Whitesides, TN 9-9-63
Wilcox 12-7-63
Wildcat Battlefield 10-20-62
Wilder, John Thomas, Col.
    9-18-63, at Chicamauga
Wiley, William 8-21-64
Willich, August, Gen. 5-15-64,
    wounded; 11-25-63, brigade
Wolford, Mrs. 11-24 & 25-62
Wood, Thomas J. Gen.
    10-10-63, assumes command
    11-25-63; 8-1-64; 9-2-64;
    10-26-64; 12-3-64; 12-23-
    64; 5-9-65, general order
Wood, Lt. 9-19-63, lost
Woodbury. TN 7-5-63
Wood's Division 10-16-62; 6-5-
64
Young Ladies' Magazine 10-21-
62
Yount, John M. Lt. 3-12-64
Zollicoffer, Felix Kirk, Gen. CSA
    10-20-62; 10-28-62-